DEEP DOWN FAITH

CORNELIUS PLANTINGA JR

FAITH ALIVE®
Christian Resources

Grand Rapids, Michigan

We are grateful to Bob Rozema for his work writing new content, updating pedagogy, and helping to shape the transformation of *A Sure Thing* into *Deep Down Faith*. A long-time editor for Faith Alive/CRC Publications, Mr. Rozema has worked on many projects over the years and continues to serve the church through his writing and editing.

We are also grateful to Dr. Cornelius Plantinga Jr. for his work on the original *A Sure Thing*. Dr. Plantinga has served Calvin Theological Seminary, Grand Rapids, Michigan, as its president and as associate professor of Systematic Theology. He is also the author of several books, including *Beyond Doubt: Faith-Building Devotions on Questions Christians Ask*.

We welcome your comments. Call us at 1-800-333-8300 or e-mail us at editors@faithaliveresources.org.

ISBN 978-1-59255-478-2

FSC

MIX
Paper from
responsible sources
FSC® C011935
www.fsc.org

PREFACE

Deep Down Faith is a new edition of Dr. Cornelius Plantinga Jr.'s *A Sure Thing,* originally published by Faith Alive in 1986 and reprinted in 2001. Over the years, this book has become a classic text for teaching young people the essentials of the Reformed faith. With accessible language, unforgettable illustrations, and vibrant stories, Plantinga makes these venerable and treasured doctrines sing with relevance and urgency to today's youth.

This new edition features updated language and illustrations, as well as a new online study guide. *Deep Down Faith* will be especially useful to older teens and young adults for devotional reading or as a guide for discussion in small group or one-on-one mentoring settings. It can also be used as a textbook for church education classes in Reformed doctrine, or in preparation for making Public Profession of Faith or Confirmation.

Faith Alive is pleased to offer this classic in a new edition for twenty-first century youth, trusting that it will continue to be used by the Holy Spirit to form faith for a new generation.

Rev. Leonard J. Vander Zee
Theological Editor, Faith Alive Christian Resources

CONTENTS

UNIT 1

OUR AWESOME GOD

WEEK 1

WHAT IS GOD LIKE?

GOD IS MYSTERIOUS

SCRIPTURE

(Jacob) dreamed that there was a ladder set up on the earth, the top of it reaching to heaven; and the angels of God were ascending and descending on it. And the LORD stood beside him and said, "I am the LORD, the God of Abraham your father and the God of Isaac. . . . I am with you and will keep you wherever you go. . ." Then Jacob woke from his sleep and said, "Surely the LORD is in this place—and I did not know it!" And he was afraid, and said, "How awesome is this place! This is none other than the house of God, and this is the gate of heaven."

—Selections from Genesis 28:12-17

TEACHINGS

We all believe in our hearts
and confess with our mouths
that there is a single
and simple
spiritual being,
whom we call God—eternal,
    incomprehensible,
    invisible,
    unchangeable,
    infinite,
    almighty;
    completely wise,
    just,
and good,
    and the overflowing source
        of all good.

—Belgic Confession, Article 1

> The **Belgic Confession** is a very old document of the Reformed church (1561); it consists of 37 articles or statements of Reformed doctrine.
>
> **Confessions:** organized, carefully written statements of doctrine approved by the church.

If you're a fan of horror movies, you probably enjoy that thrill of fear you get when the background music turns ominous and a creaking door heralds the entrance of something too horrible to describe. Aliens, monsters, and ghosts are the stuff of entertainment—as long as they aren't real.

But what about the *real* presence of an unmistakably powerful spirit? Scary?

Probably people have felt that way about God from near the beginning of time. Early in the Bible we find evidence of such feelings. At a place he calls "Bethel" (which means "house of God") Jacob senses that someone from beyond has mysteriously visited him. He feels haunted and afraid. The one who has visited Jacob is so strange, so alien, that Jacob probably feels like fleeing. He feels awe. And the place where he feels it, therefore, seems awesome or awe-ful.

It's hard for us to get this feeling about God. We say God's name so often and worship God so regularly and hear so much about God that he doesn't seem very awesome. God seems almost like an unseen great-uncle in another country. We get the feeling of awesomeness about God only at certain times and in certain places. If we are alone at night and hear the wind come mysteriously through the trees, we may think of God. If we attend the funeral of someone we love, we may feel the strangeness of death and the mystery of God. Or suppose we step into a large Eastern Orthodox church. We see statues and smell candles. We sense an atmosphere that is strange and awesome to us. We may feel surrounded by the secret things of God.

Multiply this a thousand times in thinking of the mystery of God. Even when we love God and trust that God loves us, we still can't see God or know everything about him. Even when we can't imagine the world without God, we are often puzzled by his ways with the world.

Still, God has made himself partly known to us. By speaking and acting, God has let us know something of who he is and what he wants. Thus we know that God is good and great and triune. We know that God wants our obedience and trust.

When we say that God is good or great or triune, we are listing some of God's *attributes.* Attributes are things true of someone. When we know some of God's attributes, we can praise and even

imitate God. We can partly understand and try to describe God.

> **Attributes of God:** God's characteristics or qualities, such as goodness and greatness. God's attributes help us understand, praise, and imitate God.

I say "try to describe" because God is in some ways indescribable. To say that God is good, for instance, is a little like saying that the Atlantic Ocean is a long swim.

To tell the truth, we will never understand some things about God. God is great beyond all our imagining and holy beyond all our power to think of him. God is terribly and awesomely real. God is indescribably good and great. God is triune.

In all these ways and more God is a mystery.

FOR REFLECTION

When have you been particularly aware of God's awe-fullness? What do you think prompted that experience?

PRAYER STARTERS

Tell God the things that make you stand in awe of him. Invite him to teach you more about who he is. Or pray along with a hymn or song about God's awesomeness.

GOD IS GOOD

SCRIPTURE

The LORD is good to all,
>and his compassion is over all that he has
>>made.

The LORD is just in all his ways,
>and kind in all his doings . . .

My mouth will speak the praise of the LORD,
>and all flesh will bless his holy name forever
>>and ever.

—Psalm 145:9, 17, 21

TEACHINGS

Our world, fallen into sin,
has lost its first goodness,
but God has not abandoned the work of his hands:
our Maker preserves this world,
sending seasons, sun, and rain,
upholding all creatures,
renewing the earth,
promising a Savior,
guiding all things to their purpose.

—*Our World Belongs to God: A Contemporary Testimony*,
paragraph 4

Attributes of God: God's characteristics or qualities, such as goodness and greatness. God's attributes help us understand, praise, and imitate God.

Our World Belongs to God, published in 1986 and revised in 2008, provides an updated look at how the Reformed faith addresses concerns facing people today.

"Good" is a word so common we use it without thinking. "How ya doing?" the cashier at the coffee shop asks. "Pretty good," you reply. A friend posts some of your favorite lyrics on Facebook. "Good song!" you comment. At work you do more than is expected of you. "Thanks," says your boss. "Good job."

A common word—*good.* But there are times when you really mean it. You've been out all day hiking, or working, or cross-country skiing. Every muscle aches with pleasant tiredness. Every bone has gone off duty. At night you climb slowly into your bed, squirm deliciously till it nests and cradles you perfectly. You whisper your prayer to God and then let everything in the world fall away into drowsy nothingness. A bed on a tired night can feel so good.

Or suppose you've been playing tennis or basketball. It's an outdoor court, and you forgot your water bottle. So you wait for a drink until you get home. Water is a common gift for most of us. But when you are really thirsty, when not just your tongue and lips and throat but your whole body craves liquid, then even water can be incredibly good. It's an overflowing fountain of good.

One more example: you settle into the sofa with a book. Sometimes you don't feel like reading, but this time you've found a book you can't close. You begin to care deeply about the characters. The places and adventures in the book make you feel new things. The whole story moves you outside of yourself in some wonderful way. A good book can be incredibly satisfying.

Goodness is what satisfies us, feeds us, fills us to the brim. That is the way we have been created by God. We have a built-in desire for beds, thirst-quenching liquids, good books, good food, even good people. What's good is whatever God created us to want.

Did you ever notice that the psalms speak of God himself as what we want? Psalm 42 compares God to water. A deer "longs for flowing streams." The deer wants water as a drink, as a bath, possibly as an escape from hunters. God, says the psalmist, is like a stream. God is like water that quenches, cools, and removes us from danger. We *thirst* for God.

> **God's goodness:** an attribute of God; it means that God satisfies the needs of all his creatures.

Another psalm (63) compares God to food. God is like a feast for some starving, hunger-crazed person. The person wants as much of God as he or she can get because God is good. We *hunger* for God. We long for God because we belong to him.

Do these sound like strange ideas? Perhaps they are. Perhaps that's because we do not hunger and thirst for God enough. But something we do in church shows our desire for God—and also shows God's way of meeting it. At the Lord's Supper believers take a piece of bread in hand and lift a cup to their lips. They say, "This is the body of Christ. This is the blood of Christ." Then they eat and drink. There is no doubt they are eating bread and drinking wine or juice. Still, in some mysterious way believers are also consuming as much of God as they can get. They are satisfying their hunger and thirst for God—because God is so good.

Psalm 145 speaks of God's goodness. The Lord is kind to the poor, just in opposing the wicked. God has open ears for our prayers and open hands to hold out to us good things. The Lord "satisfies the desire of every living thing." The Lord, in other words, is good.

But, once more, the point of saying this is not just to admire or appreciate. The point is to worship and give thanks. For whatever goods we have—beds, drink, food, good people, even God himself—are a sheer gift. A never-ending gift. God is an overflowing fountain of good.

That is why we want him.

FOR REFLECTION

Read Psalm 145, paying special attention to the specific examples of God's goodness.

PRAYER STARTERS

Thank God for specific needs he has met for you—as many as you can think of. Talk to God about an area of unmet need (in your life or someone else's) where you want to see his goodness.

GOD IS GREAT

SCRIPTURE

Praise the LORD!
How good it is to sing praises to our God;
    for he is gracious, and a song of praise is
        fitting. . . .
He determines the number of the stars;
    he gives to all of them their names.
Great is our LORD, and abundant in power;
    his understanding is beyond measure.
The LORD lifts up the downtrodden;
    he casts the wicked to the ground.
—Psalm 147:1, 4-6

TEACHINGS

I trust him so much that I do not doubt
    he will provide
        whatever I need
        for body and soul,
    and he will turn to my good
        whatever adversity he sends me
        in this sad world.
He is able to do this because he is almighty God;
he desires to do this because he is a faithful Father.
—Heidelberg Catechism Q&A 26

> The **Heidelberg Catechism** is a popular confession of the church, used primarily to teach doctrine. This 16th-century confession includes 129 questions and answers about the Apostles' Creed, the Ten Commandments, and the Lord's Prayer.

I once saw a picture of a very large firefighter bending over a very small girl. The girl had been in a house fire and had breathed in a lot of smoke. By the time she was carried out she wasn't breathing at all. So the firefighter knelt at her side, pinched her nostrils shut with his thumb and first finger, placed his mouth over hers, and breathed into her lungs the breath of life.

Sometimes we think of kneeling, stooping, and crawling as signs of weakness. A slave kneels before a master. Someone who is being humiliated in a book or movie crawls in front of his tormentor.

But kneeling or stooping can also show strength, the strength of goodness. The small girl I mentioned above received mouth-to-mouth resuscitation from a strong man. In the same way a person who cares for a tiny pet or who rescues someone younger and smaller or who cares for someone old or sick is showing strength.

Worldly people often get this mixed up. They think of kindness as a weakness. Sometimes they sneer at goodness. But anybody who has ever been picked up by powerful arms or who has struggled to nurse a sick or dying person—anybody like that knows that kindness, goodness, and compassion are great strengths.

One of the odd and striking things about God is that his goodness so often shows itself in kneeling, stooping, and bending. Of course, God is great without doing these things. The Bible keeps telling us, for example, of God's powerful deeds in nature. God cracks open great mountains; he shakes the whole earth till it rumbles and splits. He stretches out the heavens and tramples on the waves of the sea (Job 9:8). God possesses unimaginable strength, intelligence, resourcefulness, and power. God is incredibly vast, majestically strong, galactically great. That is part of the reason people fear God.

But our psalm for today tells us that God's greatness includes his stooping, his bending toward us. "Great is our LORD, and abundant in power" (v. 5). Then, in the very next verse, the psalmist writes, "The LORD lifts up the downtrodden."

> **God's greatness:** an attribute of God; it means that God is awesome. God's greatness encompasses both power and compassion.

Some of God's children are downtrodden. People tread on them. Careless people walk all over them. The downtrodden eagerly look for friends, but others tell them to get lost. They need food, but others grab even the little they have. Lacking proper homes and education and support systems, these people always seem to have someone's foot in their face. They are like human cigarette butts. Other people like to crush or squash them.

God lifts up the downtrodden. It is part of God's *greatness* to do this. God lifts squashed people to their feet, throwing off the wicked who have been walking all over them. God's greatness is the muscle behind his goodness.

God's greatness is awesome. People fear it. But it is also kind. God bends over to feed young ravens, young children, young adults. Because God is high, he can lift up and straighten out crushed people.

For all God's downtrodden people, one day in the city of David a Savior is born. A baby is born in a cow shed. God stoops over to place a tiny child in the world.

All of heaven's greatness lies there wailing in the straw. What must we think of that?

FOR REFLECTION

Read Psalm 147. Notice the different ways God displays greatness.

PRAYER STARTERS

Think of human examples of compassionate strength. Let those examples help you praise God for his greatness. (For example, "God, I remember how my dog fought when I held her down for her shots at the vet. Sometimes I think I'm like that with you. But you don't give up; you know what's best for me even when I don't like it.") Or sing to God a song that praises God's greatness—his power and compassion. Here are a few to start you off: "How Great Thou Art," "Mighty to Save," and "How Great Is Our God."

GOD IS TRIUNE

SCRIPTURE

"I ask not only on behalf of these, but also on behalf of those who will believe in me through their word, that they may all be one. As you, Father, are in me and I am in you, may they also be in us, so that the world may believe that you have sent me."

—John 17:20-21

TEACHINGS

Q. Since there is but one God,
    why do you speak of three:
    Father, Son, and Holy Spirit?

A. Because that is how
    God has revealed himself in his Word:
    these three distinct persons
    are one, true, eternal God.

—Heidelberg Catechism Q&A 25

People often compare things. Some jokes and riddles, for example, depend on comparisons. Suppose someone asks, "When is a frog like a baseball player?" (When it catches flies.) For the joke to work, a frog and a baseball player have to be alike in some way. They have to be comparable.

In the fine work of great writers, comparisons help make stories interesting to read. In John Steinbeck's story *The Red Pony*, a boy named Jody receives a colt as a gift. Steinbeck tells us that the new pony's coat was "rough and thick as an Airedale's fur." Later, Jody brushes and curries his pony so that "his coat lay as smooth and gleaming as orange-red lacquer." Finally, Jody wants to train the red pony never to fall on top of him. Why? "He had seen that happen to men before, had seen how they writhed on the ground like squashed bugs, and he was afraid of it." In the author's mind dog's fur, paint, and bugs are interesting comparisons for horsehair and people.

The Bible is full of comparisons. God is compared to a rock. Jesus is compared to a shepherd. You and I, who are members of the church, are compared to the limbs of a human body.

One of the most mysterious things about God is that God is both one and three. There are three persons in God—the Father, the Son, and the Holy Spirit. But there is still only one God. When Christians say this, they are stating the doctrine of the Trinity. They are saying that God is triune.

Doctrine: the church's teachings, based on the Bible, about God and our salvation.

But what would that be like? What is a good comparison for the triune God?

People have thought about this for centuries. Some have suggested that God is like water. After all, water has three forms—solid, liquid, and vapor—but is still only one substance. Maybe God is like that.

Others have said that God is like a man who has three roles to play. God is like an actor. The President of the U.S., for instance, has to play the role of president. But he may also have to play the role of husband (to his wife) and father (to his children). He is therefore one man with at least three roles. Is God like that?

No. In fact, neither of these comparisons is a very good one. In the first comparison, the three forms of water are actually not very much like persons. None of them can think or love, for example. And in the second comparison, the president, even with three roles to play, is still only one person. God, on the other hand, is three persons.

Perhaps we can find a better comparison. Think of three persons in a family. They are very much alike. Marriage, birth, or adoption tie them together. The family members may look like each other. Further, they know each other deeply and love each other. They share memories, experiences, hopes, and plans. If anyone or anything (such as a mugger or a tornado) threatens them, they turn to face this threat together. They are three persons, but one family unit.

Triune: being at once a triple and a unit. To say that God is triune is to say that God is three persons (Father, Son, and Holy Spirit) but only one God. That is, God is a **Trinity**.

In a way, God is like that. God is like an extraordinarily close family. The three persons in God are only one divine family or Trinity.

But the Bible gives us the best comparison. In today's passage the Father and Son together are compared to the church. (In other places the Spirit is included.) Does this seem like an odd comparison? The church, after all, contains so many sorts of persons. And some don't seem very much like God.

Still, this is the Bible's comparison. God is three persons, but there is only one God. The church is many persons, but there is only one church. That is, across the world and across the centuries there is only one group of persons who call Jesus their Lord.

God is like the church. Or, better, the church is like God. Do you think the church ought to be even more like God than it is?

FOR REFLECTION

How is comparing the Trinity to a family or the church helpful to you? What is still mysterious?

PRAYER STARTERS

For decades John Stott, an influential Christian writer and preacher, started each day with a trinitarian prayer. Look his prayer up online and consider using it as your own.

WEEK 2

WHAT DOES CREATION REVEAL ABOUT GOD?

BUILDING A UNIVERSE

SCRIPTURE

In the beginning God created the heavens and the earth. Now the earth was formless and empty, darkness was over the surface of the deep, and the Spirit of God was hovering over the waters. And God said, "Let there be light," and there was light.

—Genesis 1:1-3 (NIV)

TEACHINGS

In the beginning, God—
Father, Word, and Spirit—
called this world into being
out of nothing,
and gave it shape and order.

—*Our World Belongs to God,* paragraph 8

We all do hundreds of things we hardly ever think about. We vibrate our eardrums, beat our hearts, pump our blood. We multiply cells, expand lungs, mix stomach juices with swallowed Big Macs. We sneeze in dusty rooms, blink in bright sunlight, yawn when someone else yawns, hiccup for no known reason.

But even though we are the ones who do these things, we seldom think about them. Why? Because they are all involuntary. That is, we do not do them on purpose. They are things we do because, like all animals, we have bodies. You could almost say that heart beating and blood pumping and cell multiplying are things we don't really *do* at all. Instead, they happen to us or in us.

But there also are a great number of things we do on purpose. We download *this* song and not *that* one. We intentionally cut a piece of cloth or wood to size. We purposely update our Facebook profile. We do such things because, unlike snails and slugs, we are persons. To be a person is to *act* in intentional and orderly ways.

When we act in these ways, we are like God! The triune God, the God of three persons, is supremely the God who acts. God the Trinity is bursting with purposeful activity. God is alive with plans, programs, and designs. Even if some of God's acts are hidden from us, even if some occur in mysterious ways, still we know from reading the Bible that God is the great actor in the drama of the universe.

The first act of God we know about is creation. As we know, the Bible begins with a simple, but magnificent, statement: "In the beginning God created the heavens and the earth." It is hard for us to grasp this. What was it like without a universe? Why did God see fit to create one? How can we imagine the great bursts of godly power that lit up the stars, swung moons into orbit, and delicately balanced the earth on its axis? How can we imagine the thoughts of the first man and woman as they gazed around at a brand-new world, watching birds and animals at play and feeling inside themselves the stirrings of life?

> The **sovereignty of God:** the attribute of God that means that God is supreme and in control.

We can't really imagine these things very well. But we do live in the world that has come from these beginnings. What a world it is! God designed and then built the universe out of his sheer intelligence and stunning power. Christians believe, moreover, that God built the universe out of nothing. There was no universal lumberyard where God had a charge account, no stone quarry, no pet store stocked with animals. The striking truth is that God made not only the universe but also the materials out of which he made it. This is part of what we mean when we say that God is *sovereign.* Sovereignty means that God is supreme and in control. The universe reveals God's attribute of sovereignty.

Think of the result! We have been created with five senses so that we may know and take delight in God's creation. In five ways we *sense* that God has acted in creation. We see a beautifully dressed autumn tree, smell a fresh loaf of warm bread, touch a puppy's velvet coat, hear the lonesome call of a bird, taste the juices of a perfectly ripened peach.

All these things—and millions more—come from God. Christians see, smell, touch, hear, and taste God's creation as if there were signs and signatures all over it that said "Made by God."

Can you understand now why the psalmists keep telling us to praise him?

FOR REFLECTION

Many people experience some of their most profound awareness of God's supremacy when they are outside, gazing at the stars or a mountain range or some other part of nature. When or where are you most aware of God's sovereignty in creation?

PRAYER STARTERS

Use Psalm 8 or Psalm 139 as your own prayer about God's creation of nature (Psalm 8) or the human body (Psalm 139).

AND IT WAS VERY GOOD

SCRIPTURE

God saw that the light was good. . . . God saw that [the land and seas were] good. . . . God saw that [the plants and trees were] good. . . . God saw that [the sun, moon, and stars were] good. . . . God saw that [the creatures of sea and sky were] good. . . . God saw that [the land animals were] good. . . . God saw everything that he had made, and indeed, it was very good.

—Genesis 1:4, 10, 12, 18, 21, 25, 31

TEACHINGS

In the beginning
everything was very good.

—*Our World Belongs to God,* paragraph 9

God acted sovereignly in creation. In an incredible explosion of activity God spread out the heavens, dug and filled the oceans, planted the great gardens and forests. God launched birds, stocked lakes with fish, and set animals free to cruise the earth. And, last, God made human beings to work and play, worship and serve, love and laugh. He made them like himself to do these things and then rest.

Why did God create? Was he lonesome? No, within the holy Trinity God already enjoyed life, zest, and an overflowing of love. Was God absentmindedly doodling in creation—the way

we do, sketching out houses and stick people to amuse ourselves when we are bored? No, the universe shows every sign of having been created on purpose. Did God tell himself he had to create or else he couldn't be God? No, God was free either to create or not to create. God is sovereign. It was up to him whether to make a universe.

> People have many different ideas about **creation.** When we speak of creation in this book, we mean the sovereign act of God by which he brought into being the whole universe from nothing. Creation shows God's sovereignty, goodness, and greatness, as well as God's image in us.

Why, then? Why did God create? We do not know all the reasons. But one reason is this: God created because he is *good.* To be good means in part that you want to share what you have with others. Couples do this when they commit to each other. Parents do this when they make room for children. They want to share their life, their love, their laughter, their faith, their home. They want to share *themselves.*

So it is with God. In creation God made room for others. God had already existed without beginning or limit. But at creation God began a great experiment. God began to share his life and existence with whales and frogs, birch trees and bluegrass. And God made persons like himself. The God who was overflowing with goodness opened his home to guests.

Many of us have been guests in somebody else's home. It can be a wonderful experience. A good host or hostess welcomes you with a restful place to sleep, nutritious and attractive food, interesting things to see and do. A host or hostess *makes room* for you in a generous way. This practice of hospitality flows out of human goodness. It is, after all, not so easy to be hospitable. You have to do extra work to make your guests feel at home. You might have to sleep on the couch. You have to take responsibility for your guests and try to protect them.

But in any case human hosts do not create their guests. They simply welcome guests that already exist. God went a step further. He made a whole universe in order to have things and persons he could love—and that would love and praise him in return. God's goodness shows itself in his creative hospitality. God has made room in his life for you and me.

Now notice one more thing. In a strange and wonderful way God passed along his own goodness to his creation. The whole first chapter of Genesis rings with the word *good*. Not only is God good; God also saw that what he had made was good. Then he saw again that it was good. And again and again. All of it good. At last God stepped back, looked over all that he had made room for, and called it *very* good.

Can you see why it is good for us in turn to make room for others?

FOR REFLECTION

What comes to mind when you think of God as a host? Of yourself as God's guest?

PRAYER STARTERS

Think of yourself as God's guest and the world as the guestroom he has provided for you. Offer thanks for specific things in the guestroom that delight you.

SIGNS OF GOD'S GREATNESS

SCRIPTURE

"Where were you when I laid the earth's foundation? . . . Who marked off its dimensions? . . . Who shut up the sea behind doors? . . . Who cuts a channel for the torrents of rain, and a path for the thunderstorm?"

—Job 38:4, 5, 8, 25 (NIV)

TEACHINGS

God formed sky, land, and sea;
stars above, moon and sun,
making a world of color, beauty, and variety—
a fitting home for plants and animals, and us—
a place to work and play,
worship and wonder,
love and laugh.

—*Our World Belongs to God*, paragraph 9

One day my family and I visited the Detroit Zoo. It was the sort of cool, clear summer day that seemed to make even caged animals glad to be alive. We watched a hippo repeatedly open its great pink mouth, as if she expected to have her four teeth cleaned and checked by a hippo dentist. A sixth-month-old polar bear cub did endless belly whoppers into a small diving pool. Seals and sea lions swam fifteen-yard freestyle races. Monkeys studied and groomed each other's fur. Prairie dogs commuted underground back and forth from the suburbs to the center of prairie-dog city. In a family of lynx the children romped and fought, their mother occasionally separating them with a large paw. The father lynx simply watched in cool aloofness.

Why are animals fun to watch? Partly because they are so much like us. Or we are like them. Also, partly because animals are so different from each other in size, color, shape, speed, and habits. Some are massive and slow, like living trucks. Others are so small and quick you wonder how the zoo people ever caught them. Some are striped, some spotted, some flecked, some dappled. The Asian giraffes we saw were marked with rust-colored rectangles on beige fur. Animals come in almost indescribable variety.

Zoologists have colorful names for groups of animals. A group of lions is called a *pride* of lions. (Perhaps we can guess why.) Then there is a gaggle of geese, a peep of chickens, a knot of toads, a parliament of owls, and a clash of rhinos. All this clashing, gaggling, peeping, knotting, and priding tell us how marvelously different animals are from each other—and what fine imaginations zoologists have.

But their imaginations are nothing like God's. It is a sign of God's greatness that he has created such incredible kinds of things. And such vast numbers of things—billions of stars, galaxies, solar systems, fiery comets, deadly rays, planets circled by moons. Countless plants and kinds of plants. Numberless birds and kinds of birds.

In a place like Canada's Banff National Park visitors can listen to a chorus of wolves or to the roaring of the Athabasca River. They can peer at awesome, soaring peaks or at the depth of sky-blue waters—or at the one reflected in the other. They can hike across places so wondrously beautiful that the Creator of the heavens and the earth seems to have settled there in all his mystery and glory. God made Banff.

And God made us. How remarkable the way he does it! Each of us starts as a single cell that comes from the union of a sperm and an egg. Then that cell divides into two, then four, then eight, then sixteen, on and on to millions and billions of cells. A great scientist once pointed out that at a certain stage in this process one particular cell appears. This one cell, as it divides, will become a human brain. Everything needed to learn to talk, to write, to play music or softball is in that one cell. All we need to learn to argue or give up an argument; every ability to be surprised, thoughtful, or bored; every raw material for thinking, imagining, or planning—all of it is in this single cell that keeps dividing and dividing until one day it becomes that trillion-cell wonder, the brain.

This is a work of God's greatness in creation.

FOR REFLECTION

What can you learn about God from the huge variety of animals he created?

PRAYER STARTERS

Celebrate God's imagination by picturing one of the animals you find amazing. Simply tell God what you notice and what you like about the creature he made. Or go to a website like *National Geographic*'s and use their slideshow or photos to prompt your prayer.

GOD'S IMAGE IN CREATION, IN YOU

SCRIPTURE

Then God said, "Let us make mankind in our image, in our likeness, so that they may rule over the fish in the sea and the birds in the sky, over the livestock and all the wild animals, and over all the creatures that move along the ground."
So God created mankind in his own image, in the image of God he created them; male and female he created them.

—Genesis 1:26-27

TEACHINGS

Made in God's image
to live in loving communion with our Maker,
we are appointed earthkeepers and caretakers
to tend the earth, enjoy it,
and love our neighbors.
God uses our skills
for the unfolding and well-being of his world
so that creation and all who live in it may flourish.

—*Our World Belongs to God,* paragraph 10

Images. They are all around you. You get up in the morning and peer into a mirror. What peers back at you is not you but your image. You look into a camera viewfinder or watch a favorite clip on YouTube. You gaze at a reflected mountain upside down in a lake. You have a dental X-ray taken or make a photocopy of your passport. In all these cases you are dealing with images.

An image is a likeness of something. Often, as in mirrors, it is a reflected likeness. Some images, as in great portraits, are beautiful. Some are funny, as in cartoons. A few (in good video games, for example) are exciting.

In addition, images are often very powerful. They can deeply influence your thinking and feeling. Why do you suppose advertisers often show a wealthy or a happy person using a certain product? Why do rulers of some countries plaster up their picture on every wall, fence, and billboard? Why does the second commandment in the Bible tell us we must not make an image of God?

After God had made day and night; after God had created land and seas, plants and trees, moons and stars, birds and fish and land animals—after all that, God did one final thing. God made an image. God made a likeness, a reproduction, a reflection of himself. God made human beings.

> **Image of God:** the likeness of God in human beings. We see the image of God in us by our ruling over creation, by our fellowship with each other, and by any right actions we do. The image of God means being like Christ.

It's a scary and difficult thought—that we humans are like God. What could it mean? After all, we have bodies and faces, but God has no body at all. So how could we look like him? Also, we are persons who often do or say wrong things. God never does. So how could we resemble God in our acts or speech?

Yet we do. Look at the Genesis verses at the beginning of this reading. One way we resemble or image God is in our *ruling.* God has made us responsible for taking good care of the earth, making sure that water and air are clean, for instance, and that forests and other natural gifts are protected. God wants us to use soil intelligently and to handle animals well. God is, of course, the ultimate ruler over all these things, but he has seen fit to share his ruling by giving us a part to play in it. We are stewards of the earth.

Now look at verse 27. Being created male and female is also part of what it means to be in the image of God. Of course, God is not male or female. God is a family of three wonderfully fellowshipping persons: Father, Son, and Holy Spirit. But we human beings can have a similar fellowship—not only with God but also with each other! Because we are male and female we can have families. We can know and love other human beings intimately. And our *loving fellowship* images God.

As a matter of fact, according to the New Testament, whenever we *act rightly*—showing kindness, for example, or helping someone who isn't attractive, or telling the truth—we are imaging God. To act like God is to show God's likeness to the world.

Have you ever noticed that it is sometimes hard to visualize a person you deeply love? Sometimes we can get a better picture in our minds of somebody we don't know very well than of a person we are very close to. God is the one we must love above all. And we cannot picture God at all. Yet at times we can see what God is like. We see God's image in the ruling, fellowshipping, and right actions of human beings. We see God especially in Jesus Christ, who is not only human but also divine and is therefore the perfect image of God.

And when we imitate Christ, we can tell what God is like not only by looking at Christ himself. We can also tell by looking in a mirror.

FOR REFLECTION

In what specific ways have you recently imaged God by your stewardship, fellowship, and right actions? How do you feel about being an example that shows what God is like?

PRAYER STARTERS

Ask God to show you ways to clearly image him. Ask for help in areas of stewardship, right actions, or fellowship where you don't reflect God very well.

WEEK 3

WILL GOD REALLY PROVIDE?

GOD PROVIDES

SCRIPTURE

"The God who made the world and everything in it, he who is Lord of heaven and earth, does not live in shrines made by human hands, nor is he served by human hands, as though he needed anything, since he himself gives to all mortals life and breath and all things."

—Acts 17:24-25

TEACHINGS

Our world, fallen into sin,
has lost its first goodness,
but God has not abandoned the work of his hands:
our Maker preserves this world,
sending seasons, sun, and rain,
upholding all creatures,
renewing the earth,
promising a Savior,
guiding all things to their purpose.

—*Our World Belongs to God,* paragraph 4

An animal shelter is a noisy and busy place. It's also a sad place. Row after row of abandoned or abused animals bark, whine, yip, howl, and meow. Nobody wants them.

Each of these animals has a history. Perhaps one of them was once given to a child as a pet. For the first few weeks everybody in the house played with the newcomer. But then school started, or people got busy some other way and the pet was gradually neglected. Nobody gave the animal a bath or a grooming. Nobody bothered to train or discipline it. No one provided the right diet or proper veterinary care. Because of such carelessness a pet that was once the center of attention in a home became an unwelcome nuisance.

Some of these animals stray away. Others are driven out into the country and pushed out of a car. Some are allowed to run the neighborhood in packs. When these abandoned creatures end up in animal shelters, a few are adopted. Most have to be killed.

One of the greatest tragedies of the world is that some children are treated in similar ways. Careless parents conceive these children but don't really want them. Some kill them before they are born. Others abandon live babies in trash cans or on the steps of churches. Still other parents allow their children to grow up in their houses but never give them strong, loving care. For example, they don't ever read to them or play with them when they are small. They don't keep them clean. They don't hug them or hold them or tell them they are important and loved. Some of these parents even smash their children in the face or lock them in dark closets for days.

These are parents who have created children but have not provided for them. Day by day their children suffer. Their minds and spirits and bodies and feelings gradually crumble because nobody takes care to nourish and support them.

To provide for someone is to show *providence*. You can show it by supporting a person's life with food, education, love, a house, even discipline.

All good providers, including our parents, learn their providence from God. God acts in creation, but then he also acts in providence to take care of his creation. God makes provision for summer and winter, springtime and harvest. God gives both rain and sunshine so that grains and fruits and green plants—and all the creatures who feed on them—may continually grow and be nourished.

> **Providence:** the care God shows for his creation. God preserves the world, rescues his people, works for good, and controls history. Providence lets us trust and thank God.

By providing these things God *preserves* his creation. He never abandons it. He never turns his back on it. Like a parent who holds a child's head above water, God faithfully upholds what belongs to him. God provides for life to reproduce, flesh to heal, humans to know and love him. God provides antibodies to fight infection, spiders to fight flies.

God even provides firefighters to combat fires. Did you ever consider why most of us live safe and healthy lives? Why do people fight fires, set broken bones, help abused children, dam floods, imprison criminals, grow beans, teach children, fix teeth, sell clothing? What if nobody were willing to do any of these things? What if nobody cared? Suppose everybody went on strike at the same time. Civilization would collapse!

But this doesn't happen because God is at work in his world. He preserves it. And he often does this by empowering *us* to do his work. Every garbage collector, every judge, every forest ranger, every teacher, every police officer is acting for God in preserving his world.

God takes care of what he has made. That is why we trust him.

FOR REFLECTION

Try naming six things that you normally take for granted in your day-to-day life, but that actually come from God and are signs of his providence.

PRAYER STARTERS

Give thanks for those six things and any other ways that God provides for you. Or use this stanza from the hymn "Great Is Thy Faithfulness" as your prayer:

Summer and winter and springtime and harvest,
sun, moon, and stars in their courses above
join with all nature in manifold witness
to thy great faithfulness, mercy, and love.
Great is thy faithfulness!
Great is thy faithfulness!
Morning by morning new mercies I see;
All I have needed thy hand hath provided.
Great is thy faithfulness, Lord, unto me.
—text: Thomas O. Chisholm, 1923; tune: Willam M. Runyan, 1923

GOD HAS PROVIDED RESCUE

SCRIPTURE

The LORD said, "I have indeed seen the misery of my people in Egypt. I have heard them crying out because of their slave drivers, and I am concerned about their suffering. So I have come down to rescue them from the hand of the Egyptians."

—Exodus 3:7-8 (NIV)

TEACHINGS

While justly angry,
God did not turn away
from a world bent on destruction
but turned to face it in love.
With patience and tender care
the Lord set out
on the long road of redemption
to reclaim the lost as his people
and the world as his kingdom.

—*Our World Belongs to God,* paragraph 18

Because of his sovereign greatness and goodness God preserves the world. But why is this necessary? Why can't the world preserve itself? To answer this we have to remember two things. One is that we are not our own. We and our world belong to God. God is the creator. We are only creatures. Even our casual language tells us that we forget this at times. Our friends wave goodbye and say, "Take care!" Clerks in stores tell us, "Have a nice day!" (Try saying back, "Sorry, I have other plans.") Actually, we can't do these things. We can't really take care of ourselves. And whether we have a nice day depends on many things and people outside our control. The truth is that we depend entirely on God.

The other thing to remember is that our world is sinful. Way back at the beginning Adam and Eve pushed their way out of God's arms in order to be on their own. They wanted to belong to themselves, rule themselves, run their own garden. Everyone feels the tragic result. Sin entered the world and began to spread like an oil slick. Since that time the human story has always included war, kidnapping, rape, murder, child abandonment, cruelty, racism, drunkenness, divorce, disease, and other miseries. God's world has been constantly threatened and at times almost wrecked by sin.

But God has kept on preserving his world. Sun and rain and fruitful seasons have continued in their rhythm. And one more thing: God has provided rescue for sinners.

We all know how a person can get him- or herself in trouble. A hiker wanders off in a wilderness area; rangers have to search for her. A drunk and disorderly man nearly drowns in a lake; lifeguards have to swim out and haul him in. A rock climber breaks all the rules of safe climbing and needs a rescue team to get her down the mountain.

Now think back over what you know of the Bible. Again and again we read similar stories. God's people get themselves into terrible trouble. Then God rescues them. Almost at once, by sin and foolishness the people again get themselves enslaved, or hurt, or miserable in some other way. And again God comes to the rescue. Trouble and rescue. Sin and salvation. Over and over that is the pattern. If the human story includes more sadness and wreckage than we can imagine, it also reveals—in a way that is equally hard to imagine—that God keeps on coming back to rescue his children.

God saved Noah from the flood. God promised Abraham blessing for the whole world. When Joseph's brothers sold him like an animal, God used this sin to save the whole family from starvation. When that family and its children got enslaved in Egypt, God "heard them crying out" and "came down to rescue them." The Israelites in the desert kept telling their children the story of this mighty exodus. But they also complained about the food. So God sent them manna. Through the years God gave them laws, a temple, priests, prophets, kings. In great battles he delivered them from enemies left and right.

When at last the Israelites went miserably off into exile, God rescued them. And to them and to the whole world God one day sent a Savior, Christ the Lord.

When human beings killed Jesus, God raised him. Since then God has poured out his Spirit, raised up his church, and equipped millions of women and men to spread the gospel and to fight sin. History is, in fact, the death struggle of the raging forces of evil on the one hand and the rescuing God on the other. And history tells us that the God who has rescued before will do it again.

In the Scripture we can read the rescue stories and believe them. Does God purposely have rescue in mind for *us*?

FOR REFLECTION

Remember the rescue worker from week 1, day 3? He was a human example of God's attribute of greatness. What do you see as the relationship between rescue and greatness?

PRAYER STARTERS

Use Psalm 105 (in which the psalmist praises and thanks God for a long list of rescues) to guide your prayer. Or compose (on paper or just in your head) a psalm of your own, identifying times that God has rescued you, whether from physical or spiritual danger.

GOD IS PROVIDING WHAT IS GOOD

SCRIPTURE

And we know that in all things God works for the good of those who love him.

—Romans 8:28 (NIV)

TEACHINGS

Q. What do you believe when you say,
     "I believe in God, the Father
     almighty, creator of heaven and earth"?

A. . . . I trust God so much that I do not doubt
          he will provide
          whatever I need
          for body and soul,
          and will turn to my good
              whatever adversity he sends me
          in this sad world.
     God is able to do this because he is almighty
          God
     and desires to do this because he is a faithful
          Father.

—Heidelberg Catechism Q&A 26

Every day you read about it online. Or see it on TV news. You read about and see evil.

Some evils are caused by human beings. We've experienced many of those personally. Someone cuts ahead of you to take the last parking spot. A person you thought was your friend spreads untrue rumors about you. A family is scarred by controlling or abusive relationships.

In the larger world that we read about or see on TV, human evils are as great or even greater. Every Christmas, it seems, we read about a family that scraped together enough money to buy their children a few gifts—only to find some night that a thief has stolen every one of them. I once read a news account of some robbers who burst into a Utah music store. One of the thugs forced customers to drink a caustic drain cleaner that burned their esophaguses and stomachs. Another stomped a ballpoint pen down through a man's eardrum into his skull.

Such things are so wicked and painful that we can hardly stand even to hear about them. But terrible events happen every day in our sinful world, and sooner or later we come to know it. One of the most notorious examples of human evil in the twentieth century is the Nazi holocaust, the slaughter of six million Jews in Europe in World War II. Some were starved or beaten or kicked to death. Others were machine-gunned so that they would topple over into the burial ditches they had been forced to dig for themselves. Some had to submit to medical experiments designed to see how much pain a human being could suffer before dying. Many, including children, were gassed and then incinerated.

Large numbers of these Jews believed in God. Over and over again they prayed. *Why?* they asked. Why is this happening? O God, why do you allow this? Some who suffered, or who saw the suffering, just quit believing in God.

While humans cause much of the evil in the world, fearful evils also happen in nature. Floods, earthquakes, tornadoes, drought, and hurricanes threaten millions. Some evils of nature happen in our own bodies. A person is born with brain damage. A child develops leukemia. A loved father or mother dies terribly of some other dreaded disease.

Once more, believers ask *why.* Sometimes they don't just ask it. They shout it or howl it or scream it into the night. If God is so great and good, if God acts in providence to preserve his children and rule his world, then *why?*

We do not always know. And it's foolish to pretend to know when we don't. We sometimes think we can tell what good reason God might have for allowing evil, but often we only guess. Maybe God allows people great freedom to do both evil and good because otherwise they wouldn't be humans at all, but only robots. Maybe God doesn't turn all guns into salami and all bullets into bubbles because then the world wouldn't be real and couldn't be counted on. Maybe God allows diseases and tornadoes to make us depend on him or to make us more courageous. Maybe God sometimes sends punishments on a whole nation. Or maybe there are times when a person's suffering—and the way he or she handles it—draws others closer to God.

It is hard to say in a particular case. Rarely, if ever, do we know exactly why God permits a certain evil. But we do know this: just as a doctor must sometimes hurt you in order to help you, so God is always working with us for good. Even when we can't see it or tell it. That is sometimes hard to accept. But no God, and no good, would be even harder to accept.

We know one more thing. Our Lord Jesus Christ himself, as he died inch by inch from his fatal wounds, shouted, "My God, my God, why have you forsaken me?"

Two days later he was alive again and speaking peace to his disciples. God *does* act against evil and for good. It is part of God's providence.

FOR REFLECTION

If you could ask God for the explanation of just one evil event, which one would it be?

PRAYER STARTERS

Ask God to provide, specifically "whatever you need for body and soul" (Q&A 26, above) or to bring something good out of an adverse experience you're currently going through.

GOD WILL PROVIDE CONTROL

SCRIPTURE

And Jesus came and said to them, "All authority in heaven and on earth has been given to me. Go therefore and make disciples of all nations, baptizing them in the name of the Father and of the Son and of the Holy Spirit, and teaching them to obey everything that I have commanded you. And remember, I am with you always, to the end of the age."

—Matthew 28:18-20

TEACHINGS

Even now,
as history unfolds
in ways we know only in part,
we are assured
that God is with us in our world,
holding all things in tender embrace
and bending them to his purpose.
The confidence that the Lord is faithful
gives meaning to our days
and hope to our years.
The future is secure,
for our world belongs to God.

—*Our World Belongs to God,* paragraph 12

If you're like most people, you are sometimes afraid. Our fears differ, but we all have them. You head off to a new job. You don't know what's there, or even who's there. You feel the flutterings of fear in your stomach. The same is true of getting used to a new home in a new neighborhood or getting used to a new stepparent.

Some people are afraid of high places, or closed-in places, or even wide-open places. They have phobias. Some kids are clutched with fear at the sight of asparagus or brussels sprouts. Some people are afraid to fly.

Many people are afraid of losing their health, or their job, or their spouse. And most of us are afraid of walking around in certain neighborhoods after dark. We're also afraid of some animals. And of some people. And of getting lost. When we are lost, a fear can rise up in us that becomes a panic if we do not fight it. In fact, it might be the panic, not the lostness, that ends up hurting us.

September 11, 2001, unleashed a new fear— new, at least, to most North Americans: terrorism. Before that day, you wouldn't have had to take off your shoes at the airport security check. You would have laughed at the idea of needing a passport to go between Canada and the United States. And Christian/Muslim relations would have been something you thought of only in the context of the Middle East—if you thought of them at all. Confronted with the images of the twin towers in flame, people who once thought,

"Nothing like that would ever happen where I live," aren't so sure any more.

One of the special treasures of the Christian faith is God's assurance that all events—even seemingly senseless acts of terrorism—are, in the end, redeemable. While God permits evil, he never causes it. God is always out to save. And God will not be thwarted. If God permits a terrorist attack, the result may be according to God's plan, though not according to his wish or desire for a perfect world. An event within God's providence can thus be in accord with his will in one way (it fits into his plan) but be contrary to his will in another (there are no senseless killings in a perfect world). Sin does strange and awful things to a world, even when a great and good God is in control.

God has acted in the past to rescue his people and continues in the present to work for good. In fact, he does both these things all the time. All along God works steadily through the rhythms of nature to preserve and support life. What God does is all part of his great world plan that centers in the work of Jesus Christ. And it stretches out into the future. God has a plan for "the fullness of time" to make sure the magnificent death and resurrection of Christ have the results God wants—peace and love and the final safety of God's people and his world.

What does this mean for *us?* It means we may be confident in spite of our fears. God is at work in our world by the Holy Spirit. God is speaking to the world by his Word. God is saving the world through his church. Over all, God is in control.

God *will* act in providence to bring his world and his children to the end he has in mind.

Will that include more terrorist attacks—perhaps even in your own neighborhood? We do not know. But we do know the world is in God's hands. We are therefore free to grow and love, marry and work, worship and serve. That is because we know that whatever happens, whatever and whomever we fear, nothing in the world can ever separate us from the love of God.

God is in control.

FOR REFLECTION

In what ways is your future "secure" (paragraph 12, above)? What gives you that confidence, or why do you suppose you lack it?

PRAYER STARTERS

Pray for God's control in specific current events. Or Google "news" and use the top stories to guide your prayer.

WEEK4

HOW CAN WE KNOW GOD?

GOD SPEAKS

SCRIPTURE

"Every valley shall be lifted up,
    and every mountain and hill be made low;
the uneven ground shall become level,
    and the rough places a plain.
Then the glory of the LORD shall be revealed,
    and all people shall see it together,
        for the mouth of the LORD has spoken."

—Isaiah 40:4-5

TEACHINGS

We know God by two means:
First, by the creation, preservation, and government
of the universe. . . .
Second, God makes himself known to us more
    clearly
by his holy and divine Word.

—Belgic Confession, Article 2

Suppose your friend calls you on the phone. Suppose the president or prime minister addresses the nation. Suppose a preacher delivers a sermon or a sports fan yells an insult or a teacher presents a lesson or a comedian tells a joke or a parent praises a child or a group discusses an idea or a sergeant barks a command or a TV announcer brings an "important message" about a new product—a combination dessert topping and floor wax.

What do all these people do? They *speak.*

Speaking is so common we don't even think about it. We begin speech so early in our lives that we cannot remember learning it. We hear so much speaking that we unconsciously tune out much of it.

Yet there are times when the power and importance of speech impress us. If you travel internationally, for instance, you may become frustrated because you cannot speak the language. Or if you have a speech or language difficulty, you may have to struggle to overcome it. If you think you must criticize something a person has said or done, you notice how important it is to choose your words carefully.

Speech is a gift of God to human beings. Animals cannot speak (or maybe it's just that they have poor enunciation). Speech lets us inform others. It lets us persuade, question, command, even entertain. By speech people have declared war, preserved history, confessed sin, preached the gospel, made promises, and greeted friends. Sometimes people speak just for the fun of it. And sometimes they misuse the powerful gift of speech by mocking another person or by taking God's name in vain or by telling a sneaky lie.

Speech is so important to how we think, feel, and act that ordinary human life would be unimaginable without it.

> **God's speaking:** God's communication to us. God speaks
> - In his world
> - In his word (including the Bible)
> - By his Son

The Bible tells us that God speaks. The same God who gives speech also speaks himself. We recall that God's speaking brings the world into existence. Over and over in Genesis 1 we read the words "And God said . . ." When God speaks, things happen.

God speaks in providence as well as in creation. Why? God wants to *get through* to his human creatures. Even after they rebel against him and fall into sin, God wants to be in touch with them, in fellowship with them. God is a personal, active, caring, saving, communicating God. And God's creatures cannot know his will or hear his plans or be frightened by his warnings or comforted by his forgiveness unless he speaks and they listen.

So the Bible is full of God's providential speaking. God gives commands and asks questions. God makes covenants and in wonderful ways promises a Savior. God calls prophets and appoints priests, judges, and kings. In the New Testament God the Father announces Jesus' birth and declares his love for him at Jesus' baptism (Luke 3:22). Jesus himself speaks for the Father and as his Son. He forgives sins, drives out demons, converses with his friends, comforts the poor, rebukes some of the Pharisees. After Jesus' resurrection the Holy Spirit teaches the disciples what to say and do.

God speaks. In creation and providence the Father, Son, and Spirit command, declare, question, comfort, teach, forgive.

But how? After all, even though our text for today says, "the mouth of the LORD has spoken," we know that God the Father does not really have a mouth. So how can God speak?

God has his ways. He arranges for people to have mysterious dreams and visions. He speaks through the beauty and design of his created world. He speaks by way of meaningful events. It seems in the Bible as though God sometimes speaks by creating thoughts in the minds of certain believers. In biblical times God spoke most often by sending someone to speak for him—a prophet, an apostle, a messenger, even his own Son. All of what these people say for God is the word of God; the part of their message that is written down in the Old and New Testaments is the Bible.

Does it still happen, do you think? Does God still speak?

FOR REFLECTION

Why does God choose to speak to us?

PRAYER STARTERS

Take time to have a conversation with God, not a monologue on your part. Ask him to speak to you and then be still, listening for God's response through the Scripture he brings to your mind.

GOD SPEAKS IN THE WORLD

SCRIPTURE

The heavens are telling the glory of God;
    and the firmament proclaims his handiwork.
Day to day pours forth speech,
    and night to night declares knowledge.
There is no speech, nor are there words;
    their voice is not heard;
yet their voice goes out through all the earth,
    and their words to the end of the world.
—Psalm 19:1-4

TEACHINGS

We know God by two means:
First, by the creation, preservation, and government
of the universe,
since that universe is before our eyes
like a beautiful book
    in which all creatures,
    great and small,
    are as letters
    to make us ponder
    the invisible things of God:
        God's eternal power and divinity. . . .
—Belgic Confession, Article 2

A young shepherd watches his flock by night. In the stillness of the long watch he leans on his staff and gazes into the evening sky. He sees hundreds of stars, maybe as many as two thousand. As always, some seem bright, some faint, a few hazy or milky. A number of stars appear to be doubled up with others. Parts of the sky look like great fields of stars, the individual lights combining into a huge cluster.

Here and there the shepherd thinks he spies star patterns that look like dippers, dragons, camels, or hunters. He observes that certain familiar stars appear in a different place than they did only a few months earlier. But from long experience he knows that when the seasons come around again, these stars will be back in the same section of sky where they used to be.

This particular night, while the shepherd watches, an eerie thing happens. Near the top of the quarter moon a brilliant star disappears behind the darkened part of the moon, only to reappear on the light side of it a few minutes later. The shepherd is awed, humbled, impressed. And into the Judean night he whispers the name of God.

As the hours pass, the shepherd waits for the sun to rise and his watch to end. Gradually the sky in the east lightens and blushes pink. Then the great flaming ball of light begins its climb. It seems full of fire and excitement for a new day. It is like an eager runner, straining at his starting blocks. Or it is like a joyful young husband who comes out of his dark tent and stretches his arms toward the sky and the new day in his life. Glancing at the climbing sun that will soon bathe everything in its inescapable heat, the shepherd once more turns his thoughts to God.

Day and night. Light and darkness. Sun and stars. The shepherd thinks about them. Are not these the things God made by speaking at creation? And now here they still are for us to see and feel—great, silent things full of God's mystery and beauty. They are so regular you can plan your life by them. Surely something of God comes through in the watches of the night or in the heat of the noontime. At last the shepherd sits down to turn his thoughts into a song:

The heavens are telling the glory of God;
    and the firmament proclaims his handiwork.
Day to day pours forth speech,
    and night to night declares knowledge.

So it is for us. God speaks in his world. In the design of the evening sky, in the color and variety of 685,000 kinds of insects, in the growth of 250,000 species of plants, in the birth of a human child whose tiny ears are shaped to catch the sound of a mother's voice—in all these things, and in countless others, God speaks.

God speaks his power in the endless crashing of surf against coastal cliffs. God speaks his reliability in the regular rhythm of day and night, light and darkness. God speaks his providential care in the design of grasshoppers that look like leaves to their enemies and in the hitchhiking of young beetles who get to their homes on the backs of bees. A number of Christians have suggested that God speaks his sense of humor in the design of the duckbilled platypus, one of the earth's oddest-looking mammals.

God speaks in his world. And his world includes us. From the incredible complexity of our brains to the simplicity of our little toes our bodies reveal the thought and work of God. But God also speaks in our thoughts and feelings. That is why we long for him even when we do not know it. That is why we do not find it hard to believe in God even though we cannot see him. That is why we know the difference between right and wrong.

God speaks in us.

FOR REFLECTION

If God speaks through creation, why doesn't everyone believe in him?

PRAYER STARTERS

Think back on your day. Where in God's world today have you seen evidence of God's speaking to you? Give thanks and praise for those things.

GOD SPEAKS IN HIS WORD

SCRIPTURE

"For as the rain and the snow
　　come down from heaven,
and do not return there
　　until they have watered the earth,
making it bring forth and sprout,
　　giving seed to the sower and bread to the
　　　　eater,
so shall my word be that goes out from my mouth;
　　it shall not return to me empty,
but it shall accomplish that which I purpose,
and succeed in the thing for which I sent it."
—Isaiah 55:10-11

TEACHINGS

Second, God makes himself known to us more openly
by his holy and divine Word,
as much as we need in this life,
　　for God's glory
　　and for our salvation.
—Belgic Confession, Article 2

As we have seen and heard, God speaks in the world. In the beauty, order, and caretaking of nature God declares his goodness, greatness, and sovereignty. In our own human longing for God and in our knowledge of right and wrong, God says that we belong to him and that he wants us to act like his children. In other words,

God's speaking and acting reveal who God is and what God wants.

God speaks in his world. But he also speaks in his Word. Are the two kinds of speaking connected?

They are. We can see how they are connected by looking at the Bible text for today.

> **God's Word:** What God says in his speaking. Some of what God says is written down in the Bible. That's why the Bible is sometimes called "God's Word."

In the Isaiah text for today, God first talks about rain and snow, and about the water that descends from the clouds. What does it do? It moistens the dry earth so that corn, wheat, rye, soybeans, and other nourishing things can sprout and grow. The grains we eat in cereals and bread come up from the earth because water comes down from heaven. One *purpose* of rain is the watering of crops. If the earth is saturated, the water that collects in ponds and field puddles does not ordinarily evaporate back into the atmosphere until it has done its life-giving work. The falling and rising of water tell us that God is good and that he wants to preserve life on the earth.

In the same way, says God in verse 11 that his word comes to earth from heaven, accomplishes its purpose, and then returns to him. In world and word there is the same pattern. Things come from God, do their work, and return to him. Their mission is accomplished.

But what is the purpose or mission of God's speaking in his Word? Why doesn't God just speak in his world? After all, we can tell a great deal about God from what he says in his world. Isn't that enough?

No. The reason it isn't enough can be stated simply and sadly: human beings have sinned and fallen away from God. They have lost their ability to see and hear God clearly in his world.

One of the terrible things about sin is that it blinds us to God's glory in creation and providence. It also deafens us so that we can no longer hear God speak. That is why people look at the starry sky without thinking of God. Or people listen to the wind moving mysteriously through the trees and do not hear the voice of God.

Sin has blinded and deafened us to God. But the fall into sin way back at the beginning of history has also interfered somehow with creation itself. Things in nature are no longer perfectly good. The rain and snow that come down from heaven sometimes cause terrible floods. Or sometimes they quit coming altogether. Then fields dry up, topsoil blows away, and people suffer from drought and famine. We and all the rest of creation have been badly damaged by sin.

That is why God speaks not only in his world but also in his Word. God wants to get through to us. So he sends prophets and preachers to warn us, challenge us, comfort us. More clearly than nature can, these people tell us who God is and what he wants. They spell it out. They especially tell us something nature never could—how we can be saved from sin. They bring the saving Word of God. Isaiah is a prophet who does this. Your own pastor is a preacher who does it. Isaiah preaches in the Bible. Your pastor preaches from the Bible.

God speaks in his Word. By influencing certain human beings to say what he wants them to say, God addresses us. He questions and commands. He announces his rescue plan. Then we respond to God by answering, obeying, and praising him.

In this way the Word of God accomplishes its purpose. It does not return to God empty but accomplishes what he desires and achieves the purpose for which he sends it.

FOR REFLECTION

If you didn't have God's Word and the only way you could learn about God was through his world, what misconceptions might you have about God?

PRAYER STARTERS

Psalm 119 is one long prayer about God's Word. Use one of the sections as your prayer. Or imitate the psalmist by writing out what you want to say to God.

GOD SPEAKS BY HIS SON

SCRIPTURE

In the beginning was the Word, and the Word was with God, and the Word was God. He was in the beginning with God. . . . And the Word became flesh and lived among us, and we have seen his glory, the glory as of a father's only son, full of grace and truth.

—John 1:1, 2, 14

TEACHINGS

God gives this world
many ways to know him.
The creation shows his power and majesty.
He speaks through prophets, poets, and apostles,
and, most eloquently, through the Son.
The Spirit, active from the beginning,
moved human beings to write the Word of God
and opens our hearts to God's voice.

—*Our World Belongs to God,* paragraph 31

When poets want to compare two things, they often use a metaphor. They say things like this: "The road was a ribbon that wound around the mountain." Or, "Morning is a new sheet of paper for you to write on." Or even, "The Lord is my shepherd."

A metaphor compares two things that are otherwise not very much alike. Poets aren't the only ones who use metaphors. Everyone does. In fact, some metaphors have become so common we hardly notice that they are comparisons: "He's a star." "He's a pig." "This car's a lemon." "You're off-base" (or off-track, or off your rocker). "It's in the bag." "This reading is a piece of cake." Such metaphors must be puzzling to those who are just learning the English language!

But, puzzling or not, metaphors are useful things. When they are new to us, they help us see an object or a person in a fresh way. They delight us with a pleasing or surprising comparison.

The Bible is full of metaphors. Our bodies, for example, are called "temples of the Holy Spirit" (1 Cor. 6:19). The Word of God is compared to a "double-edged sword" that cuts us to the heart (Heb. 4:12). Faith is said to be a "shield" against everything Satan can throw at us (Eph. 6:16).

Some of the best and most interesting metaphors in the Bible have to do with God and God's Spirit. For example, as stated above, "The Lord is my shepherd" is a famous metaphor. But in the Bible God is also compared to a rock (Ps. 18:2); to flowing streams of water (Ps. 42:1); to fire (Heb. 12:29); to a bird (Ps. 17:8); to a nursing mother (Isa. 49:15); to a husband (Hos. 2:16); and to human fathers, kings, judges, and lords. The Spirit of God is compared to a wind (John 3:8).

So it is with Jesus Christ. The Bible uses a number of metaphors for him, especially in the gospel of John. Jesus is "the light of the world" (1:9). He is "the bread of life" (6:35). He is a grapevine (15:1). And, as our text says, Jesus is the Word of God.

What could that metaphor mean? How could a person be like a word?

Let's see. Suppose someone said, "Do you want to know what intelligence is? Think of Albert Einstein!" "Do you want to know what wickedness is? Think of Hitler!" "Do you want to know what honesty is? Think of Abe Lincoln!" Do you see what is going on here? We connect a person with a certain word if the person is a striking example of what the word means. A word can be *lived out* or *embodied* in a person. Honesty, for instance, was embodied in Abe Lincoln.

Jesus as God's Word: Everything important about God is "lived out" by his Son, Jesus Christ. That's why he is sometimes called the Word of God.

Now let's try some of our questions again. Do you want to know what truthfulness is? Think of Jesus Christ. All the words and qualities—all the attributes—that apply to God may be seen in action in the life of Jesus. Love, goodness, and greatness are embodied in him. These qualities, as the Bible puts it, "became flesh and lived for a while among us." In fact, whatever God wants to say to us is said by the life and teaching of Jesus. God's *Word* to us is this person. God speaks by the Son of God.

What does God say by way of Jesus? When Jesus calmed a storm, it was God's way of saying he is sovereign over nature. When Jesus multiplied bread and fish to feed a great crowd, it was God's way of saying that he would nourish his people and care for them. When Jesus was nailed to a tree by wicked people, God told how great human sin is. But he also tells us that his love and power to overcome it are even greater.

God speaks in his world. God speaks in his Word. God speaks especially by his Son. And what God says by his Son is the greatest story ever told.

FOR REFLECTION

Stanza 31 at the beginning of this reading says that God speaks "most eloquently through the Son." In what ways is Jesus a "more eloquent" revelation of God than creation and the Bible?

PRAYER STARTERS

Use Psalm 119:9-16 to shape your prayer (again, if you used it with the previous reading), replacing "word" with "Jesus."

WEEK 5

WHAT'S THE GOOD WORD?

THE BREATH OF GOD

SCRIPTURE

But as for you, continue in what you have learned and have become convinced of, because you know those from whom you learned it, and how from infancy you have known the Holy Scriptures, which are able to make you wise for salvation through faith in Christ Jesus. All Scripture is God-breathed.

—2 Timothy 3:14-16 (NIV)

TEACHINGS

We confess that this Word of God
was not sent nor delivered "by human will,"
but that "men and women moved by the Holy
　　Spirit spoke from God,"
　　as Peter says.
Afterward our God—
　　with special care
　　for us and our salvation—
commanded his servants, the prophets and
　　apostles,
to commit this revealed Word to writing.

—Belgic Confession, Article 3

During the Vietnam War many American soldiers were captured and imprisoned by the enemy. One group of soldiers told part of their story when they were finally released. They told how they had been painfully beaten up. They described stinking food and miserable sleeping conditions. They recalled how many times they had prepared themselves to die, certain that their enemies would either torture them to death or else casually shoot them through the brain.

One additional agony these prisoners suffered was loneliness. Their captors purposely kept them apart so they could not encourage each other or plan escapes. Each prisoner had to sit in his own cell. There was nothing to do, nothing to read, nobody to talk to.

But a number of these prisoners were Christians. And as they sat on the floor of their cells, fearful and lonely, they tried as hard as they could to recall passages of Scripture they had memorized when they were young. One man could recall Psalm 23. Another knew several other psalms and the Beatitudes. A number of prisoners remembered John 3:16. And a few knew a lot more.

Gradually they worked out a system of communication. They would tap in code on the walls that separated their cells. At first they tapped names, addresses, and simple greetings. Then they tapped encouragement. They tapped warnings. And they tapped out as many Bible verses and passages as they knew, each man adding as much as he could recall to the general treasury of Scripture.

By the time these Christians were released, they had put together hundreds of verses of Scripture. They had assembled their own Bible. One of them later said that this activity saved their sanity and probably their lives.

The apostle Paul knew what it was like to be in prison. He also knew what it took to encourage another Christian. So Paul writes to Timothy, "Continue in what you have learned . . . how from infancy you have known the Holy Scriptures." Then he adds a strange claim. "All Scripture," he says, "is God-breathed."

The first few words present no problem. "Scripture" means writing, and "Bible" means book. The Bible is therefore a book of writings. It's the part of God's Word that is written down and treasured by the church.

But what does that second part of Paul's sentence mean? "All Scripture is God-breathed." Does Paul picture God as taking a big breath and then exhaling the words of Scripture? Or does he picture the Scriptures as already written and then God blowing into them the breath of life to make them lively and helpful? Whatever picture Paul has in mind, he is talking about the *inspiration* of Scripture.

> **Inspiration of Scripture:** the process by which God "breathed" into the biblical writers what he wanted them to write. God moved, influenced, inspired them by the Holy Spirit. The same Holy Spirit now inspires us to receive and believe the Bible.

What he means is this: for over a thousand years God breathed his thoughts and words into human writers. From the earliest book of the Bible to the latest, God inspired the Bible's writers. Some were history writers. Some were poets. Some wrote laws and lists or put down collections of wise sayings. Some wrote about the life of Jesus. Others were letter writers. None of these writers was perfect. All used their own language and style. Each colored what he wrote with some of his own personality. But deep in the hearts and minds of these writers God was at work, influencing them, moving them, inspiring them.

The result is God's breathed-out Word, the Bible. Just as a lifeguard resuscitates a nearly drowned swimmer, so God breathes life into dying human beings by his written Word. The Bible tells people of God's presence, God's purpose, God's Son, and our salvation.

That is why prisoners of war struggle to recall it. That is also why it speaks to you and me. The Scriptures are the very breath of God.

FOR REFLECTION

If you were isolated in a POW camp, how much of the Bible would you be able to recall? Are there any passages that you would find especially meaningful in that situation?

PRAYER STARTERS

Ask the God who inspired Scripture to inspire you to hear him speaking through that Scripture.

LISTEN! GOD IS SPEAKING

SCRIPTURE

Above all, you must understand that no prophecy of Scripture came about by the prophet's own interpretation of things. For prophecy never had its origin in the human will, but prophets, though human, spoke from God as they were carried along by the Holy Spirit.

—2 Peter 1:20-21(NIV)

TEACHINGS

We receive all these books
and these only
as holy and canonical,
for the regulating, founding, and establishing
of our faith.

—Belgic Confession, Article 5

New Englanders tell a story about an old man who lived outside a certain town. This man was an expert electrician. In fact, when he was young, he designed the electrical system for the town. He figured out how lines and circuits could best be arranged to bring cheap and plentiful electrical energy to the town's citizens.

But the townspeople did not treat the man well. When he got to a certain age, they fired him and replaced him with younger electricians. In effect, the town told the old man to get lost. So he moved out to a nearby woods. Nobody saw him or heard from him.

Then, one day, the town's power failed. Lights flickered and went out. Refrigerators warmed up. Heaters cooled down. TV sets went dark and silent. The town was in a panic. And none of its young electricians seemed to know how to solve the problem.

Then one of the town commissioners remembered the old man in the woods. Possibly *he* could find a way to restore power. He was an authority on the town's electrical system. After all, he had thought it up in the first place.

So the old man was brought to the central power plant. He walked around slowly for a few moments, shining his flashlight here and there. Finally he pulled a little hammer out of his pocket, walked over to one main circuit, and tapped on it. Instantly the lights went on and power surged through the whole system. The old man went back to his home in the woods.

Three weeks later the mayor received a bill. On it the old man charged the town $1000.05 for his work. This is how he listed the charges:

$0.05 tapping
$1000 knowing where to tap

The old man was an authority on the town's power system. Why? Because he was its author. The system *came* from him.

The Christian church says the Bible is the authority for our faith and our lives. Why? Because God is its author. The Bible gets its authority from its author. What the Bible says, God says. That is why the Bible is an expert on how we must think and act. That is why the Bible has power to influence and help us. That is why the Bible has the right to give us orders that we must obey. *God* speaks through the Bible. And of course God is the supreme authority in the universe. After all, he thought it up in the first place.

> **Authority of Scripture**: The power of the Bible to influence our believing and acting. Because the Bible is our authority, it can even give commands that we must obey. The Bible is authoritative because God is its author and because only in the Bible do we find Jesus Christ, our rescuer.

The Scriptures are like one of the speakers in a radio or TV set. If the president or prime minister addresses us, we hear the address through one or two of those speakers. But the speaker by itself is not authoritative for us. The real authority is instead the person who communicates to us *through* the speaker.

So it is with the Scriptures. As our text says, the Scriptures do not come just from people. Human writers do not themselves have the power to help or command us. Instead, prophets "spoke from God" as they were carried along, or inspired, by the Holy Spirit.

That's why Christians study the Bible and take it so seriously. It's God's speaker. It speaks with God's authority. Christians are people who stand in the world with this *book* in their hands. We obey its commands. We open ourselves up to its comfort. We thrill to its great passages of hope. And through the Bible we come to know Jesus Christ, our Savior.

Even Jesus himself read and obeyed the Bible. So must we. It is our authority because of its author.

FOR REFLECTION

Not everyone appreciates authority—at least when someone else has authority over them. What are some positive things about the authority of Scripture?

PRAYER STARTERS

Ask for the grace to submit to God's authority through the Bible.

THE BOOK THAT CANNOT FAIL

SCRIPTURE

Jesus answered them, "Is it not written in your Law, 'I have said you are "gods"'? If he called them 'gods,' to whom the word of God came—and the Scripture cannot be set aside—what about the one whom the Father set apart as his very own and sent into the world?"

—John 10:34-36 (NIV)

TEACHINGS

Therefore we must not consider human writings—
 no matter how holy their authors may have
  been—
equal to the divine writings. . . .
For all human beings are liars by nature
and more vain than vanity itself.
Therefore we reject with all our hearts
everything that does not agree
with this infallible rule . . .

—Belgic Confession, Article 7

The marathon is a twenty-six-mile race for endurance runners. It tests a person's speed, stamina, courage, and even intelligence. To win a marathon a person obviously needs speed. But a marathon runner needs stamina as well. He or she also needs courage to endure pain. And a marathon runner needs intelligence in order to make up and follow a "race plan"—that is, a strategy that will actually win the race.

But runners are only human. Some make mistakes in their race plan. Others follow their race plan perfectly—except for the part at the end that calls for them to cross the finish line first. These runners simply lack winning speed, stamina, or courage. So a few of them try to cheat. In the 1972 Olympics at Munich, a runner sneaked into the race at mile twenty-five. He had not bothered to run the first twenty-four miles. This, of course, gave him a small advantage. He used it to cross the finish line first, but he did not win the race. He was disqualified as a cheater.

The fact is that most runners do not win. By cheating, or by making a strategy mistake, or simply by failing to keep up, a runner can easily fall short of his or her goal. Runners are not *infallible*.

The Bible is. When the church says in its confessions that the Scriptures are infallible, it means three things. It means, first, that the Bible does not cheat or deceive us. It means, second, that the Bible makes no mistakes in bringing God's Word to us. In the third place it means that the Bible does not fail to reach its goal. The Bible, if we may say so reverently, is a winner.

> **Infallibility of Scripture:** the quality of the Bible that means it will not fail. By the Bible's unfailingness or infallibility we mean that it does not deceive us, make mistakes in presenting God's word, or fail to reach its goal of helping people get saved and then lead thankful lives.

Let's take these meanings of infallibility one at a time, First, the Bible does not cheat or deceive us. It is honest and truthful. In this respect the Bible differs from a lot of other books. Many books, after all, tell us lies. Some say it is OK to hurt someone if it will help you get what you want. A number of books suggest that making a great deal of money is the best thing to do with your life. Some books give twisted accounts of love and sex. Human beings often lie. Some of the clever ones publish their lies in books.

But the Bible is truthful. It comes from human beings, but ultimately it comes from God. And God doesn't lie. We can therefore depend on the Scriptures.

Second, the Bible makes no mistakes in bringing God's Word to us. It makes no error in doing this. We therefore say that it is "inerrant." Like a runner who makes and follows a perfect race plan, the Scriptures faithfully present Jesus Christ and God's rescue plan for fallen people.

This does not mean, of course, that there are only plain, boring facts in the Bible and no personal interpretations of these facts or interesting stories about them. As we know, the Bible uses parables, stories, and metaphors. Matthew, Mark, Luke, and John offer four accounts of Jesus, each a little different from the others. And we know that the Bible writers lived in the ancient world. They believed that the sun revolves around the earth and that the earth is flat. No matter. So far as the message of the Bible is concerned, its Scriptures make no mistake.

Third, the Bible does not fail or fall down in reaching its goal. It achieves God's purpose of helping to save believing women, men, children, and teens of every race and of all times and places. That is, besides being honest and accurate, the Bible is effective. It works. People get rescued by taking the Bible's message to heart. They also learn how to please and thank their rescuer.

The Scriptures, as our text says, cannot be "broken." They cannot fail, or fall, or falter, or be false. They are the infallible Word of God.

And they are meant for you and me.

FOR REFLECTION

Can you identify from your own experience evidence that the Bible is infallible—that is, true, without error, and effective? Is there anything in the Bible that makes you question its infallibility?

PRAYER STARTERS

The early church father Jerome (c 347–September 30, A.D. 420) translated the Bible from Greek and Hebrew into Latin. He also gave us this prayer:

Lord, thou hast given us thy Word for a light to shine upon our path;
grant us so to meditate on that Word, and to follow its teaching,
that we may find in it the light that shines more and more until the perfect day;
through Jesus Christ our Lord.

OUR GUIDE FOR LIVING

SCRIPTURE

All scripture is inspired by God and is useful for teaching, for reproof, for correction, and for training in righteousness, so that everyone who belongs to God may be proficient, equipped for every good work.

—2 Timothy 3:16-17

TEACHINGS

The Bible is the Word of God,
the record and tool of his redeeming work.
It is the Word of truth,
breath of God,
fully reliable in leading us
to know God
and to walk with Jesus Christ
in new life.

—*Our World Belongs to God,* paragraph 32

One of my friends told me about a man who was packing for a long trip. The man's wife asked him if he was ready to go. "Almost," he said. "But there is still a corner in one suitcase to fill with what's left: a guidebook, a lamp, a mirror, a hammer, a book of good poetry, a bundle of old letters, a hymn book, a sharp sword, and a small library of sixty-six volumes."

"But how will you get all *that* in your suitcase?" his wife asked. "Like this," said the man, as he placed his Bible in the few inches of remaining space and then closed the suitcase.

What this story tells us, of course, is that the Bible is many things at once. And it has many *uses:* it guides us, lights up the world through which we walk, reflects the face of God like a mirror, teaches us the early history of Israel, and so on.

Some people use the Bible in ways never intended by its writers. For example, some people carry a pocket Bible for good luck. Some treat the Bible as though it were a magic crystal ball or a deck of fortune-telling cards: they close their eyes, flip Bible pages at random, and let their finger drop blindly to a place on some page. Underneath their finger is the text they will use to guide their decisions for the day. (What do you do if the text says something like "And Uz was the brother of Buz"?)

A few people spend their time fooling around with the Bible, thinking, for example, about who was the shortest man in the Bible (either Bildad the Shuhite, or else the Roman soldier who slept on his watch). Some people even make up sports quizzes about where the Bible refers to such things as tennis ("Joseph served in Pharaoh's court") or baseball ("In the big inning"), and so on.

But all this is foolishness. Responsible Christians do not use the Bible for things outside its purpose. The Bible is not a handy guide to boat building, animal habits, astronomy, or the exact age of the earth. Surely the Bible is not our magic book or fortune teller.

So what *is* the Bible for? What are its proper uses?

First, the Bible tells us the truth about God, the world, and how they are related to each other. The Bible is a kind of tourist's guide to the universe. We read the Bible to become informed, to get good information about who God is and who we are in God's world. Our task is to receive and believe this information.

Second, the Bible tells us not only what to believe but also how to behave. The two are connected. For instance, it is because we believe that God is great and good that we worship him and seek to imitate him by being good to others—especially those who are unpopular and weak. As our text for today says, the Bible teaches and trains us in righteousness. It is like an athlete's training manual or a runner's race plan. Our task is to follow the manual.

Third, the Bible lifts us and helps us with our problems. The same Holy Spirit who inspired the Scriptures now inspires us when we read them so that we are filled with hope. The Bible encourages believers. Our task is to take such encouragement to heart.

Fourth, as we mature, the Scriptures guide us to become intelligent citizens, to spend our money properly, to choose a job and mate in a Christian way, and so forth. Of course, the Bible cannot answer all our questions. For example, it cannot tell us which person to marry or whom to vote for in an election. But it can tell us what sort of person to marry or vote for. In this way the Bible is a guide to all of life. Our task is to let it lead us.

Finally, the Bible is the book that helps us become personally close to God, our Father, and Jesus Christ, our Savior. We must therefore trust them and give ourselves over to them.

For all these reasons we must read and know the Scriptures. The Scriptures are the main place in which the God of the universe speaks. And when God speaks, we must listen and believe.

FOR REFLECTION

How are you using the Bible?

PRAYER STARTERS

One of the uses of the Bible is to encourage us and help us with our problems. Bring those problems to God now, asking him to bring you help and encouragement through his Word during the coming week.

UNIT 2

OUR NEED FOR A SAVIOR

WEEK 6

WHAT IS WRONG WITH US?

WHAT IS WRONG WITH US?

SCRIPTURE

So when the woman saw that the tree was good for food, and that it was a delight to the eyes, and that the tree was to be desired to make one wise, she took of its fruit and ate.

—Genesis 3:6

TEACHINGS

In the beginning of human history,
our first parents walked with God.
But rather than living by the Creator's word of life,
they listened to the serpent's lie
and fell into sin.

—*Our World Belongs to God,* paragraph 13

Something is wrong with us human beings, and we know it. All we need to do is catch the daily news on TV or online to know things aren't right. On a quiet summer afternoon in my hometown, a man driven by anger and drugs murders his wife and daughter and then guns down five others before killing himself. Halfway around the world in Kabul, Afghanistan, a Taliban suicide bomber rams his vehicle into a crowded NATO bus, killing seventeen people. A Wall Street broker bilks investors of millions of dollars. A prominent politician posts explicit pictures of himself online. A drunk driver careens over a curb and smashes into a child on a tricycle.

On it goes, day after day, year after year, all across the country, all around the world. We are talking, of course, about sin and misery. Together they make up what we call *evil.* Nobody can miss evil. Everybody knows about it. As a matter of fact, all of us who read this know about evil from our own experience. Sometimes we suffer from it; sometimes we make others suffer from it.

> **Evil:** the combination of sin and misery that we see in the world around us. Evil originated in the angel world but comes to us through the fall of Adam and Eve.

Why? After all, everybody knows that evil things are hurtful. So why don't people just stop doing them?

Experts guess at the reasons. Some say the reason we hurt each other is that we are ignorant people, unaware of how to live the right way. Education, they insist, is what we need to make us more fully human.

But that is not the right answer. As we know from our own experience, people know some of the things they do are hurtful but do them anyway. And education is not the solution to our problem. Wrongly used, it just turns dull criminals into smart ones.

Others say that what's wrong with us is our inability to get what we want—money, for example, or a feeling of power over others, or personal freedom to do as we please. So we are frustrated and angry and show it by the hurtful ways we act. These people believe that more money or power or freedom will solve our problems.

But that is not right either. In the first place, if people want money or power or freedom, they will have to take them from others. Then *those* people will be frustrated and angry. In the second place, most people who get what they want are still not satisfied. They keep wanting more money or power or freedom, thus raising the same old problem all over again.

Christians believe what the Bible teaches—that there is a better and deeper explanation of human trouble with sin and misery. The first human beings were created good. In fact, they were made to image God by being powerful rulers, loving companions, and joyfully obedient children of God.

But they sinned. They stumbled and fell. And like a chain of dominoes, all of us who come after them have been toppled by their fall. We stand or fall together.

> **The fall:** the event in which our first parents disobeyed God and thus brought evil into the world.

Or think of it like this: parents pass on certain traits to their children. Your eye, skin, and hair color, for instance, come from your parents or, through them, from your grandparents. Even some diseases can be inherited.

The tendency to do wrong instead of right is something like that. Like a hereditary disease, it is passed down through the generations. We are born with it. And every day we see, read about, or suffer the symptoms of our human disease: lying, stealing, murder, war, terrorism, divorce, ridicule.

Here is yet another way to think of it: the human race is like a great palace in ruins. We were built by a master builder. You can still see some of the soaring greatness and noble goodness that were built in. In fact, that is why everybody in our world wishes things were different from the way they are. People remember what our house used to be like.

But we have wrecked our house. We now see crumbling, sagging, rusting, and ruin. And we seem powerless to fix these things. Every repair we make needs repairs itself.

If only the master builder would come back! Without him, the human story can only be called a tragedy.

FOR REFLECTION

What evidence of sin and misery do you see in your own world: your community, workplace, school or campus, home?

PRAYER STARTERS

Talk to God about areas of your life that are plagued by sin and misery, about concerns that trouble you today. Ask for God's healing, grace, and mercy.

LISTENING TO THE GREAT DECEIVER

SCRIPTURE

But the serpent said to the woman, "You will not die; for God knows that when you eat of it your eyes will be opened, and you will be like God, knowing good and evil."

—Genesis 3:4-5

TEACHINGS

In the beginning of human history,
our first parents walked with God.
But rather than living by the Creator's word of life,
they listened to the serpent's lie
and fell into sin.

—*Our World Belongs to God,* paragraph 13

Have you ever noticed that evil is frequently advertised as good? When people want you to do something wrong, they hardly ever say, "Try it! You'll hate it! It's a rotten thing to do!" They never suggest that you lie or cheat or steal or hook up with someone just because it's wrong and hurtful. They never advertise some foolish or useless thing as being foolish and useless.

No, people dress up evil as good. They put a good face on it. They say, "Try it! You'll like it!" They say, "Let's do it just for the fun of it." They say that if you lie you'll protect yourself. If you steal you'll enrich yourself. If you cheat you'll get ahead. If you hook up with someone you'll have all the fun of sex without the hassle of commitment. To complicate the situation, it's true that fun, protection, riches, getting ahead, and sex *can* all be good things.

Evil imitates good. It cannot show its true face. Evil always wears a mask. We see this already near the beginning of the human story. Part of the tragedy of the fall is that Adam and Eve listen to the Great Deceiver. (Genesis calls him a serpent, but according to Revelation 12:9 he is really Satan or the devil.) The Great Deceiver's best trick is to make evil sound good. He could sell kryptonite to Superman.

As we know, the first human beings were free and full of bliss in loving and serving God. The only thing God did not permit them to do was eat fruit from a mysterious tree called "the tree of the knowledge of good and evil."

It is on this tree that the Great Deceiver centers his sales pitch. Look, he says to Eve, God wants to keep all the power for himself. *God* wants to decide what's good and what's evil. That is why he put this tree off limits. If God says eating its fruit will be the death of you, he lies. God just wants to protect himself. God is a liar, says Satan, "for God knows that when you eat of it your eyes will be opened, and you will be like God, knowing good and evil" (Gen. 3:5).

Can we step back from these familiar words and see what is going on here? It's the oldest trick in the world. It's dressing up evil as good. Satan, the Great Deceiver, points out all the good things you will get if you disobey God. "Your eyes will be opened" and you will "know good and evil." What Satan means is that you will be able to *decide for yourself* what is good and what is evil. You can make your own rules, run your own garden, do what you want.

In this, says Satan, "you will be like God." And who doesn't sometimes want to play God, or be God, or be like God? It's the top position in the universe! Satan conveniently forgets to mention, of course, that Adam and Eve are already like God. They have been made in God's image and likeness.

> **Tragedy of the fall:** the fact that the fall happens not to less important creatures (whose fall wouldn't matter so much) but to people made in God's image. The fall is also tragic because it includes trickery, foolishness, and pride and has disastrous, long-term consequences.

So the Great Deceiver sets his trap. The bait is something that, like all bait, looks good. The well-being of the human race now depends on whom Eve believes. Will she trust the God who made her and who awakened her to all the light, peace, and joy of life in God's world? Or will she trust the devil, who is all dressed up in his borrowed Halloween costume?

We know what happened. We also know it still happens all the time. Evil imitates good. Kidnappers disguise themselves as trusted adults, perhaps as police officers or family friends. Child molesters tell their victims they love them and that the two of them share a special secret. Liars insist they are telling the truth. Thieves and cheats pretend they are winners. Blogs present silly or violent people as heroes.

Satan himself, says Paul, still "masquerades as an angel of light" (2 Cor. 11:14). When you trust and obey the Great Deceiver, sooner or later you become his slave. This too is part of the human tragedy.

FOR REFLECTION

What parts of your life are most vulnerable to lies and evil masked as good?

PRAYER STARTERS

Ask God to help you unmask deception and evil, so that you can see it as it really is. Look to God for the only true good to be found in the world.

GREAT PRETENDERS

SCRIPTURE

Pride goes before destruction,
    and a haughty spirit before a fall.

—Proverbs 16:18

TEACHINGS

Fallen in that first sin,
we prove each day
that apart from grace
we are guilty sinners. . . .
Looking for life without God,
we find death;
grasping for freedom outside the law,
we trap ourselves in Satan's snares;
pursuing pleasure,
we lose the gift of joy.

—*Our World Belongs to God,* paragraph 14

Satan is a great deceiver. But humans are great pretenders. Everyone pretends now and then to be someone she isn't. Most of the time this is harmless or fun. You imitate someone else's voice or style of clothing. You imagine yourself winning the Boston Marathon or the national lottery. You talk confidently about a subject you really know nothing about. Do any of these things, and you are a pretender. Actors are pretenders. Some politicians are pretenders. Some students who say they're late for class because their alarm didn't go off are pretenders.

Pretending is often full of good humor. But sometimes it isn't. When most countries had kings instead of presidents or prime ministers, pretenders were a problem. It was very important to protect the king (especially if he was a good one) from pretenders. Who were these dangerous people? They were persons who tried to unseat the king and enthrone themselves. Sometimes pretenders would gather an army and try to fight the king. Sometimes they would make foolish campaign promises to the people. A pretender would lay claim to the king's throne. That is, he would pretend to be king himself. A good example of a pretender in the Bible is King David's handsome son Absalom.

The story of the fall in Genesis is the story of human pretenders to God's throne. This is one of those times when pretending is not funny. The Great Deceiver tells our first parents that they can "be like God, knowing good and evil." As we have seen, this is a promise that they can decide for themselves what is good and what is evil. That is, it is a promise that Adam and Eve can take God's place.

Trembling with ambition, our first parents pretend to be God. The sad result of this foolishness is the fall heard 'round the world. It turned out Adam and Eve could not handle the position of

God. They were not up to it. They were, after all, only human.

What is so tragic about this? Adam and Eve pretend to be someone they are not. Like someone who boasts about his sky-high SAT score—and then has to admit that he was stretching things more than a little—the first human beings try pathetically to go beyond their limit. They are tripped up by pride. They fall for pride. That is, they try to go beyond who they are (*images* of God) and be someone they are not (God).

Pride goes before destruction,
    and a haughty spirit before a fall
        (Prov. 16:18).

We have seen this kind of falling all around us. Someone boasts that he has a date lined up with one of the most popular women on campus; skeptical friends find out she has never even heard of the would-be Romeo. A friend claims to know exactly how to rid your computer of its virus but succeeds only in passing along the malware to everyone in your address book. A Facebook profile grossly exaggerates someone's athletic feats or musical ability. And on it goes.

We human beings want so much to be great that we fool ourselves into thinking we are like God. This is a sad and sorry part of the human tragedy. For the truth is that we *are* great if only we do not try to be great pretenders.

Our greatness shines out instead when we reach for God and call him "Father."

FOR REFLECTION

In what area are you tempted to "be" something you're not?

PRAYER STARTERS

Read Philippians 2:5-11. Think about how Christ, the Lord of heaven and earth, "humbled himself." Ask God to help you set aside your pride. Then lift your hands to God and simply say "Father," acknowledging that you are God's son or daughter.

NAKEDNESS AND CLOTHING

SCRIPTURE

And the man and his wife were both naked, and were not ashamed. . . . Then the eyes of both were opened, and they knew they were naked; and they sewed fig leaves together and made loincloths for themselves. . . . And the LORD God made garments of skins for the man and for his wife, and clothed them.

—Genesis 2:25; 3:7, 21

TEACHINGS

In their rebellion
they tried to be like God.
As sinners Adam and Eve feared
the nearness of God
and hid.

—*Our World Belongs to God,* paragraph 13

The fall brought shame. The texts above tell us how it happened and what God did about it. These texts show us the history of the human race. They tell us of creation, fall, and redemption. They tell us about perfection, then tragedy, and then rescue. The texts tell us about nakedness, shame, and graceful clothing.

Adam and Eve are at first perfectly innocent and unembarrassed in their nakedness. They have nothing to fear, nothing to hide, nothing to cover up. In their nakedness and in their innocence the man and the woman can look at each other and see that they belong together. They are a perfect match. There is nothing to laugh at, no one to hurt. Their nakedness is a sign that nothing is wrong. When Adam and Eve look at each other, all they see is a person to love. That is the way God made them—to be together in his image. The man and the woman are as free in their nakedness before each other as they are in their nakedness before God.

But then the fall. The first blush of shame spreads across the face of the human race. We all know what shame feels like. Shame is a red face, a downcast eye, an awful feeling of being all wrong. Here is its very beginning. Adam and Eve disobey God "and then the eyes of both of them were opened, and they knew that they were naked; so they sewed fig leaves together and made coverings for themselves."

As a wise Christian once said, nakedness looked good on perfect human beings. But now things change. With great sorrow and mystery the Bible writer tells us that "they realized they were naked."

What does this part of the fall mean? It means much more than just physical nakedness, much more than embarrassment. Adam and Eve discover shame—shame before God, shame before each other, shame as each looks at the self he or she had never really seen before.

Now they feel like hiding from God. Now they scramble to pin the blame on someone else. Now they frantically cover up so they can no longer see their own shame. "They sewed fig leaves together and made loincloths for themselves."

Shame: a sense of humiliation after sin. People who are ashamed feel as if they'd like to crawl under something or have some covering hide them from view. The fall brings shame into the human race.

Clothing is born. It is still with us. We wear clothing not only for warmth and comfort, not only for color and shape to delight us. We wear clothing to cover up. We need a covering. We need physical secrets. Why?

Because we are no longer good enough to be naked. Public nakedness is too dangerous. It tempts us to hurt other people or to use them for selfish pleasure. Public nakedness would tempt us to ridicule each other. In a perfect world it would not matter if your body were fat or thin or unusually shaped. We would rejoice in such differences the same way we enjoy the difference between a banana and a pear. But in a world that mocks and hurts we need clothing.

Ashamed of themselves, Adam and Eve do the best they can to cover up. They weave pathetic little garments out of fig leaves.

And then a strange and wonderful thing happens. The God they have disobeyed comes back to them. The God they have tried to get rid of brings a gift. The God whose grace is deeper than our sin "made garments of skin for Adam and his wife and clothed them."

Can we see what a wonderful thing this is? Can we see what a surprising and graceful God we have? The man and the woman find themselves naked and ashamed in a suddenly cold and frightening world. Pathetically they shiver in their homemade clothes. *They should never have needed any clothing at all.* But here comes God with better and more durable clothing for their shame. Life in sin will be hard and painful. God knows the man and the woman will need good clothing for it. So the Lord God makes graceful clothing for guilty people.

This is the God to whom we are not enemies but loved children. This is the God of amazing grace in the midst of human tragedy.

FOR REFLECTION

How does God make "graceful clothing" for you when you feel shame over something you've done? Or, put another way, how have you experienced God's amazing grace in your life?

PRAYER STARTERS

"Amazing Grace" is one of the best-known and best-loved hymns of our times. Look up the words to that hymn (if you don't already know them), then sing the hymn or use it as your prayer of thanks to God.

WEEK 7

WHAT'S SO BAD ABOUT SIN?

ALL HAVE SINNED

SCRIPTURE

Therefore, just as sin came into the world through one man, and death came through sin, and so death spread to all because all have sinned.

—Romans 5:12

TEACHINGS

We believe
that by the disobedience of Adam
original sin has been spread
through the whole human race.
It is a corruption of the whole human nature—
an inherited depravity which even infects small
    infants in their mother's womb,
and the root which produces in humanity
    every sort of sin.

—Belgic Confession, Article 15

Suppose you like to draw or paint. Your art teacher has you learn art technique by making pencil copies of interesting photographs. You look at something already done and do it all over again. You do a photocopy.

Now suppose you become skillful enough to enter an art contest. The rules forbid copies, saying that you have to hand in "an original pencil drawing or watercolor." An *original*. It means, of course, something you invent. It means something that begins with you. This watercolor or drawing must arise from your own brain, your own imagination. Then it must pass through your nerves and hands and fingers onto a surface. You must come up with something original.

The Christian church speaks of original sin. We mean the sin that had its origin or beginning in Adam and Eve. Sin started with them, but, sad to say, it did not end with them. Adam and Eve's sin is reproduced in all of us. Their sin is the original photograph. Our sins are the reprints, the reproductions, the photocopies.

> **Original sin:** the corruption and guilt that the human race has inherited from Adam and Eve. The doctrine of original sin tells us that sin is universal, that it keeps reproducing, and that it is extremely hard to get rid of.

Of course, an art student can choose whether or not she wishes to copy a photograph. There seems to be much less choice with sin. We do not choose to imitate Adam and Eve when we sin; we just *do.* It is as though we cannot help it. It is as though we are infected with sin while we are still in our mother's womb. We are born with the tendency to sin.

Have you ever noticed, for instance, that little children are naturally selfish? A two-year-old will sometimes try to grab all the toys in the room, even if he cannot possibly hold them all at once. Children have to be shown and told and taught how to share generously with others. Selfishness comes naturally; generosity must be learned. That is why Shel Silverstein's "Child's Prayer" is only half-funny:

> Now I lay me down to sleep.
> I pray the Lord my soul to keep.
> If I should die before I wake,
> I pray the Lord my toys to break.
> So no other kid can play with 'em.

There's more: just as an original drawing comes from inside a person, so sin comes out of our own hearts and minds and imaginations. Sin is imitation of others, all the way back to Adam and Eve. But it is also more than that. For when sin comes from the inner self, from that deep inner place where we are proud or angry or envious of others, then sin is original all over again.

Let me try to say this another way. When we sin, we do copy others at times. We see how they cheat or put someone down, and we imitate them. But when we *want* to do that, when we decide to lie or put someone down, the sin becomes ours. Something old and bad and deep inside us awakens. And the sin that appears is our original sin.

It is as though a hundred students made drawings of one photograph. Each did it in his own way. Each added her own touches. The result would be a hundred *original copies.*

That is the terrible thing about sin. Sin reproduces itself in countless new ways. Sin makes copies. Sin has children and grandchildren. Sin is a root with a thousand branches. Sin is a river with a million side streams. Sin is a contagious disease with a billion new victims. Sin, in other words, corrupts the whole world with wickedness, sadness, and guilt. And it finds a home in us.

The doctrine of original sin tells us that sin is universal, that it reproduces itself in original copies, and that it is miserably hard to get rid of. When we understand that, and when we begin to understand our own guilt for sin, then we can start to see why the Christian church speaks with longing for a savior.

FOR REFLECTION

How are our sins like "original copies"? How does understanding sin in this way affect you?

PRAYER STARTERS

Be honest with God about the mess sin has made in your own life and your need for Jesus, who came into the world to save sinners.

CORRUPT MINDS AND CONSCIENCES

SCRIPTURE

To the pure all things are pure, but to the corrupt and unbelieving nothing is pure. Their very minds and consciences are corrupted.

—Titus 1:15

TEACHINGS

Q. Then where does this corrupt human nature come from?

A. From the fall and disobedience of our first
        parents,
    Adam and Eve, in Paradise.
    This fall has so poisoned our nature
        that we are all conceived and born
            in a sinful condition.

—Heidelberg Catechism Q&A 7

The Bible has a big vocabulary for sin. It uses metaphors and colorful language to describe the many ways in which sin reproduces.

For example, sometimes the Bible writers think of sin as *unfairness* or *injustice.* Perhaps you recall the word *iniquity*, which means the same thing. Here sin means not treating others as equals. As in the prophet Nathan's parable to King David, sin is grabbing and killing a poor man's single lamb. You do it because he is poor and weak and you are rich and powerful. It is unfair.

Sometimes sin is *trespassing* or *transgressing*. God's holiness or God's law is pictured as a piece of land. When we step across its border, we trespass. We tread on holy ground. We go beyond our limits. We sin as Adam and Eve did in trying to be as God.

Or sometimes sin is pictured as missing a target, or stumbling and falling, or getting all dirty, or wandering off the right path and getting lost.

What the Bible writers are telling us with this rich language is that sin is everywhere. Sin seeps into every part of the human house, like an overflowing sewer that cannot be plugged. It is not just that we commit wrong acts (we trespass). It is also that we fail to do right acts (we miss the target by a mile). We commit wrong and omit right.

It's not just that our acts are wrong (like pushing around a smaller and weaker person). It is also that our words are often wrong: we lie, for example, or brag, or mock someone who is socially clumsy. And it is not just that our words and deeds are often wrong. Even our thoughts show that sin has seeped in. We secretly think we are better than others, for instance, even if we don't dare say it. Or we envy someone who is smarter or richer. Or we wickedly look down on a person of another race.

To sum up, sins can be of thought, of word, and of deed. There are sins of omission (failing to do what we should do) and commission (doing what we should not do). A sin is in fact anything at all that displeases God and does not match up with his will for us.

But the Bible writers do not talk just about sins in the plural. Often they talk instead about sin, in the singular. They see sin as a huge force or power that floods into human life like an army—destroying kindness, smashing justice, deceiving children, hurting old people, wrecking families, drowning the poor, pulling down good rulers and propping up bad ones, bribing the police, and ruining everything good.

When this power shows itself in our own homes, when it conquers us as persons, we think, talk, and act like sinners. In fact, it is not only that we are sinners because we sin. It is also that we sin because we are sinners. When sin is inside us, when it floods our hearts, then sins flow forth from sin. Sin is the sewer; sins are all the gunk and junk that flow from it.

> **Corruption:** the seeping or flooding power of sin. Sin seeps into every part of human life, staining and spoiling thoughts, words, deeds, feelings, and inclinations.

The word for this seeping, flowing power of sin is *corruption*. Original sin corrupts us.

Of course, hardly anybody ever shows the worst of such corruption. If all human sewers gushed full force all the time, life would end in a miserable flood of evil. That is why God checks the floods. He holds them back. He partly plugs our sewers. As an army corps of engineers controls the pollution of an oil spill in the ocean, so God controls human pollution by laws and civilization, by customs and teachings and the good influence of believers. When God does this, we say he gives common grace. Common grace controls corruption.

> **Common grace:** God's way of partly stopping corruption so that human life can continue. Common grace explains why unbelievers often show good behavior—better than that of some Christians.

Still, corruption makes us guilty and miserable. And common grace will not save us. That is why Jesus Christ must be the Savior not only for our sins but also for our sin. He must rescue us from the corruption of original sin.

FOR REFLECTION

What evidence of God's common grace do you see in the world today?

PRAYER STARTERS

Thank God for holding back sin in our world. Thank Jesus for dying to take away *your* sin.

OVERWHELMED BY GUILT

SCRIPTURE

LORD, do not rebuke me in your anger
 or discipline me in your wrath. . . .

My guilt has overwhelmed me
 like a burden too heavy to bear.
—Psalm 38:1, 4 (NIV)

TEACHINGS

God requires that his justice be satisfied.
Therefore the claims of this justice
must be paid in full,
either by ourselves or by another.
—Heidelberg Catechism, Answer 12

Q. Can we pay this debt ourselves?
A. Certainly not.
 Actually, we increase our debt every day.
—Heidelberg Catechism Q&A 13

Every so often you read about a person who has done some terrible thing but feels no remorse. Perhaps this person murdered a whole family in the middle of the night. But he is not sorry, not remorseful, not even very interested in what he did.

Decent people are shocked by such accounts. They find it hard to believe that a person would do something as wicked as mass murder; and they are very upset when such a murderer shows no remorse. It's frightening. It's not normal.

If a person can feel no love and no guilt, he or she may have a psychopathic personality. Psychopaths are deformed human beings.

Ordinary human beings feel guilty when they do wrong. Some sensitive people feel guilty even when they haven't done anything wrong. Did you ever wake up from a dream feeling guilty but unable to remember why?

Occasionally people feel guilty when they just come close to wrongdoing. Children, for example, sometimes feel terribly guilty when their parents divorce—even though these children had nothing to do with the tragedy. Police officers who shoot someone in self-defense may afterward feel so guilty that they get sick. Some are even tempted to commit suicide. Even though their use of a gun was entirely justified, they still feel *unclean.*

These examples help us see that being guilty and feeling guilty are different things. Usually they go together: if a person is guilty of a crime or sin, she will feel guilty. But not always. A murderous psychopath is actually guilty but feels no guilt at all. On the other hand, the child of divorcing parents may feel awfully guilty but actually be innocent.

I think we all know what guilt feelings are. We have felt them. But what is guilt itself?

To be guilty is to have broken a law, human or divine. It is to be responsible or blameworthy for a crime or sin. In a court of law nobody asks at first whether you *feel* guilty. People want to know instead whether you plead guilty and whether you are guilty. That is, they simply want to know whether you did the crime you are accused of having done.

> **Guilt:** what we have when we break God's law and deserve the law's penalty. Guilt includes not only what we have when we do wrong; it also includes what we have when we fail to do right. When we fail to do right, guilt is called debt.

Original sin includes guilt. In fact, original sin has two parts. One is corruption, the poisoning or polluting of humanity by sin. The other is guilt. We are originally *guilty*. That is, our original sin deserves a judge's guilty verdict and a court's penalty.

The Heidelberg Catechism uses an interesting word for our guilt. The catechism calls it *debt*. Think of it like this: because we belong to God, we owe him our time, our energy, our service, our total obedience. Think of all this as worth, say, a million dollars a day. The first day we hardly think about God. By the next day we therefore owe God not only a new million but also the old million dollars plus interest! In only a few weeks our debt would overload our calculators. In several months it would make the national debt look like pocket change. Our debt, growing heavier and heavier every day, would soon be staggering. Its burden would break our backs and buckle our knees.

Who on earth could pay this debt? Who in heaven's name could step in to lift our burden?

FOR REFLECTION

Recall a time when you've felt guilty about a specific sin. Did your guilt help you turn to God for relief? Do you have freedom from guilt today, thanks to God's forgiveness?

PRAYER STARTERS

Consider using parts of David's prayer in Psalm 38 (from *The Message*) as your own:

Take a deep breath, God, calm down—
don't be so hasty with your punishing rod. . . .
My bones are brittle as dry sticks because of my sin.
I'm swamped by my bad behavior,
collapsed under gunnysacks of guilt.
Lord, my longings are sitting in plain sight,
my groans an old story to you. . . .
What I do, God, is wait for you,
wait for my Lord, my God—you will answer!
Don't dump me, my God, don't stand me up.
Hurry and help me;
I want some wide-open space in my life! Amen.

THE POWER OF MOMENTUM

SCRIPTURE

The LORD saw how great the wickedness of the human race had become on the earth, and that every inclination of the thoughts of the human heart was only evil all the time.

—Genesis 6:5 (NIV)

TEACHINGS

Q. But are we so corrupt
   that we are totally unable to do any good
   and inclined toward all evil?
A. Yes, unless we are born again,
   by the Spirit of God.

—Heidelberg Catechism Q&A 8

When you watch a basketball game on TV, you may hear the commentator say something about momentum. Suppose the Magic are playing the Lakers. The Magic have been winning. Their defense has been tight and stingy. Their shot selection has been wise. And they have been intercepting passes by "magic." But then, in a seven-minute stretch in the third quarter, the Lakers begin to get their act together. They start swishing baskets from impossible angles. They launch lightning-fast breaks. Their defense becomes even stickier and stingier than that of their opponents.

And the commentator says, "The momentum has changed."

He means, of course, that the game is now going the Lakers' way. It's as though someone has tipped the court so that everything naturally flows toward the Lakers' basket. The Magic, meanwhile, find themselves facing an uphill battle.

Momentum is an amount or quantity of motion. You know that if a car—or especially a train or ship—is just barely moving, it may still be extremely hard to stop. It's so large. It's so heavy. Even when moving slowly it has a great deal of momentum.

Human life has a kind of momentum as well. For instance, suppose you've got a part-time job preparing burgers at your local burger emporium. At first it's slow going, as customers trickle in and time drags. Then, suddenly, the rush begins and you are swamped with orders. Soon you find yourself getting into this cool motion of gracefully flipping burgers, taking them off the grill, and slapping them into buns. Your hands fly as you add the requested catsup, pickles, tomatoes, and lettuce and then wrap each burger in a blur of motion. You lose all track of time. You turn into a super-efficient burger-making machine. Your boss smiles and you dream of opening your own burger joint some day.

You've got momentum.

In fact, work, sports, schoolwork, home chores, networking with friends, good deeds—all these things succeed when you get into the swing of them, when you get moving, when you gain momentum.

Unfortunately, human life includes not only good but also bad momentum. Once a person is going in the wrong direction, they are hard to stop. It's hard for a smoker to smoke just one cigarette. It's hard for a dieter to eat just one potato chip. It's hard for a liar to stop lying. These people have bad momentum going.

Original sin in its corruption and guilt has bad momentum. Our debt to God snowballs. Our corruption increases. A whole society can gain bad momentum.

I think we can see why this is so. It is because the things in us that can go right or wrong are all hooked together. These things are our thoughts, words, deeds, and feelings. It's as though all these things are hooked together by cables, gears, and pulleys. For example, if we hate someone, we might also dream about some deliciously bad thing happening to him or her. We might also want to curse this person or spread some nasty rumors online about him or her. If things get even worse, we might join with others in physically bullying this person. Feelings are tied to thoughts. And thoughts are tied to words and deeds.

Strangely, we not only hurt people we hate. We also hate people we hurt. If we hurt someone, we have to tell ourselves that she had it coming.

Why? Because she's so hateful. So we begin to hate this person even more. And so on, round after round.

The Bible says we do this because our hearts are "inclined to evil." We have evil at our core. We have evil in the inner place where our feelings, thoughts, words, and deeds come from and where they are tied together. Bad momentum is the result of a heart that is inclined or tipped away from God.

That is why the Bible says we need surgery. We need a heart transplant. To have a new heart is like being born again.

FOR REFLECTION

Where have you seen evidence of "bad momentum" in your relationships with parents or siblings or classmates or team members?

PRAYER STARTERS

When you sense "bad momentum" taking over in your relationships, here's a simple prayer (from David In Psalm 51) that could make your own:

Create in me a pure heart, O God,
and renew a steadfast Spirit within me. . . .
Restore to me the joy of your salvation
and grant me a willing spirit, to sustain me.
Amen.

WEEK 8

WHAT DOES HUMAN MISERY LOOK LIKE?

MISERY: THE FALLOUT FROM THE FALL

SCRIPTURE

Lamech said to his wives:
"Adah and Zillah, hear my voice;
    wives of Lamech, listen to what I say:
I have killed a man for wounding me,
    a young man for striking me.
If Cain is avenged sevenfold,
    then Lamech seventy-sevenfold."
—Genesis 4:23-24

TEACHINGS

Q. How do you come to know your misery?
A. The law of God tells me.
—Heidelberg Catechism Q&A 3

Some time ago, the news told the story of a man who shot four teenagers in New York. The man was on his way home from work on a subway train. Four teenagers surrounded him. First they asked him for the time. Next they asked him for a match. Finally they asked him for five dollars. "Sure," said the man, "I've got five dollars for each of you." Then he pulled out a gun and shot the four youths, one after another. All had to be hospitalized. One is still paralyzed from damage to his spinal cord.

When the man who did the shooting gave himself up, he discovered that he had become a hero. People sent him money and promised legal help.

Reporters said the man had done something terribly necessary. Strangers wrote to say they would have done the same thing. People are, after all, sick and tired of being hassled and threatened in public places. They feel trapped and frustrated when streets and subways are unsafe. They hate it when young toughs mug them. Finally an ordinary man had done what a lot of citizens would have liked to do. An ordinary, soft-spoken citizen blew four muggers away.

A bit later, more of the story came out. The subway "hero" had been mugged once before, and his muggers had gotten off with small jail sentences. This angered and frustrated the man so much that he bought a gun, carried it illegally, and waited for a chance to use it. If the law would not take revenge on bullies and thieves, then he would have to do it himself.

Meanwhile, as it turns out, all four of the teenagers had been wanted by the police. Three of them were carrying sharpened screwdrivers. All had mugged before. They were dangerous people.

More has come out: the youth who is paralyzed comes from a Christian home. His own father was killed by muggers years ago. So the boy's mother tried to raise him herself—but soon ran into trouble. The young man began to hang around with a street gang. He became a thief. And one day he got himself shot on a subway train. Now his mother prays for him and for the man who shot her son.

> **Misery:** the pain and suffering that come from sin; the fallout that comes from the fall. Among the fallen world's miseries are disorder, estrangement, and death.

This situation is full of misery. Misery is the pain, the suffering, the wretchedness that comes from sin. Misery is the fallout from the fall.

Anyone can see the misery in the case we are describing. The paralyzed teenager lies miserably in a hospital bed. He'll never walk again. His mother is wretched. The citizens who live in fear of muggers are miserable. Even the "hero" who shot the teenager ended up in jail for taking the law into his own hands. Misery all around. In sin nobody wins.

From the time of the fall the world has been full of misery. Much of it is caused by violence. One person injures another. So the second person injures the first person back—only more so. Then the first person gets revenge—on and on in endless rounds of violence, revenge, and misery. Sometimes people even boast of the revenge they have taken and the misery they have caused—like Lamech, the Bible's first terrorist:

I have killed a man for wounding me,
    a young man for striking me.
If Cain is avenged sevenfold,
    then Lamech seventy-sevenfold.

Does this sound as if it might have happened in a subway?

The reason we hate sin and misery is that we know their opposites. We know what's right and joyful. We know that God says, "Do not steal" and "Do not kill." We know Jesus Christ says, "Love your neighbor as yourself."

How do we come to know our misery? The law of God tells us.

FOR REFLECTION

When have you felt the pain of being "miserable"? What caused your misery? How did you deal with it?

PRAYER STARTERS

Think of one "miserable" situation you know about. It could be an item from the news or something closer to home, perhaps involving someone you know. Say a prayer that God would show mercy to those involved in that situation.

THE MISERY OF DISORDER

SCRIPTURE

I do not do the good I want, but the evil I do not want is what I do. . . . For I delight in the law of God in my inmost self, but I see in my members another law at war with the law of my mind, making me captive to the law of sin that dwells in my members. Wretched man that I am!

—Romans 7:19, 22-24

TEACHINGS

All spheres of life—
family and friendship,
work and worship,
school and state,
play and art—
bear the wounds of our rebellion.

—*Our World Belongs to God,* paragraph 16

Misery comes in many kinds. The pain that comes from violence and revenge is miserable. So is loneliness, especially the feeling of being cut out or shut out. Poverty, divorce, unemployment—all of these are miseries. In fact, as our confession says, every sphere or area of human life shows the wounds of our rebellion.

Today I want to focus on the misery of disorder.

As we recall from the story of creation, God did his great work one step at a time. God did things in order. Each time God called his creation "good," he meant that it had turned out as he intended. It was a custom creation, made to order. As God arranged things, each part of creation meshed smoothly with the others. Sun, moon, and stars traced the pattern God had drawn for them. Animals grazed and romped together. The human beings loved God and clung to each other. Everything was in harmony. All was at peace. The whole creation was orderly and at rest.

Sin brought disorder. It disturbed the peace. Sin brought noise into the music of creation. It caused disorder between God and Adam and Eve. The human beings who had been created to walk with God and lean on God began instead to fear God and to hide from him (Gen. 3:10).

> **Disorder:** the loss of harmony and right relation in the universe. Disorder shows up in relations between God and humanity, between some humans and others, between humanity and nature, and even within individual human beings.

Sin also caused disorder between the man and the woman. They had trusted each other. They had been companions. But after the fall they began instead to blame and accuse. And the man began the long, sinful history of bossing his wife around (Gen. 3:12, 16).

Sin caused disorder, too, between human beings and the rest of creation. God's original order was for Adam and Eve to keep the earth—sowing, tilling, and reaping good food from it. But after the fall, thorns and thistles began to crowd out the crop. Soil got rocky and dry and hard to cultivate.

Sin even caused disorder inside each human being. The man and the woman began to feel the terrible difference between what they should do and what they did do. In our text for today Paul talks about the same thing. It is something we have all felt. Paul talks about how we know what's right; we even want what's right. But somehow we still end up doing what is wrong. It is as though there are two persons inside us, each battling the other for control. Paul is finally so frustrated with being a battleground for these two persons that he roars out his misery: "Wretched man that I am!" The misery of disorder.

What God ordered in creation humans have disordered by sin. Why, still today, do meetings and courtrooms have to "come to order"? Because our natural inclination, after the fall, is toward unruliness. Why do police and military commanders have to give orders? Because if everybody did what he or she wanted, there would be chaos—a lot of people would get drunk and be disorderly, for instance. Why does a basketball referee have to keep control of a game? Because we cannot even *play* well unless rules are obeyed. Why do citizens sometimes demand a return to "law and order"? Because otherwise a whole society can turn into a riot.

God likes things done decently and in good order, as the Bible says. God's law is in fact a way of restoring order to a fallen creation. When God says, "Love me above all and your neighbor as yourself," he is calling us to order. God is calling us to trust and obey. For there's no other way to be happy than within God's law and order.

FOR REFLECTION

Where in your daily living are you especially aware of the pain of "disorder"? Is there anything you could do to restore harmony in that situation?

PRAYER STARTERS

Focus on one situation in which you see the misery of disorder. It could be something like pollution of a local river or lake; it could be a strained relationship between two people; it could be an out-of-control situation at school or on campus; it could be something you see in yourself. Talk to God about this situation and what you or others might do to help restore order and harmony.

THE MISERY OF ESTRANGEMENT

SCRIPTURE

So the LORD God banished him from the Garden of Eden to work the ground from which he had been taken.

—Genesis 3:23 (NIV)

TEACHINGS

Although Adam and Eve were expelled
from the garden
and their days burdened
by the weight of sin,
the Lord held on to them in love.
and promised to crush
the evil forces
they had unleashed.

—*Our World Belongs to God,* paragraph 19

On the news you sometimes hear an item like this: "An east-side man barricaded himself in his home today and held off police for three hours after slaying his estranged wife and her lover."

His "estranged" wife. Who is that?

An estranged wife is a woman who has become separated from her husband. There has been some terrible break in the marriage, and the couple has split up. Each person becomes in some way a stranger to the other. The husband and wife are therefore *estranged.*

Estrangement is a human misery that comes from the fall. It is an example of disorder. We were meant to be at home with God, with others, and in God's world. But now, without Christ, people are strangers to each other, and to God, and even to nature.

> **Estrangement:** a disorder in which persons or things that ought to be friends become strangers instead. For example, when people are estranged from God, they see God not as a loving father but as an embarrassment or even an enemy.

When Adam and Eve sinned, the Bible tells us they were "banished" from the garden. To be banished is to be put out, thrown out, sent away. To be banished is to be estranged. The person who is banished is treated as an enemy instead of a friend, as a foreigner instead of a citizen, as a stranger instead of a son or daughter. When the Bible tells us that Adam and Eve were banished from the Garden of Eden, it is not just saying they were removed from a piece of real estate. No, the Bible writer is telling us that the human beings were separated from all that is bright and joyful and welcome and secure. Adam and Eve were banished from *home.* And they were estranged from *God.*

Many of us have only a tiny hint of what this might be like. Thank God, many of us have loving homes. And we know that God loves us. We don't feel so terribly estranged. We have hardly ever been banished from any place but the refrigerator.

Still, if we think back to times of loneliness, we can start to get the feeling. Suppose there is a group you want to be with. But they don't want you to be with them. Whether politely or not, they tell you to get lost. You pretend you don't care. But you do. It hurts. It hurts a lot. You feel cut out, unwanted, banished, estranged.

Or think what it's like to have deeply wronged a close friend. You said hateful things you really didn't mean. Now your friend is understandably hurt and seriously angry with you. Your conscience bothers you. You realize that unless you get matters cleared up, you'll feel estranged from your friend and somehow even from yourself.

Now multiply this feeling a hundred times. It is the human misery of estrangement. People are estranged from God: they flee from God, or fight God, or find talk of God embarrassing.

People are estranged from each other—parents from children, husbands from wives, friends from friends, races from races, countries from countries. The misery is not just separation but what separation brings with it: estranged people often fear and try to hurt each other. And that causes more misery.

We are even estranged from nature. We have driven numerous creatures to the brink of extinction and not a few over the brink. We spew so much carbon dioxide into the air that the polar icecaps are melting at an alarming rate and scientists warn that global warming threatens the future of the planet. We are not at home in God's world.

We are even estranged from ourselves. Sometimes we can't believe we actually do and say the things we do. We take ourselves by surprise. We disappoint ourselves. We are sometimes strangers to ourselves.

The Bible tells us about these estrangements, but it also shows us how they are overcome. In fact, Jesus himself shows us. For example, he purposely loves strangers and enemies—a scuzzy little sinner named Zacchaeus, a prostitute, a demon-possessed lunatic. Jesus loves people whom others hate. And one day Jesus tells the story of a young man who ran away from home and became a stranger to everybody who loved him (Luke 15). The prodigal (or lost) son, as he's called, is a picture of the misery of estrangement. But in the prodigal's father Jesus also shows us a picture of the amazing grace of God, who opens his arms and his home to welcome us back and welcome us in.

Estrangement. Homecoming. This is the good news of the gospel.

FOR REFLECTION

Have you ever felt estranged from God? What does this look and feel like? What kinds of things can cause it? How can we overcome it?

PRAYER STARTERS

Think of all the ways God has of keeping you close to him. Thank God for these things and ask God to never be far from you.

THE MISERY OF DEATH

SCRIPTURE

And the LORD God commanded the man, "You are free to eat from any tree in the garden; but you must not eat from the tree of the knowledge of good and evil, for when you eat from it you will certainly die."

—Genesis 2:16-17 (NIV)

TEACHINGS

Looking for life without God,
we find death.

—*Our World Belongs to God,* paragraph 14

People hate death. Except when people are very old or very depressed or in terrible pain, they do not want to die. They cling to life. They shrink from death. People pray and struggle and spend money and see doctors. They try everything they can think of to ward off death.

Even Jesus hated death. When Jesus' friend Lazarus died, Jesus did not explain that this was necessary. He did not try to accept Lazarus's death. Jesus wept. And when Jesus turned to face his own death, he wept again. He struggled with God. Jesus showed that he himself feared and hated death.

Why? The reason is that death is an enemy. Death is an enemy because it is a kind of estrangement. And estrangement is a kind of disorder. And disorder is a kind of misery.

It is true, of course, that people also find death interesting. They read about it. They make and watch plays and movies about death. They wonder about what lies beyond death. For example, in Stephen Crane's *The Red Badge of Courage,* the hero, Henry, pauses in battle to peer into the open, staring eyes of a dead man. Crane writes that Henry is "trying to find the answer to *the* question." That is, Henry is trying to read in the dead man's eyes the answer to the question of whether there is life after death.

People think about death more than they admit. Even some children's prayers have a central place for death:

If I should die before I wake,
I pray the Lord my soul to take.

And some old children's songs are really about death, even though you wouldn't notice it at first:

Ring around the rosies, pocket full of posies,
Ashes! Ashes! We all fall down!

Dust to dust. Ashes to ashes. We all die.

But even though death fascinates people, it also frightens them. Why? Death brings pain. People often suffer before they die. People always suffer when their loved ones die. Some of us have had to suffer the death of a mother or father or brother or sister. It hurts more than anyone could ever explain. You never know how much you love a person until the person has died. Then you know.

Even those of us who have not lost a loved one can begin to imagine what it must feel like. For when we imagine one of our parents or siblings dying, we feel like weeping. It is too painful even to think about.

Death brings pain. That is because death is an estrangement. Death is a separation, a ripping, a tearing of life. *Death should never have happened.* If Adam and Eve had not sinned, and if we would not sin, we human beings would not die.

Death is a misery that comes from sin. The penalty for disobeying God in the Garden of Eden was death. We are talking here not only about physical death but especially about *spiritual* death—the estrangement from God that people experience when they try to live without him. Spiritual death includes loneliness, fear, guilt, violence, suspicion, and a feeling that life has no meaning. The name for final spiritual death is hell.

> **Spiritual death:** the estrangement from God that people experience when they try to live without him. Hell is the ultimate spiritual death.

But once more God has a way past this misery. God's solution to death is another death! Jesus dies and rises so that we will never spiritually die. We will never be estranged from God. Nothing in the whole universe, says Paul, can separate us from the love of God (Romans 8:38-39).

Think once more of the parable of the prodigal son. At the end, why does the father want singing and dancing and feasting? Why is there a great, noisy, joyful party?

It is because a son who was dead has come alive again. For the misery of death this is the good news of the gospel.

FOR REFLECTION

When you think about your death or the death of loved ones, what comforts you?

PRAYER STARTERS

Express your feelings about death to God. Then be silent for a minute or two before the God who has promised that even though we die, we shall still live forever.

WEEK 9

HOW DOES GOD RELATE TO SINNERS? (COVENANT OF GRACE)

THE SHINING FACE OF GOD

SCRIPTURE

"The LORD bless you
    and keep you;
the LORD make his face shine on you
    and be gracious to you;
the LORD turn his face toward you
    and give you peace."

—Numbers 6:24-26 (NIV)

TEACHINGS

While justly angry
God did not turn away
from a world bent on destruction
but turned to face it in love.
With patience and tender care
The Lord set out
on the long road of redemption
to reclaim the lost as his people
and the world as his kingdom.

—*Our World Belongs to God*, paragraph 18

Some years ago in Tennessee a girl was born without a face. There was a story about it in the *Reader's Digest*. The newborn girl had a healthy heart and lungs, strong arms and legs, and a well-formed digestive system. But where her face was supposed to be there was only "a shapeless mass of wet mucous membranes, with only a ragged opening for breathing and feeding."

People who saw this child were stunned into silence. Some shielded their own faces with their hands and turned away. Others gasped or cried.

Then, one day, a hospital supervisor called a meeting of all those who took care of the faceless child. "I don't want to hear any more talk about this baby's appearance," said the supervisor. "Her name is Alice, she has a purpose in this world, and we're going to treat her like any other newborn patient."

These were brave words. The truth was that Alice's road toward happiness would run uphill. Alice's mother was a frightened, unmarried teenager. Alice's father wanted little to do with his daughter. Other relatives thought of Alice as "an evil omen."

But one strong and kindly woman took an interest in Alice. This woman, Thelma Perkins, was a nurse in the hospital where Alice spent much of her early life. Mrs. Perkins often held and cuddled the child that others feared. She talked to Alice and patiently fed her through the opening in her head. "I've held enough babies to know when they wanted love," she said, "and Alice needed a lot of it."

Mrs. Perkins was right. Alice's own mother was not mature enough to care for her daughter. After all, Alice would need years of patient, skillful attention. She would need at least a dozen operations. For example, surgeons would have to build a whole new mouth for Alice and try to form a nose—both of those from "extra" bones and tissues in Alice's body. For years Alice would look strange. She would need strong, loving parents to help her cope with pain, frustration, blindness, and cruel comments. She would need protection. She would need caring people to teach her, help her, and tell her again and again that she was loved. Alice's mother couldn't handle all this.

Therefore, Thelma Perkins and her husband, Ray, agreed to become Alice's foster parents. Ray Perkins patiently taught Alice how to walk. After many months Alice could explore the house by "hooking her thumb in Ray's pocket and walking beside him." Thelma Perkins helped the blind child learn to get around in the house and yard without getting hurt. Both helped her deal with the thoughtlessness of people who care too much about what a person looks like on the outside. As a matter of fact, other children have sometimes been kinder to Alice than adult strangers have been.

At Sunday School one morning, a woman seeing Alice for the first time blurted out, "Who's that monster?" "That's just Alice, ma'am," said a little girl standing nearby. Then she took Alice by the hand and led her off to class.

The main people in Alice's life are Ray and Thelma Perkins. They have shown grace: that is, they have shown loving kindness to a person in misery. They have acted like God. Alice has no eyes. She cannot see their faces. But if she could, she would see the shining of graceful light and love.

> **Grace:** loving kindness to a person in misery, especially when a person is miserable because of his or her own sin. Grace is then undeserved favor or kindness.

After a number of years, Mr. and Mrs. Perkins legally adopted Alice as their own child. "She's always been my little girl," said Thelma. "The paperwork just made it official."

That paperwork is what we call a covenant of grace.

FOR REFLECTION

What does it mean to you that you are God's adopted child?

PRAYER STARTERS

Thank God that you are his adopted child. Then turn the words of the blessing from Numbers 6 into a prayer ("May the Lord bless me and keep me," and so on).

COVENANTS: OFFICIAL LOVE

SCRIPTURE

I will establish my covenant between me and you, and your offspring after you throughout their generations, for an everlasting covenant, to be God to you and to your offspring after you. And I will give to you, and to your offspring after you, the land where you are now an alien, all the land of Canaan, for a perpetual holding; and I will be their God.

—Genesis 17:7-8

TEACHINGS

The Lord promised to be God to Abraham, Sarah, and their children, calling them to walk faithfully before him and blessing the nations through them.

—*Our World Belongs to God,* paragraph 21

Suppose a man and a woman get married. On their wedding day the two people stand solemnly before God and their families and friends, and they make promises to each other. Each promises to love the other till death. Each promises to help and encourage the other, even if one of them gets hurt or ugly or sick. Then they exchange rings. The ring is a sign of their love and a seal (guarantee) on their promises. And they kiss. The public kiss is also a sign of their love and a seal on their promises. After the kiss the minister declares them husband and wife.

"What God has put together," says the minister, "let nobody else pull apart."

The man and woman have made a *covenant.* That is, they have made a solemn agreement with each other. You could also call it a *pact.* The main idea is that they bind themselves to each other with vows, or promises. To make the binding strong they do it in public. They do it in front of witnesses—including God. They give each other signs and seals of their pact. They receive a marriage certificate that makes their pact legal. Neither could say later that they were just kidding.

As anyone can tell, marriage is a very serious thing. It is joyful, of course. But it is also weighty and deep. Two people who know each other and love each other do this serious thing. They make their love official. They make it legal. They have it signed, sealed, and witnessed in public. They make a covenant.

Why? Why not just live together? Why risk public promises? Why bother with rings and kisses?

People marry because this covenant helps to make their love secure. People are weak and sinful. If they did not bind themselves together with weddings, the woman might leave as soon as she saw someone she liked better. Or the man might leave if his wife got injured or lost her job.

People need security. They need to know the other person will not abandon them. They need to be able to trust and depend on their spouse. If they are going to share all their secrets; if they are going to trust another person not to dump them when they fail; if they are going to give themselves in love to another person; if they are going to make plans, and children, and a home, and a life together—then they will need as much security as possible.

That is why God made marriage. And adoption. And many other covenants. In fact, in the Bible God is making and renewing covenants all the time. God himself makes covenants with people he loves. With God the situation is like that with Mrs. Perkins and Alice. You remember that Mrs. Perkins said Alice was always her little girl. The paperwork just made it official.

Think of covenants in the Bible in this same way. Genesis 15 and 17 tell us that God made a covenant with Abraham. That covenant is renewed with Moses at Mount Sinai (Ex. 19-24) and fulfilled in the New Testament by the work of our Lord Jesus Christ. The Bible tells us of other, smaller, covenants too. Some are like adoptions. Like a parent, God rescues his children and then makes a solemn promise to take care of them. He adopts them. The rainbow covenant with Noah is like this (Gen. 9:8-17).

> **Covenant:** a solemn agreement or pact. In a covenant there are always promises on one side and often obligations on the other. Covenants are usually signed and sealed, sometimes by specific actions.

But sometimes a covenant looks more like a marriage. In the book of Hosea, for instance, it is as though God marries his people. Sometimes a covenant looks like a pact between a king and his subjects. He will be their protector and helper. He will help them grow and prosper. Meanwhile, they must obey him. The covenant has two parts: one part is the promise made by God the King. The other part is the duty of people to obey.

This arrangement, like a wedding or an adoption, makes love official. It allows for security. It also allows for blessing. In fact, God's blessing falls on those who are secured and protected by the covenant.

FOR REFLECTION

Why does God make covenants with the people he loves?

PRAYER STARTERS

King David offered a beautiful prayer of thanks after God made a covenant with him to establish his throne forever. Use or adapt David's prayer, below, to thank God for making a covenant with you.

Who am I, my Master God . . .
that you have brought me to this place in life?
What can I possibly say in the face of all this?
You know me, Master God, just as I am.
You've done all this not because of who I am
but because of who you are—out of your very heart!
This is what makes you so great, Master God!
There is none like you, no God but you. Amen.
—2 Samuel 7:18-22 (The Message)

THE GRACIOUS PROMISES OF GOD

SCRIPTURE

"I will make of you a great nation, and I will bless you, and make your name great, so that you will be a blessing. I will bless those who bless you, and the one who curses you I will curse; and in you all the families of the earth shall be blessed."
—Genesis 12:2-3

"The promise is for you and your children and for all who are far off—for all whom the Lord our God will call."
—Acts 2:39 (NIV)

TEACHINGS

God holds this world
with fierce love.
Keeping his promise,
he sends Jesus into the world. . . .
—*Our World Belongs to God*, paragraph 5

As we've seen, Adam and Eve's fall into sin brought misery into the world. Life fell apart. Humans became strangers to God and to each other. People even became estranged from themselves. And death entered the world. Cain killed Abel, Lamech sang his terrorist song, and the flood drowned wicked people. Then, by the end of Genesis 11, all the proud people who tried to crowd God out of the world by building the Tower of Babel—all these people were scattered in confusion across the earth. The early part of the Bible shows us sin, disorder, estrangement, death, and scattering.

What is astonishing is that God does not give up or get out. God does not say, "To hell with this world." No, the world is not sent to hell. Like an adoptive parent, or a spouse, or a just and kindly king, God comes not with hell but with grace.

Grace is loving-kindness for miserable people. It comes even to people who are miserable because of their own sin. Grace is undeserved favor for sinners. And God specializes in grace.

There are plenty of examples of grace in our own lives. Suppose you forget to pay your car insurance. There's usually a grace period of thirty days during which you may pay it. Suppose you "say grace" before a meal. It's a way of saying thanks for food you do not really deserve. Suppose someone insults you. You later do something strange: you bring that person a gift. That's grace (and maybe self-protection!).

Take a more serious example. Suppose you shoplift something from a department store. Shoplifting is wrong, and you know it. Still, in some crazy, dangerous mood you do it anyway. And a store detective catches you.

You feel miserable. The detective vividly describes what happens to shoplifters in the legal system. He calls your parents and tells them what happened. Finally the store detective stands up and says, "I'm going to let you off with a warning. Don't ever try to steal anything again." Grace. You should have been punished, but you weren't.

Later, your father says, "I'm really disappointed in you and very upset about what you did. But I know you're sorry. And I still love you. And I promise to always love you, no matter what." Grace. A graceful promise.

All such graces are learned from God. When God makes a covenant of grace with Abraham, he makes his love official. God's is a saving love that people do not deserve. It is offered in promises. These promises are packages of grace that are to be opened in the future. (One of them is opened on Christmas Day.) The first promise package appears in Genesis 3:15. God promises Adam and Eve that he will "crush the serpent's head." This means that God will finally crush the misery they and we deserve.

> **Covenant promises:** God's promises in the covenant of grace that he will love his people, protect them, and help them. God also promises to bless the whole world through his people.

In Genesis 9:11-17 God promises Noah that he will never again destroy the whole earth with a flood. In Genesis 12 God promises Abraham that the great nation of Israel will come from him and that God will provide a wonderful land in which this nation can grow. God also promises that by means of this nation in this land he will bless other nations. That, in fact, turns out to be the most important promise of all. God wants to save

and bless the whole world! He wants to bless all who are scattered, all who are "far off."

God is a promise maker. Unlike some human beings, God also keeps his promises. What God says he will do, he actually does.

We depend on this. As a matter of fact, a thoughtful Christian by the name of Lewis Smedes once said that only one thing in the world tells us that we will never be abandoned or left alone. Only one thing tells us that our world will not end in a smoking ruin. Only one thing tells us that God wants to forgive our sins and make us clean. That one thing is the promise of God. It is the main part of the covenant of grace.

If we can't count on God's promises, then we can't count on anybody's.

FOR REFLECTION

Reflect on some of the promises God has graciously made to you. If you wish, look up some of these promises in these passages: Genesis 17:7; Isaiah 9:6; Matthew 28:20; John 14:2; John 14:16-17; Acts 2:17; Hebrews 13:5; 1 John 1:9.

PRAYER STARTERS

Thank God for each of the promises made to you.

WHAT WE OWE TO GOD

SCRIPTURE

Then God said to Abraham, "As for you, you must keep my covenant, you and your descendants after you for the generations to come. This is my covenant with you and your descendants after you, the covenant you are to keep: Every male among you shall be circumcised."

—Genesis 17:9-10 (NIV)

TEACHINGS

As covenant partners
set free for joyful obedience,
we offer our hearts and lives
to do God's work in the world.

—*Our World Belongs to God,* paragraph 6

The covenant of grace has two parts. One part includes all the graceful promises of God. God will never leave us or forsake us. God will supply graceful clothing when we are naked, guilty, and ashamed (Gen. 3:21). God will bless all the nations through Israel and, now, through Jesus Christ and the church. God will bring the world to a just and loving end.

God promises all this in his covenant of grace. It is his way of making love official. This is the "paperwork" that Mrs. Perkins talked about. God always loves his people. But because God wants us to feel secure—like an adopted child, or a marriage partner, or a person devoted to a just ruler—God makes his love official. God makes promises. God covenants with his people. A covenant is God's way of planning and controlling our future. He does this by promising his love and then signing and sealing his promise with the strange ceremony of circumcision in the Old Testament and baptism in the New Testament.

So what do we have to do? Do we simply say thanks? Do we just take God's gifts and ask for more? Do we simply notice how gracious God is and let it go at that?

No. Covenants, as I said earlier, have two parts. The first part is God's. But the second part is ours. True, in some covenants (like the one with Noah) God makes the promises and that's it. But in the main covenant in Scripture (the one with Abraham) we have a role to play as well. This is true not only in the Old Testament, where Moses acts for God's people (Ex. 19-24). It is also true in the New Testament, where Jesus Christ takes the place of Moses in acting for God's people (Heb. 3:5-6). In both cases there is something that we, God's people, have to do.

In Genesis 17 God tells Abraham what this is. God lists again all the gifts he offers: children, land, blessing to the nations. Then God turns to Abraham. "As for you . . . ," he says. "As for you." What must Abraham do?

"As for you, you must keep my covenant—you and your descendants." Covenant making is God's part. Covenant keeping is ours.

What does that mean? It means that we have obligations. But what are those obligations?

Covenant obligations: the duties God's people owe to God. These are especially obedience (because God is Parent and King), trust (because God is Savior), and thanks (because God shows grace).

Suppose someone does a kind deed for another person. The person who has been helped might say, "Much obliged!" I'm obliged to you. I have an obligation to you.

An obligation is something you owe. If you hurt someone, you owe that person an apology. You are obliged to say, "I'm sorry." If you are late with a library book, you owe a fine. It's your obligation. If you are a son or daughter (and who isn't?), you owe your parents obedience. And when someone does a kind deed or shows grace to you, you owe them thanks and gratitude.

So it is with Abraham and us. God gives grace. We have obligations. God makes a covenant. We must keep his covenant. We do our part through obedience, trust, and thanks. Because God is Parent and King, we owe God obedience. It is our obligation. Because God is our Savior, we must trust him. Because God is graceful, we owe him thanks. Obedience, trust, and thanks are our covenant obligations. As we will see later in our study, we can fulfill these obligations especially by prayer and by keeping God's law.

For now, simply notice how the two parts of the covenant are signed and sealed. To Abraham, God says, "Every male among you shall be circumcised." In the New Testament Peter says, "Repent and be baptized!" (Acts 2:38). Like a wedding ring or a wedding kiss, these two acts are signs and seals of promises and obligations.

FOR REFLECTION

Obeying God as parent and king, trusting God as savior, and thanking God for the grace shown to us are our key covenant obligations. Think about each of these responses. How are they evident in your life?

PRAYER STARTERS

Talk to God about how you truly want to be obedient, trusting, and grateful in your daily life. Ask for God's help in doing this.

UNIT 3

OUR WAY OUT: GOD PROVIDES SALVATION

WEEK 10

WHO IS THIS? (INCARNATION)

WHO IS THIS?

SCRIPTURE

He said to his disciples, "Why are you so afraid? Do you still have no faith?" They were terrified and asked each other, "Who is this? Even the wind and the waves obey him!"

—Mark 4:40-41 (NIV)

TEACHINGS

Remembering the promise
to reconcile the world to himself,
God joined our humanity in Jesus Christ—
the eternal Word made flesh.

—*Our World Belongs to God,* paragraph 23

In the movies, it is not uncommon for a hero who is being tortured by the enemy to stretch out his or her arms as though being crucified. It doesn't matter whether the hero acts at all like Jesus Christ. Hollywood simply wants us to connect the hero to Christ—to think of this person as suffering for his or her people. The filmmakers can make more money that way.

That's because Jesus Christ is the most famous person in the world. Thousands of books, plays, essays, and poems have been written about him. Hundreds of paintings and sculptures depict him. Billions of people know his name, even if only as a pair of curse words. People sing about him; children pray to him; politicians claim him for their cause. All history snaps like a twig at his birth, so that events are measured according to whether they come before Christ or after him. And more than two billion people across the world, including you and me, are named after him.

Yet there is a lot of confusion about Jesus Christ. Some people think of him as a kind of socialist rebel. Others believe he was more like an American businessman. Some think of him as a good man but not a great one, a pretty good teacher who was clearly right about many things but wrong about others. A number of unbelievers see Jesus Christ as a magician, or even as a madman. A few people even believe that Jesus never existed—that he is a mythical figure like Hercules or Robin Hood or Superman. And then, in every age since Jesus' birth there have also been many who have believed in him, who have turned to him and whispered, "Lord."

Why all the confusion? One reason is that people are not always perfectly honest. They do not want to believe what is true if it will not help them make money or act important or feel right about what they are doing. So they turn Jesus into a handsome movie star or a hard-driving CEO or someone who promises his followers wealth and success. Such people want a Play-Doh Jesus who can be twisted and shaped to become whatever god they like.

But another reason for uncertainty about Jesus Christ is that he is frankly a mysterious person. The gospel of Mark shows us that people were confused about him from the beginning. Some people who saw or heard Jesus thought that Elijah had returned. Others got Jesus mixed up with John the Baptist (Mark 8:28). His townspeople assumed he was nothing more than the local carpenter (6:1-6). Enemies dismissed him as a demon-possessed lunatic (3:22). And everywhere Jesus went, he seemed to astonish and bewilder people, even his own disciples. They kept saying things like "What is this?" and "Who is this?" (1:27; 4:41).

The Bible gives a hundred answers to these questions. Who is this? He is both the lamb of God and a shepherd. He is a suffering servant but also a lord. He is a convicted criminal but also a judge. He is the savior who did not save himself, the defender of the weak who did not defend himself. He is the living water who almost died of thirst. He is the king of creation whom soldiers pinned helplessly to some two-by-fours. He is the light of the world who was snuffed out—only to flame up gloriously again. He is our Lord and our God.

Who is this? Out of all these biblical answers we'll look together at three that are especially important to the church: that Jesus is the *Christ,* that he is *Immanuel,* and that he is *one of us.*

FOR REFLECTION

Do you agree that Jesus Christ can be "a mysterious person," even to those who follow him? Why or why not?

PRAYER STARTERS

Praise Jesus, using some of the names he is given in the Bible. Or use this prayer to Jesus from the multitudes before his throne (Revelation 5:12-13, NIV):

"Worthy is the lamb who was slain,
to receive power and wealth and wisdom and
    strength
and honor and glory and praise! . . .
To him who sits on the throne and to the Lamb,
be praise and honor and glory and power,
forever and ever."
Amen.

JESUS IS THE CHRIST

SCRIPTURE

Jesus went on with his disciples to the villages of Caesarea Philippi; and on the way he asked his disciples, "Who do people say that I am?" And they answered him, "John the Baptist; and others, Elijah; and still others, one of the prophets." He asked them, "But who do you say that I am?" Peter answered him, "You are the Messiah."

—Mark 8:27-29

TEACHINGS

God holds this world
with fierce love.
Keeping his promise,
he sends Jesus into the world . . .

—*Our World Belongs to God,* paragraph 5

For centuries they dreamed about it. In the deserts and villages, along the seas and hills, Israelites told of a coming time when God would make things right. With a mighty arm God would shake his people free again, just as he had in the exodus. God would burst the chains that bound his people to the Babylonians or Romans. God would arrest all the terrorists who had hijacked his loved ones.

In Israel itself the rich would no longer squeeze blood money out of the poor. The strong would no longer make tracks across the faces and chests of the weak. People who were lame would leap and dance. People who were blind would gaze hungrily at a world they had never seen before. People who were deaf would listen with wonder to the songs of larks and lyres. Deserts would be turned into fragrant gardens, bayonets into gardening tools, enemies into friends. Jerusalem would be at the center of the world, and all the kings of the earth would come there to bow and pay their respects. Covenant promises and obligations—broken and forgotten—would at last be fulfilled. A *messianic age* was coming.

> **Messiah:** the Hebrew word for "the anointed one." In the Old Testament this person was an expected warrior king, suffering servant, or even God himself. He would bring reconciliation, peace, and prosperity. The Greek word for Messiah means "the Christ."
>
> **Messianic age:** in the Old Testament, the age to come, when God would make things right by means of his anointed one, or even by his own appearance.

The Israelites got this idea from prophets. The prophets got it from God. But the prophets did not speak only of a coming messianic age. They spoke also of a particular person, an individual, who was to come. It was from this person that the age to come took its name. For over the years people began calling this expected person "Messiah."

Who was this person and why was he called "Messiah"?

The prophets described Messiah in many ways. Sometimes they talked of the one to come as though he would be a great warrior king. As David had slain the Philistines, so the Messiah, the new David, would slay God's enemies (Isa. 63:1-6). On the other hand, the one to come would be a man of sorrows who would be slaughtered like an animal for the sins of others (Isa. 53). He would be a king or a servant, but in any case he would be "anointed." That is, like kings and priests in the Old Testament, he would have oil poured over him as a sign that God had picked him out for special work. Or, like a prophet (Isa. 61), Messiah might be anointed with the very Spirit of God poured out on him.

The important thing to know is this: the Hebrew word that was used for the person to come, *Messiah*, means "the anointed one." Greek-speaking Jews used the word *Christ* instead. No Jewish child of God could hear one of those words without a lump forming in her throat. The Messiah was coming! The Christ! The anointed one! He would be the greatest of men, a kind of twig growing out of the trunk of David that would finally dwarf David himself.

Or else, as the prophets sometimes put it, the one to come would be a branch growing out of *the Lord* (Isa. 4:2). Messiah would be the "Mighty God" (Isa. 9:6) or God-with-us (Isa. 7:14) or the Lord himself suddenly coming to his temple (Mal. 3:1).

Messiah, in other words, might be human or he might be divine. In either case he would be brilliantly great.

Centuries later a traveling teacher talks with his followers. People have been asking about him and his miracles. "What is this?" they ask. And "Who is this?" At last the teacher turns to look at his own disciples. There is perhaps a pause and a silence. Then the question comes—a question like a shot to the heart: "Who do *you* say I am?"

The answer that comes back carries the weight of centuries. Isaiah and the prophets are in the answer. The longing of the generations is attached to it. Peter's own life depends on it. Peter's answer has become famous and has become our own. *"Su ei ho Christos,"* he says. "You are the Christ."

Who is this? He is the one who was to come. He is the Christ. Messiah has arrived at last.

FOR REFLECTION

It's the most important question you will ever be asked. It's the same question Jesus asks of his disciples: "Who do you say that I am?" What is your response to Jesus? Please give a personal (and honest) answer, writing out your response if you wish.

PRAYER STARTERS

You may want to use this phrase to shape a prayer to Jesus: "Jesus, to me you are . . ." Conclude your prayer with thanks to Jesus for all that he is to you.

JESUS IS IMMANUEL

SCRIPTURE

Therefore the LORD himself will give you a sign. Look, the young woman is with child and shall bear a son, and shall name him Immanuel.

—Isaiah 7:14

TEACHINGS

He is the long-awaited Messiah,
one with us
and one with God,
fully human and fully divine,
conceived by the Holy Spirit
and born of the virgin Mary.

—*Our World Belongs to God,* paragraph 23

A man named Walpole once wrote a fairy tale called "The Three Princes of Serendip." In this tale the princes make a number of wonderful discoveries by sheer accident.

Today similar wonderful accidents are named after the princes. Finding a delightful thing you were not looking for is now called "serendipity." You call a wrong number—and make a lasting friend. You hunt for a lost golf ball—and find a twenty-dollar bill instead. You sit down to solve some math problems—and discover to your amazement that you are having fun. Serendipity.

Something like that happened when Jesus Christ appeared. God's people had been longing and looking for Messiah. Hundreds of years earlier, the prophets had pointed to a warrior king or a suffering servant or even God himself as the one to come. But gradually the last two of these possibilities began to fade from people's minds. By the time of Jesus' birth most people thought Messiah would be a politician. They believed the Christ would be a mighty, royal man who would lead a revolt against the Romans. He would be a revolutionary war hero who could make things hot for Herod and Caesar.

We can imagine, then, why people did not at once recognize Jesus as Messiah. He certainly didn't look or sound much like a royal rebel. He seemed to speak more of peace than of war. He advised trigger-happy young rebels to love their enemies. He stated that the meek, not the mighty, would inherit the earth. And when he entered Jerusalem on Palm Sunday, he sat on the back of a borrowed donkey.

It was like a president or prime minister arriving for a summit conference and waving to the crowds from a rusted, Rent-A-Wreck junker.

What is this? Who *is* this?

Gradually it began to dawn on people—first the disciples and then others—that this carpenter from Nazareth was no ordinary man. He did not teach the way the scribes did—repeating old answers year after year. He taught as one who had real and personal authority. In addition, he forgave not only sins committed against himself but also those committed against other people. (To understand how unusual that is, imagine somebody stole your new smart phone and a stranger came up to the thief and said, "I freely forgive you.")

Jesus healed people who were hopelessly crippled or blind. One time he performed an exorcism—the casting out of a demon—and the demon-possessed man seemed strangely to *know* him from somewhere: "What do you want with me, Jesus, Son of the Most High God?" (Mark 5:7, NIV). Jesus had calm control over the powers of nature: "Who is this? Even the wind and waves obey him" (Mark 4:41, NIV). Yet his life seemed to end in ruins. He was simply erased by the Romans. His very dead body was laid to rest by heartbroken followers.

A couple of days later two women made their way through the dawn to his tomb. They were carrying things that would keep death from smelling like death.

Suddenly Jesus met them and said, "Greetings!" And they came to him, took hold of his feet, and worshiped him (see Matt. 28:9).

Later the man who has become famous as "Doubting Thomas" (as though "Doubting" were his first name) met the risen Jesus. With a deer-in-the-headlights look Thomas choked out his confession: "My Lord and my God!" (John 20:28).

Women worshiped him. Thomas called him "God." A prophet had said the Christ would be Immanuel—that is, "God with us." But people had forgotten all about these words.

Immanuel: Hebrew word that means "God with us."

Now for the disciples and us it is the world's greatest serendipity. People had looked for a man. They got God-in-disguise, the second person of the Holy Trinity in flesh and blood. People had looked for a man who could become king. What they got was a King who had become a man. Before he left, the King told his disciples he was Immanuel: "I am with you always, to the end of the age" (Matt. 28:20).

Who is this? Jesus is Immanuel to the end of the world.

FOR REFLECTION

What does it mean to you that "Jesus is Immanuel to the end of the world"?

PRAYER STARTERS

Jesus promises to always be with you (Matt. 28:5). Where, in the coming week or two, would you especially want Jesus to go with you? Talk to him about it.

JESUS IS ONE OF US

SCRIPTURE

For we do not have a high priest who is unable to sympathize with our weaknesses, but we have one who in every respect has been tested as we are, yet without sin.

—Hebrews 4:15

TEACHINGS

As the second Adam,
Jesus chose the path we had rejected.
In his baptism and temptations,
teachings and miracles,
battles with demons
and friendships with sinners,
Jesus lived a full and righteous human life before
    us.

—*Our World Belongs to God,* paragraph 24

Some things cannot be understood until we experience them. Take hunger, for instance. We read of it or see hungry people on TV. But few of us understand hunger from the inside. Few of us know what it feels like to crave potato peelings; or to gnaw on shoe leather; or to fill our stomachs with leaves, grass, and dirt.

Or take fear. Most of us have been startled. We have had uneasy nights during tornado watches or violent thunderstorms. But what about people who have been hijacked by terrorists? What about a teenager who is abducted by a kidnapper or rapist? What about small children who are beaten almost to death by their own parents? They know the sick feeling, the paralysis, the silent scream of real fear. We do not.

Years ago a reporter by the name of John Howard Griffin wrote a book about his experiences in the southern United States. Griffin was a white man who knew the wickedness of racism only by reading about it or by seeing the signs that said things like "Whites Only" or "Colored Waiting Room." Griffin knew that gas stations often had three restrooms: "Men," "Women," and "Colored." He knew all this but did not fully understand it because he did not know how a victim of racism feels.

So Griffin arranged to get his hair and skin dyed black. The job was done well enough that he could pass for a black man. He also learned to talk and act the way a black man was expected to talk and act in those days. He then set out across the South.

The results were predictable—and yet Griffin *felt* them for the first time. Stupid young toughs called him "nigger." The word hit him like a hammer. People pushed him around. Police and others looked at him suspiciously, as if being black made it somehow likely that he was a wanted criminal. One white man with whom Griffin hitchhiked told him dirty stories; he seemed to think black people were especially fond of them.

As a black man Griffin began to understand what it is to be humiliated, or else to have people look right through you—as if you were a windowpane instead of a person. Some things cannot be understood till we experience them.

Earlier we learned that God speaks by his Son. Jesus Christ is the Word *incarnate,* that is, the Word made flesh. We have just been reminded that he is the Christ and Immanuel. What we must now bring to mind is that Jesus is a human being of flesh and bone and blood. He knows from the inside what it is to be human.

Incarnation: the Christmas event in which the eternal Son of God took on human flesh.

The eternal Son of God, who already had a glorious divine life, took on our flesh. He was born from a human mother in a cow shed in Bethlehem. A person who was already divine became a person who was human as well. Christmas is the celebration of the incarnation of the eternal Son of God.

Why did he do it? Why did the Son of God become man? The Bible does not tell us in so many words. One reason may be that if humans fell into sin, then it would be fitting for a human to pay the price to get us out of sin again. A second Adam ought to pay the debt run up by the first Adam.

But there is more to it than that. As a human being, Jesus could show us how to live, how to serve God perfectly. As a bird can show other birds where food is without scaring them away, so the human Son of God can safely lead us to our heavenly Father.

Finally, the Son of God became man to share our condition with us. He experienced what it means to be tempted by pride and power. He learned obedience to God. He learned, like John Howard Griffin, what it's like to be taunted, shoved aside, and beaten up. He was crucified, died, and was buried.

Perhaps God could not understand us from the inside if he were not a man. Certainly we could not understand very much of God unless one of our race were also divine. Some things cannot be understood unless they are experienced.

Who is Jesus? Who is this? He is the divine Son of God incarnate. He is one of us.

FOR REFLECTION

Read Hebrews 4:15 two or three times, slowly and thoughtfully. What does Jesus becoming "one of us" mean to you personally? How does it (could it) help you?

PRAYER STARTERS

"In Christ Alone" is a song that beautifully captures the themes of this week's readings. If you know the song, use it for your prayer. If you're unfamiliar with it, see it performed on YouTube.

WEEK 11

HOW CAN WE BREAK THE GRIP OF SIN AND GUILT? (ATONEMENT)

THE MIGHTIEST SACRIFICE

SCRIPTURE

He is the atoning sacrifice for our sins, and not only for ours but also for the sins of the whole world.

—1 John 2:2 (NIV)

TEACHINGS

Q. What do you understand by the word "suffered"?

A. That during his whole life on earth,
    but especially at the end,
    Christ sustained
      in body and soul
        the anger of God against the sin
          of the whole human race.
  This he did in order that,
    by his suffering as the only atoning
      sacrifice,
    he might deliver us, body and soul,
      from eternal condemnation . . .

—Heidelberg Catechism Q&A 37

We have seen and heard of it so often it no longer surprises us. But it is strange. Planted like a scarecrow in the center of our religion is an ugly, humiliating thing. People wear it on a chain like a charm. Churches mount triple-sized replicas of it twenty feet off the ground. Two-year-old Catholics learn how to touch out the pattern of it on their own heads and chests. We have gotten used to it. But it is still a strange and ugly thing.

A torture rack is the main symbol of the Christian faith: a cross. Christians see Jesus Christ not just as Messiah, but as crossed-up Messiah. He is not just Immanuel, but God with black eyes and a split lip and a beard matted with other men's spit. He is not just one of us, but a scapegoat for all of us.

This is all very strange. The apostles went up and down the Mediterranean basin preaching "Christ crucified." People thought they were crazy. Who else would dream of *celebrating* the death and humiliation of their God? Who else would think there was universal power in a rubbed-out preacher, dead weight hanging from spikes on a dreary afternoon?

It is strange, but true. God deals with sin by the sin of Romans and Jews. God conquers death by death within the holy Trinity. God overcomes misery by the misery of his Son. Because of the capital punishment of Jesus Christ, last-minute pardons are issued for us. By his scarred hands and spiked feet we are healed.

The whole process is called *atonement*. It means putting right what sin puts wrong. It means repairing a broken relationship. It means making amends for sin, paying the price to cover the damages. The Bible and the church, in fact, use a number of words for what happens in atonement—words like *reconciliation*, *redemption*, *satisfaction*, and *sacrifice*.

Atonement: the process by which Jesus Christ puts right what sin puts wrong. Christ's suffering and death are an atonement, a making amends, for sin.

Sacrifice: the act of giving up something of value in order to get something of even greater value. Jesus sacrificed his life in order to win ours.

Today let's take the last one: *sacrifice*. Jesus Christ's death on the cross is an atoning *sacrifice*.

We know the idea of sacrifice from various areas of human life. Somebody wants to sell a two-year-old car below book price. Her newspaper ad says, "Owner anxious to sell: will sacrifice." A dying patriot declares, "My only regret is that I have but one life to sacrifice for my country." A young Olympic swimmer sacrifices her social life in order to swim endless laps of backstroke, dreaming of medals and glory. A baseball player comes to the plate in a tied game, the bottom of the ninth, with a runner on first and nobody out. He lays down a sacrifice bunt.

When you sacrifice, you give up something of value in order to get something of even greater value.

Throughout the Old Testament we read of God's people bringing their sacrifices to God as an atonement for sin. They would give up something of value—an animal that might otherwise have been a meal—in order to get something of greater value: forgiveness and peace with God.

And so, on Good Friday, Jesus Christ groans and suffers through the hours of official torture. He is pinned, probably naked, to a Roman crosspiece. Pontius Pilate's joke in three languages is tacked up over his head. He suffers heat and flies and searing pain. He suffers the sneers of bystanders—the kind of people who like to crack jokes and munch popcorn at an execution. He suffers a terrifying sense of abandonment by God his Father. At one point he recites the words that begin Psalm 22:

My God, my God, why have you forsaken me?

The Son of God sacrifices his life for something he wants more: the lives of you and me. This is the strangest event in the history of the universe.

But for us it is also the mightiest and most gracious.

FOR REFLECTION

What does Christ's atoning sacrifice for you say to you about God? About yourself?

PRAYER STARTERS

How does the atonement and Christ's sacrifice on your behalf make you feel? Express those feelings to God in your prayer today.

GIVING GOD HIS DUE

SCRIPTURE

God presented Christ as a sacrifice of atonement, through the shedding of his blood—to be received by faith. He did this to demonstrate his justice.

—Romans 3:25 (TNIV)

TEACHINGS

We believe that Jesus Christ is a high priest forever . . .
and that he presented himself
in our name
before his Father,
to appease his Father's wrath
with full satisfaction
    by offering himself
        on the tree of the cross
    and pouring out his precious blood
        for the cleansing of our sins,
        as the prophets had predicted.

—Belgic Confession, Article 21

We believe that God has revealed himself as the one who wishes to bring about justice and true peace among people.

—Belhar Confession

Belhar Confession: a 1986 declaration of racial reconciliation, Christian unity, and justice written by black Dutch Reformed Churches of South Africa against apartheid.

Justice means giving a person what he or she has coming. If a customer gets a meal from a restaurant, the customer ought to pay the bill. It's owed. It's due. The restaurant has it coming. If a citizen breaks a law, the citizen will have to "pay her debt" to society. Obedience to law is what society requires; it is what society has coming. A disobedient citizen will have to satisfy her debt some other way—by paying a fine, for instance, or by going to jail. She has it coming.

We all have a sense of justice. From the time we are small children we have an idea of what is right and fair and we speak of it, especially when it's to our advantage to do so! We sense that goods ought to be handed out in a fair way. We know that punishments ought to be deserved and ought to be measured to fit the offense. That's justice. It means giving a person what he has coming—no more and no less.

We receive many of our ideas about justice from Scripture. The Bible teaches that God is supremely just. For instance, he does not want rich and powerful people or nations to hog all the earth's goods. He wants a fair share to go to the weak and poor. Further, God hates sin. His justice requires that sin be punished and avenged. God punishes Cain, for example, because God hears the cry of his brother Abel, whom Cain has unjustly killed. Abel's shed blood cries out to be avenged. It cries out for satisfaction.

God's justice demands that when someone sins, someone must pay. From Genesis through Leviticus to Revelation, this truth is written in blood across the Bible. God cannot overlook sin. God will not go soft on sin. The axe must fall. Payment must be made. The blood of sacrifice must be shed. When someone sins, someone must pay—even if it is not the sinner himself.

Why? Why must someone pay? The Bible never explains this so that we understand completely. Still, we can *feel* a sense of justice. We ourselves feel deeply that a cheater ought not to get away with cheating. We ourselves feel deeply that a murderer should not get away with his crime. Why? Because justice is right. Because only then is the debt paid, the wound healed, the emptiness filled up again.

Now think of God as a person to whom we owe obedience (like society, or like a parent). Disobedience robs God of what he has coming. Disobedience is unjust. Disobedience creates, so to speak, an empty place in God that ought to be filled up again.

To satisfy God's justice is to offer what we owe. It means making amends, balancing things out on the scale of justice. It means filling God's empty place by returning the obedience that God has coming.

There is, however, one small problem. We owe but cannot pay. God has our obedience coming, but we can't deliver. God's justice requires satisfaction, but we can't come through with it. Our bill has come due, but we are bankrupt.

The Bible and the Christian church describe a remarkable solution to this problem. Already in the Old Testament sacrifices, God himself provides a way to satisfy his own justice. A sinner could sacrifice an animal to take her place. And the Bible says that the aroma of roast lamb is to God what a good meal is to a hungry eater: satisfaction. God's justice demands satisfaction, but God's mercy provides a substitute so that the sinner herself does not have to pay.

> **Satisfaction:** giving someone what he has coming, so as to "fill up an empty place" in him. Through his death Christ satisfies God's justice by obeying God perfectly, as we cannot, and by suffering the penalty for our disobedience.

That is where the cross of Jesus Christ fits in. A sacrifice is made in order to satisfy God's justice. Our Savior is therefore a kind of priest, offering a sacrificial victim to God. But this time the victim is not a sheep or an ox. This time the victim is the priest himself who lies on a cross and thus turns it into an altar.

When someone sins, someone must pay. And the wages of sin is death, even for God.

FOR REFLECTION

What does God's justice demand? What does God's mercy provide?

PRAYER STARTERS

Use the words of the familiar hymn "Amazing Grace" as your prayer today.

THE LONG ROAD OF REDEMPTION

SCRIPTURE

You know that you were ransomed from the futile ways inherited from your ancestors, not with perishable things like silver or gold, but with the precious blood of Christ, like that of a lamb without defect or blemish.

—1 Peter 1:18-19

TEACHINGS

While justly angry,
God did not turn away
from a world bent on destruction
but turned to face it in love.

With patience and tender care,
The Lord set out
on the long road of redemption
to reclaim the lost as his people
and the world as his kingdom.

—*Our World Belongs to God,* paragraph 18

Until 1865 most African Americans in the South were sold or born into slavery. A *Time-Life* book, *Brother Against Brother: The War Begins,* tells about them.

By age twelve most slaves had to begin a life of backbreaking field work. A workday was from "can see" to "can't see." If the moon was full, a slave might have to keep working the rows and hauling cotton until midnight. His diet included little more than fatty salt meat and a little corn. Housing consisted of drafty, dirty, one-room shacks, usually occupied by six to twelve people. Unruly ones were sometimes viciously whipped by professional "slave-breakers."

Most slaves were sold at auction at least once in their lives. I suppose none of us can understand what a vile and degrading experience that must have been. White shoppers would sometimes make slave men and women hop or jump to see whether they were lively. Like horses, slaves would have their teeth inspected and their rib cages poked. A few slaves turned out to be hard to sell because their backs were a mass of scars and old welts from a slave-breaker's rawhide whip.

Couples were separated, children forcibly removed from parents. Some slaves were treated better than others. But all were property, like animals, to be used or sold as their owners liked.

A few slaves managed to escape to the North by means of the Underground Railroad—a network of routes, rest places, and safe houses that led to freedom. A number of courageous blacks and whites tried to help the desperate fugitives make a good escape. But it was dangerous work. If those who helped were caught, they could expect rough treatment. It cost a lot to free slaves.

Slave funerals were seldom sad. Often the relatives and friends of a dead slave would sing or dance, as though attending a wedding or graduation. Christian slaves longed for heavenly rest the way a thirst-crazed desert traveler craves water. When a slave entered his or her rest, those who were left would celebrate. After all, the only way most slaves could be set free was through death.

Come to think of it, there was one other way. Some slaves were set free in this life. They were freed by a person, Northern or Southern, with a conscience, someone who bought them at an auction. After paying the price she set them free.

The name for this glorious work is *redemption.* Redemption is a liberation word. It means to rescue by ransom. That is, it means delivering someone from evil by paying the required price.

The Bible often speaks of liberation, ransom, and redemption. In the Old Testament God redeems his slave people "out of Egypt, out of the land of slavery." Later, God provides animal sacrifice as a redemption from sin: the animal is the ransom provided by God and then offered to God, so that the person offering it can be set free from guilt. In addition, psalmists sometimes pray to be redeemed from the hand of their enemies and from the power of death.

But, as we know, the Bible's great word about redemption is its word about Jesus Christ, our Savior. In a mysterious and powerful way, Jesus' life and death *redeem* us.

> **Redemption:** to rescue someone by paying a ransom. Just as God redeemed Israel from the land of Egypt, so Jesus Christ redeems us from the slavery of sin and death by paying the ransom price of his lifeblood.

From what? Sometimes the Bible writers (such as Paul) speak of our slavery to sin. Sin has a stranglehold on us. In a frustrating and maddening way sin is a kind of slave driver that first tempts and then brutally punishes us.

Sometimes the Bible speaks of redemption from the fear of death, or from the guilt of having broken God's law, or from the emptiness of an aimless life. Occasionally it speaks of the devil and the powers of this world as our slave drivers.

We do not fully understand redemption. But we do know this: the price paid at auction for us is not just money, not just silver and gold. Like a courageous member of the Underground Railroad, our Redeemer pays with his life. We are redeemed by the ransom payment of blood.

It costs a lot to redeem slaves.

FOR REFLECTION

Sometimes our salvation can seem like a bit of a yawner to us. Yes, we are set free from sin by Christ. Yes, he paid the price for our sins. We've heard it so often that maybe it has lost some of its meaning. How does the comparison of sin to slavery help us appreciate the cost of Christ's redemption?

PRAYER STARTERS

Make a mental list of the things from which Christ has set you free. Then say a prayer along these lines: "Thank you, Lord, for setting me free from. . . ." Repeat for each item on your list.

OUR LINE TO GOD

SCRIPTURE

"If only there were someone to arbitrate between
 us,
to lay his hand upon us both."
—Job 9:33 (NIV)

TEACHINGS

We find all comforts in his wounds
and have no need to seek or invent any other
means
to reconcile ourselves with God
than this one and only sacrifice . . .
—Belgic Confession, Article 21

In Job 1 Satan appears one day in heaven. God and Satan begin to talk over how things are going on earth. "Say," says God, "I wonder if you've noticed my man Job. Have you seen how God-fearing he is? Have you noticed how perfectly he serves me and turns away from evil?"

Satan is unimpressed. "Sure," he says. "Sure, I've seen Job." Then Satan counterthrusts with a hard question: "Does Job serve God for nothing?"

"Look," says Satan, "you've *bought* Job's faith. You've made him rich. Every time he says the Apostles' Creed you send him a check. Of course he'll serve you. He's no fool. You think he doesn't know who writes the checks?

"But suppose we change the rules. Suppose you stretch out your hand and take away everything you've given him. He'll curse you to your face."

"You're on," says God. "I bet he won't."

So Job is thrown out onto the game board to be moved around by God's prosecutor, Satan. Satan is an accuser, a prosecuting attorney, a powerful adversary. God lets him out on a tether, just close enough to take some swings at Job but not close enough to kill him.

Job himself knows nothing of this. He's not in on any of it. All he knows is that the sun begins to set on his happiness. Job's world turns suddenly cold and dark and miserable. His possessions are stolen. Lightning strikes his sheep. His servants are slaughtered in a terrorist attack. Then, one day, a cyclone comes across the wilderness and the house falls in on Job's seven sons and three daughters. Finally Job himself is laid low with a disgusting sickness. Job sits on a pile of manure, nursing his oozing sores and cursing the day of his birth.

What does a person do when God seems to have become hostile? What does a person do when he can no longer make any sense of what God permits to happen in the world? Job knows God exists—that's not the problem. But something has suddenly gone wrong with God. Some wire in God has gotten crossed. Some miniature circuit has gotten overloaded. Some terrifying personality change has come over God.

Job cannot understand it. He keeps wondering *why*. Why must he suffer so much? How has he gone wrong with God? Why all this evil? Through all the banks of storm clouds Job keeps searching for one ray of light. He keeps wondering and storming and hunting for God.

The problem is that God is so silent, so invisible, so far away, so untouchable. If Job could only see God! If he could only somehow lay hold on God, maybe even talk to God!

But there you are. Job knows as well as you do that wishing doesn't make a thing true. And the fact is that God seems to have gone off duty. He seems unavailable for comment. There isn't any way to get to God, to get through to him.

But that's how it is. We have no line to God and he has none to us. There is nobody between us, says Job to himself.

An idea suddenly leaps into Job's mind: "If only there were someone to arbitrate between us, to lay his hand upon us both!" Job is thinking of a third party between God and humanity. This third party would be like a labor arbitrator, a person who gets a company and its workers reconciled during a strike. He would be a kind of umpire, a kind of mediator. He would be someone, says Job, "to lay his hand upon us both."

Who on earth could be an arbitrator? Where, for heaven's sake, could one find a mediator? Who could reconcile a fallen and hopeless human race with a high and awesome God? Who could represent humans by taking our case to God? And who could represent God by appearing among humans?

> **Reconciliation:** restoring peace and harmony to estranged parties. Jesus Christ brings peace and reconciliation by acting as arbitrator, or mediator, between God and humanity.

Someone, says Job, "to lay his hand upon us both." One nail-torn hand placed on a broken Job, sitting there on the manure pile. One mangled hand upon the King of heaven.

"If only there were someone to arbitrate between us, to lay his hand upon us both." God and humanity reconciled because of the coming of an arbitrator.

Could that ever happen?

FOR REFLECTION

How are we like Job? What does it mean to be reconciled to God?

PRAYER STARTERS

Do you wonder about things that don't seem right in your life? Maybe it's something that doesn't seem fair, like the chronic illness of someone in your family. Maybe it's something that continues to hurt you in some way, like a special friend who has dumped you. Whatever it is, picture Jesus laying one hand on you and the other on God. Ask Jesus to help bring you closer to God, to give you peace.

WEEK 12

HOW CAN WE BE RIGHT WITH GOD? (JUSTIFICATION)

WHAT GOD DOES FOR US

SCRIPTURE

He was delivered over to death for our sins and was raised to life for our justification.

—Romans 4:25 (NIV)

TEACHINGS

He carried God's judgment on our sin—
his sacrifice removed our guilt.
God raised him from the dead:
he walked out of the grave,
conqueror of sin and death—
Lord of Life!
We are set right with God,
given new life,
and called to walk with him
in freedom from sin's dominion.

—*Our World Belongs to God,* paragraph 25

Tom was a thief. He hadn't been a thief for long, but he had become very good at thievery. He was smart, quick, and daring. He also happened to have the kind of job that gave him opportunities for theft.

Tom worked as a student assistant to the school custodian. He washed tabletops, swept floors, pushed desks back into neat, straight rows. He also raided students' lockers and teachers' desks, stealing small change and valuables. For, although Tom was never given a master key, he knew where one was kept. And he knew how to use it quickly and return it.

Over the weeks and months students and teachers grew more and more annoyed at their losses. Usually the missing amounts were small, but once the money from candy and ice cream sales at basketball games was stolen. That amounted to quite a lot of cash. Another time a tenth grader left all her birthday money in her locker and found it gone on Monday when she returned.

Meanwhile, Tom was trying hard to get as much mileage out of his thefts as he could. He shopped for good clothes, hoping to impress his classmates with them. He talked his parents into letting him buy the latest smart phone. And he bought things for students he admired. Sometimes they would accept his gifts. Other times they'd just look at him strangely and walk away. In either case, Tom didn't seem to gain the friends he craved.

Tom knew he had a time bomb ticking in his life. One of these days he would be caught and it would blow him up. True, while he was actually in the middle of a risky theft, Tom didn't reflect on what he was doing. After all, his heart was racing as fast as his larcenous hands. But the nights—the nights were bad. The conscience that Tom had taught to shut up so it wouldn't shout at him began to whisper insistently at night. Some nights Tom could hardly get to sleep. Other nights he was troubled by nightmares.

Then one Thursday he was caught. As he was going through Mr. Gunst's desk, Tom was startled by a voice. Mr. Gunst, the history teacher, had suddenly materialized behind him and was asking in a quiet voice what Tom was doing. Tom tried to imagine some innocent reasons why he would be searching Mr. Gunst's desk, but he couldn't think of any. He could tell from the tone of Mr. Gunst's voice that *he* couldn't think of any either.

So they talked.

Mr. Gunst was one of those teachers you didn't exactly like but you always respected. He never joked around with students; he was a firm man. But he was also fair.

At first Tom tried to lie about all the other thefts. But by now he was feeling tired and small and guilty. Besides, Mr. Gunst was remarkably hard to lie to. Tom ended up admitting everything. He even admitted the reason for his stealing: he told Mr. Gunst he felt unaccepted and out of the center of things and was trying to get in.

Mr. Gunst's attitude was interesting. He was firm about what Tom had done. It was plain wrong. Stealing could not be justified. Somehow Tom would have to repay every penny of the stolen money. And Tom would have to make friends some other way, some right way.

On the other hand—perhaps because Tom was so miserable and felt so wrong and guilty—Mr. Gunst was incredibly kind to Tom himself. He acted as if, although Tom had done something all wrong, Tom himself was all right. Mr. Gunst did not justify what Tom had done, but he did justify Tom. That is, he accepted Tom, forgave him for going through his desk, and tried to arrange things so that Tom could be reconciled with the school community.

In doing these things, Mr. Gunst acted like God.

FOR REFLECTION

What do you think of what Mr. Gunst did for Tom? Does it help you understand what God does for us?

PRAYER STARTERS

Reflect on how Tom felt toward Mr. Gunst after he accepted and forgave Tom. How do you feel toward God after he accepts you and forgives you? Offer a prayer that reflects your feelings.

YOU ARE FORGIVEN

SCRIPTURE

God was reconciling the world to himself in Christ, not counting people's sins against them. And he has committed to us the ministry of reconciliation.

—2 Corinthians 5:19 (NIV)

TEACHINGS

Q. What do you believe
    concerning "the forgiveness of sins"?
A. I believe that God,
        because of Christ's satisfaction,
    will no longer remember
        any of my sins
        nor my sinful nature
            which I need to struggle against all
                my life.
    Rather, by grace
        God grants me the righteousness of Christ
        to free me forever from judgment.

—Heidelberg Catechism Q&A 56

It's an old movie, but if you've seen it, it's hard to get the terrible images out of your mind: two men terrorizing, beating, raping, and murdering two kids out on a date, sickeningly proud of themselves for the power they hold over the teenagers. In fact, in the movie, the images haunt not only us but also Matthew Poncelet—who waits on death row to serve the punishment for his crime.

While Matthew Poncelet's name is fictional, his character isn't. The movie *Dead Man Walking* is based on a true story and, since its release in 1995, has become something of a classic. Those terrible things depicted in the movie really did happen, and the man really was executed for his brutal crime.

What the movie focuses on, however, is not the crime but the relationship between Poncelet and Sister Helen Prejean, who became Poncelet's spiritual adviser during the last two months of his life. While many eagerly awaited his death, saying that he was getting what he deserved, Sister Helen offered friendship and love to one of the most detestable human beings we could imagine. Never excusing his actions, but loving him as a person, she demonstrated forgiveness.

Forgiveness of sins is one of the main parts of justification. God never justifies sins—that is, he never excuses or accepts them. Someone has to pay for them. But God does justify sinners—that is, because of Christ's atonement, God excuses his sons and daughters from the punishment they deserve and accepts them as children he loves. Sin is unacceptable to God; sinners can be accepted.

Look at it this way: sin is a problem to God as well as to us. Sin is like a virus that turns a hard drive into garbage. It's like bad breath in a friendship or fleas on the family dog. Sin is something that stands between persons like a cactus stalk. God wants to receive and accept us, but sin is *in the way.*

We recall (week 9) that in his covenant of grace God promises to forgive our sins and make us clean. Like Tom in yesterday's story or like Matthew Poncelet, we don't deserve to be forgiven. What we deserve, frankly, is punishment and trouble. And like Mr. Gunst and Sister Helen, God is no pushover. It is a deadly mistake to picture God as a sort of heavenly wimp. God is rock firm against sin and terrifyingly strong in hating and condemning it. Sin must be punished. Somebody must suffer for it.

The gracious solution to the problem, as we learned in week 11, is that the Son of God himself suffers and atones so that we might have forgiveness and peace with God. A name for this forgiveness and peace is justification. John Calvin thought justification was so important that he called it "the main hinge on which religion turns."

Justification: God's acceptance of unacceptable people. Justification includes the forgiving of our sins and the adding to us of Jesus' righteousness.

What, exactly, is justification? It can be described in many ways. It is that which makes us right with God. It is the act of God that makes peace between God and ourselves, that reconciles us to God. But perhaps the best description of justification is that it is "God's acceptance of unacceptable people." Sin has made us unacceptable. But in a stunning move of grace God accepts us anyhow. Because of the mighty, painful work of Jesus Christ, God does a kind of

gracious arithmetic to solve the problem of sin. He subtracts our sin from us; then he adds the righteousness of Jesus Christ in its place. God himself makes us acceptable to him. God himself gets rid of the stubborn problem that is in the way.

Forgiveness of sins: the subtracting, or putting away, of sins so that they are no longer held against us. When God forgives our sins, we can be at peace with him.

The subtracting part of the program is what I have been talking about: the forgiveness of sin. Sin is subtracted from us. It is taken away like a smaller number from a greater. And God bears no grudges. He never again holds our forgiven sin against us.

In fact, when you and I come mysteriously before God on the final judgment day, the person who presides—the person who holds our fate in his hands—is none other than the Lord Jesus Christ, who sacrificed himself for us.

Like Sister Helen, he says to us, "Look at me. I want the last face you see to be a face of love."

FOR REFLECTION

How does it feel to be accepted and forgiven by God? What makes us acceptable and forgiven in God's sight?

PRAYER STARTERS

To have our sins "subtracted" or "put away" by God, we need to ask for God's forgiveness. Will you make asking for forgiveness a regular part of your prayers this week?

YOU ARE RIGHTEOUS

SCRIPTURE

He [God] is the source of your life in Christ Jesus, who became for us wisdom from God, and righteousness and sanctification and redemption.
—1 Corinthians 1:30

TEACHINGS

Q. How are you righteous before God?

A. Only by true faith in Jesus Christ.
  Even though my conscience accuses me
    of having grievously sinned against all
      God's commandments,
    of never having kept any of them,
    and of still being inclined toward all evil,
  nevertheless,
    without any merit of my own,
    out of sheer grace,
  God grants and credits to me
  the perfect satisfaction, righteousness, and
      holiness of Christ,
    as if I had never sinned nor been a sinner,
    as if I had been as perfectly obedient
      as Christ was obedient for me.
  All I need to do
  is accept this gift with a believing heart.
—Heidelberg Catechism Q&A 60

The United States has a Declaration of Independence—a claim that the U.S. will no longer be a colony of Great Britain but will be a nation on its own. Ever since 1776, U.S. citizens have thought of this freedom as an improvement. Nations like to be independent.

So do individuals. But we have to wait for independence. When we were in our mothers' wombs, we were totally dependent on them for our health and well-being—in fact, for life itself. If our mothers ate the right foods and drank the right liquids, we thrived. If they ate junk, we suffered. If they got drunk, we got drunk. If they took certain drugs or caught certain diseases, it was as though we ourselves took those drugs or caught those diseases. We were totally dependent on them.

But, of course, one day we were born. A physician snipped the umbilical cord and we began to breathe. People think of this as an improvement. We ought to put away childish things.

As we grow older, we do put them away. We learn to walk on our own two feet. We learn to feed ourselves. And as we become teenagers, we try for still more independence. We want increased freedom to spend time and money as we see fit. We want to put away childish things. We want independence—and we should.

Up to a point.

As a matter of fact, we never outgrow some dependencies. For example, as long as we live, we depend on God's creation for nourishing food and thirst-quenching drink. Further, we depend on other people for friendship, fun, marriage, safety, and countless other things. We depend on the life and strength and gifts of others.

This is especially true where righteousness is concerned. To be righteous is to be holy, just, and good. Because of original sin (and our own original copies of it) we are not very good at righteousness. We cannot create righteousness on our own; we can only gather and use the righteousness of another.

Justification is God's acceptance of unacceptable people. As we have seen, it includes the forgiveness of sins. But it also includes something else: the addition of alien righteousness. Something old is subtracted; something new is added. What is added is the righteousness of Jesus Christ.

> **Alien righteousness:** the holiness of another. We do not have our own holiness, so the holiness of another (an alien) must be given to us to make us acceptable to God. Jesus is the alien.

Jesus loved his friends and treated them perfectly. He spent time and energy on unpopular people. He firmly resisted temptation. He criticized self-righteous people but accepted unrighteous people. He was willing to die rather than go against the will of God.

In justification all this is mysteriously transferred to us—as though we had acted in just the same way. Jesus' holiness is added, or granted, to us. Having alien righteousness is like shopping with someone else's credit card. It is like getting past a checkpoint in someone else's uniform. It is like being carried in the divine womb, blood-rich with the very life of God.

In fact, we now have perfect lives. We cannot *live* perfect lives, but if we repent of sin and trust our Lord, God sees Jesus' life when he looks at us.

Try to be independent of God, and you die. It is like a declaration of independence from oxygen. But depend on the alien righteousness of Jesus Christ, and you become freer, more alive, more splendid than you could ever imagine.

For the alien is our loving Savior.

FOR REFLECTION

Reread Q&A 60 at the top of this reading. Find a phrase that means the same thing as "justified." What comfort can we find in Q&A 60 when we think we've sinned too much for God to forgive us?

PRAYER STARTERS

Modify Answer 60 into your personal prayer. Start it like this:

Dear God,
Thank you for making me right with you
by giving me true faith in Jesus Christ.
Even though my conscience accuses me . . . .

Continue personalizing the answer into your own prayer.

YOU ARE ACCEPTED

SCRIPTURE

Who will bring any charge against those whom God has chosen? It is God who justifies.

—Romans 8:33 (NIV)

TEACHINGS

Q. What is your only comfort in life and in death?

A. That I am not my own,
   but belong—
      body and soul,
      in life and in death—
   to my faithful Savior Jesus Christ.

—Heidelberg Catechism Q&A 1

All of us hunger for acceptance. It is one of the things we depend on for happiness. If people we admire accept us, we grow like a watered plant in sunshine. If people we admire reject us, we wither and die inside.

How can we tell that people accept us? By their words and actions and even by the look in their eyes. If people use our names in a warm way, we feel accepted. If they invite us to join them for a game, or an overnight, or a party, or a prank, we feel accepted. If they are hurt by what we do but painfully forgive us for doing it, we feel accepted. If they look at us with care, with a light in their eyes that says we are important to them, we feel wonderfully accepted.

The hunger for acceptance is so deep and keen in most of us that we will do almost anything to get it. We will wear certain clothes, comb our hair in certain ways, use just the right language, and try for the friendship of particularly acceptable persons. We will do all these things rather than risk the pain of rejection. For if we taste rejection just once, we never want to taste it again. So we work and sweat and struggle and try for acceptance. We think we cannot accept ourselves unless we are acceptable to others.

It takes very strong and secure persons to live life the right way without worrying too much whether others will like and accept them. You probably know people like this. They seem happy and friendly in the "wrong" clothes. They choose their friends because they like them, not because their friends have a certain status. They seem relaxed, confident, outgoing. And they care about people who feel rejected.

Where do such people get this attitude and this approach to life? They get it from God. Like Mr. Gunst and Sister Helen, these people feel deeply accepted by God. They feel *justified.* They know their sins are forgiven and that when God looks at them he sees the perfect life of Jesus Christ.

A person like that also feels *free.* A person who knows she is accepted by God is free to accept others and to accept herself. She may still dress, talk, walk, and act in a certain way peculiar to her group or school. But she doesn't worry about it or feel desperate about it. After all, she doesn't depend on these things to accept herself. She depends instead on God's love, on knowing that God treasures her so much that Jesus Christ died to set her free.

When God accepts us, we can accept ourselves.

Spanish author Miguel de Cervantes tells a story that helps us understand acceptance. He tells about Don Quixote, a brave but awkward knight. In one episode Don Quixote comes into a little village inn, where he meets the village prostitute. She *is* a prostitute. There can't be much doubt about that. After all, everybody in the village says she's a prostitute. And everybody treats her like a prostitute. Most important, when people look at her with scorn, she reads "whore" in their eyes.

But the strange and brave Don Quixote doesn't see a prostitute when he sees this young woman. He sees a noble lady. He tells her she is a great and noble lady. He treats her as though she is royalty. And most important, when he looks at her, she sees in his eyes the image of a great and respected person. When she sees this image in Don Quixote's eyes, she recognizes it as her real self.

So she starts acting like the image she recognizes. She stops acting like a prostitute and starts acting like a great and respected person. She becomes Don Quixote's noble lady.

> **Acceptance:** the receiving and welcoming of another. Acceptance is the heart of justification. Accepted people often, then, begin to act acceptably.

This is what acceptance can do for unacceptable people. The God who comes for us in Jesus Christ is forever looking at people like you and me and saying not only with his lips and eyes but also with his life the words "son," "daughter," "noble lady," "my child." The same terrifying cross on Golgotha that tells us we needed someone to die for us also tells us that God thinks we were *worth* dying for.

If God accepts us, who are we to condemn ourselves?

FOR REFLECTION

"When God accepts us, we can accept ourselves." What does this mean to you personally?

PRAYER STARTERS

Talk to God as the Father who totally accepts you and calls you his child. Ask God to help you feel and act as an accepted and free person. Thank God for making you his child.

WEEK 13

WHAT DOES FAITH LOOK LIKE?

GET GRAFTED

SCRIPTURE

But if some of the branches were broken off, and you, a wild olive shoot, were grafted in their place to share the rich root of the olive tree, do not boast over the branches.

—Romans 11:17-18a

TEACHINGS

Q. Are all people then saved through Christ just as they were lost through Adam?

A. No.
Only those are saved
who through true faith
are grafted into Christ
and accept all his blessings.

—Heidelberg Catechism Q&A 20

Grafting is one of the most wonderful possibilities in creation. A person who has been badly burned in an accident can be saved from constant infection and excruciating pain by means of a skin graft. A strip of tissue from a healthy part of the body is surgically removed and transplanted to the burned area. There a surgeon carefully fastens the skin transplant to the surrounding tissue with special stitches. Gradually, if the graft "takes," skin from a healthy thigh or inner arm will begin to grow at the burned site.

Bones can be grafted too. In fact, sometimes a bone from one person is grafted onto the fresh end of someone else's bone. There are even bone banks that keep various bones on deposit till an injury or disease calls for them.

Perhaps most common of all grafts are those that people perform on plants. An expert once described the process to me. A person slices a twig from one tree and carries it to another. There he cuts a V-notch, or "envelope," that can receive the new twig. The roughened end of the twig is inserted into the notch. The joint is then snugly sealed with grafting wax or tape to hold the graft securely and to keep out disease organisms. The joint will always be a little knobby and funny looking, but if the graft takes, nourishing food and water will soon run through the tree's "plumbing system" into the newly attached twig.

Why bother with grafts? Plant experts graft in order to produce more and better fruit. If a certain kind of tree (say, an apple tree) doesn't take root well or produce many new seeds, the expert can graft a twig from it onto the fast-growing, well-rooted, disease-resistant stem of another tree and get the best of both. One has fast growth and good roots; the other has the kind of fruit people want.

Interestingly, Romans 11 and the Heidelberg Catechism speak of human grafting. Persons can be grafted. You and I can be united to Jesus Christ in order to share in his nourishing food and drink. We can then produce the special fruit that God wants to harvest from each of us.

What is meant by this? How does it work?

You recall from last week that justification means two things: it means that our sins are forgiven and that Jesus Christ's righteousness is added to us. But how do we actually *receive* his righteousness?

We receive it by faith. Faith is the grafting wax or tape that bonds us to Jesus Christ. He is the one with the fast growth and the good roots. We are the ones who, apart from him, are rootless and fruitless. Across the world God wants a vast orchard of fancy fruits: fairness, compassion, honesty, kindness, and so on. Above all, he wants to see us blossom with love for him and for others. To get all these fruits, God has arranged to graft millions of his children into the one perfect vine, or stem. When faith attaches us to Christ, it is as though his rich blood is transfused into us, flowing through us like nourishing plant food and water. Love and other wonderful things then begin to bud and burst on all of us who are united to him. He is the vine; we are the grafted branches.

> **Union with Christ:** the bonding or attaching of persons to Christ. All of us are united to Christ by being members of his church, but the union is finally secure only when we are personally grafted to Christ by true faith.

In fact, either we share in Christ's nourishing life or we wither. Either we are united to Jesus Christ by faith or else, day by day, we begin the terrible process of spiritual death.

How are we justified? By God's grace alone. How do we receive this gracious justification? Only through true faith that grafts us to Jesus Christ.

FOR REFLECTION

How does the grafting idea help us understand how we are bonded to Christ? What part does faith play in that bonding? What results from the grafting?

PRAYER STARTERS

Ask Jesus to give you faith or to strengthen your faith, so that his goodness may flow into you.

BELIEVE IT TO SEE IT

SCRIPTURE

Now faith is the assurance of things hoped for, the conviction of things not seen.

—Hebrews 11:1

TEACHINGS

Q. What then must a Christian believe?

A. All that is promised us in the gospel, a summary of which is taught us in the articles of our universal and undisputed Christian faith.

—Heidelberg Catechism Q&A 22

Walk through any grocery store checkout lane and you can't help but see those tabloids with the weird headlines: "Boy, Two, Turns into Woman Overnight"; "Family of Wolves Raises Midget"; "Woman Kidnapped by Aliens Claims She's Pregnant with Alien Baby."

Most of us do not believe such stuff. We know that some unscrupulous publisher is only trying to make money.

Disbelief can be valuable. It may save us from being fooled or cheated. For instance, it may protect you from opening an e-mail that promises you a new computer in return for completing a survey. As honest people sometimes say, if someone offers you something too good to be true, it probably is.

But disbelief can also cut us off from things that are true and from persons we desperately need. People told Columbus he was loony when he said he could get to the East by sailing west. He claimed that the earth was round; the disbelievers all knew perfectly well that it was flat. Bystanders nearly died laughing when those crazy Wright brothers said they would fly; everyone knew God wanted humans to soar no higher than they could jump.

When Jesus acknowledged that he was the Christ, people told him he was a liar. These people were standing in the presence of their only Savior. But in their disbelief they knew better. So they erased him.

Belief and disbelief are so important that our religion is often simply called "the Christian Faith." For it is faith that ties us to the person we desperately need and faith that receives his justifying gifts.

Faith includes two parts: one of them is belief; the other is trust. Today I want to talk some more about the first of these.

What is belief? Christian belief is the acceptance of the truth of the gospel. Christian belief means accepting as true the promises of God. Christian belief, says Hebrews, "is the assurance of things hoped for, the conviction of things not seen."

What do we hope for? Some of the things we hope for never come. We hope for a B but get a C. We hope for a date with someone we admire but get turned down. We hope to get into the college of our choice, but settle for one that's less expensive and closer to home.

But beyond these small hopes is a large one. Christian people hope for the triumph of right over wrong, of good over evil, of God over his enemies. In other words, we hope for the coming of the kingdom of God. All the promises of God, all the truths of the gospel, can be summed up in the coming of the kingdom. The coming of the kingdom is the big thing we hope for and the main thing we are certain of, even though we cannot yet fully see it. By faith we believe that God's kingdom will come; by faith we also believe in Christ the King, who has come and is coming again.

Reverend Frederick Buechner, in *Telling the Truth,* illustrates this with an example from the *Wizard of Oz.* At the end of the Yellow Brick Road Dorothy and her friends are awestruck by "the great and terrible Oz," whose booming voice resounds throughout the castle. But in the end his stage props are removed and Oz turns out to be only a little bald guy in disguise. He wants to help, but he has only human help to offer. Appearances are deceiving.

The promises of the gospel go just the other way. The gospel is Oz in reverse. For the gospel tells us that the unknown carpenter from Nazareth, seemingly helpless against the Roman soldiers who pin him to a cross, is actually God in disguise. Behind his human weaknesses, behind his humiliating torture and painful death, the Lord of life is powerfully at work, muscles rippling to save us. Appearances are deceiving.

You have to believe it to see it.

FOR REFLECTION

What is meant by the last line in the reading?

PRAYER STARTERS

Tell God why you believe. You may want to use this sentence starter: Dear God, I believe in you because . . . ."

DEEP DOWN TRUST

SCRIPTURE

"Do not let your hearts be troubled. Trust in God; trust also in me. In my Father's house are many rooms; if it were not so, I would have told you. I am going there to prepare a place for you."

—John 14:1-2 (NIV)

TEACHINGS

Q. What is true faith?

A. True faith is
    not only a sure knowledge by which I hold
        as true
        all that God has revealed to us in Scripture;
    it is also a wholehearted trust,
        which the Holy Spirit creates in me by
            the gospel,
        that God has freely granted,
            not only to others, but to me also,
            forgiveness of sins,
            eternal righteousness,
            and salvation.
        These are gifts of sheer grace,
        granted solely by Christ's merit.

—Heidelberg Catechism Q&A 21

Faith has two parts: belief and trust. We believe *that* Jesus Christ will return, for instance. But we believe *in* Jesus Christ himself. Again, we believe *that* God exists. But that is not enough. Even the devils believe that God exists, says James 2:19, and shudder at the thought! Besides believing *that* God exists we must also believe *in* God. To believe in a person is to trust him, depend on him, perhaps even be willing to risk ourselves for him. To believe in God, or in Jesus Christ, is to go further. It means to give ourselves into his safekeeping. It means to turn over, to hand over, our very self to this other person.

"Trust in God," invites Jesus. "Trust also in me."

> **Faith:** the bond to Christ from our side. Faith includes belief in the promises of God and trust in Jesus Christ. Faith *receives* justification.

If we think for a moment, we can see how the two parts of faith, belief and trust, are connected. Suppose your basketball coach tells you to shoot more with your fingertips than with your palm. Or suppose your coach teaches you to dribble with your head up. Neither of these things feels natural at first. You wouldn't be likely to believe that fingertip shooting and heads-up dribbling were the way to go unless you *trusted* your coach. If you trust someone, you tend to believe what he or she says.

Or suppose, on the other hand, that you are walking alone in Chicago or some other large city and a young man approaches you on the street. Weeping, he begins to tell you a sad story about how his wallet was stolen. Now he urgently needs fifty dollars to buy medicine to treat his diabetes. If he doesn't get the medication soon, he'll go into shock and die, he says. He pleads with you to help him. Although he seems sincere, you do not believe his story because you do not and cannot trust this stranger.

Disbelief often comes from mistrust, just as belief often comes from trust. If we trust God, then we believe what the Scriptures say, for example. They are, after all, God's Word. But the reverse is also true: trust often comes from belief. Thus, if you believe what the Scriptures say, you will tend to trust God. Belief and trust, in other words, usually reinforce each other.

Still, they are different things. And trust is often harder for us than belief. A gifted minister, Clarence Boomsma, used to tell students a story that helps us understand the difference between belief and trust. This true story is about a man named Blondin, who was a famous high-wire performer many years ago. Blondin once proposed a remarkable feat. He announced that he would walk a tightrope stretched across Niagara Falls.

On the fateful day huge crowds gathered on both sides of the falls. Sporting men bet large sums on Blondin's chances. High above the deadly torrent the great performer started slowly along the thin wire. Foot by agonizing foot, leaning against the wind, Blondin made his way across the whole length of tightwire.

Then Blondin came up with an even more outrageous stunt. He announced that he would attempt a crossing with a man riding on his back.

Bigger crowds gathered; larger sums were bet. Blondin set out with his precious cargo. As he inched along, several of the men who had bet strongly against him began to fear that he might succeed. So they reached for the guy ropes that braced the main wire and cut one of them. Halfway across the span Blondin at once felt the wire beneath him beginning to sway dangerously. And Blondin began to *run* to the far side, his human freight bouncing along on his back! Once more he succeeded. He actually made it!

But now let me ask you the two questions Rev. Boomsma used to ask. Do you *believe* that Blondin could do this? Suppose you do. Then you are like the spectators. You bet on Blondin.

But now the harder question: would you have *trusted* Blondin enough to get on his back?

FOR REFLECTION

"Trust is often harder for us than belief." Do you agree? Why or why not?

PRAYER STARTERS

Ask Jesus to help you trust him more and more. Or say this prayer: "Lord Christ, it is easy for me to say I believe what you have said and done. But give me also the trust that lets me place myself in your hands. Amen.

CHOSEN TO CHOOSE HIM

SCRIPTURE

"You did not choose me, but I chose you. And I appointed you to go and bear fruit, fruit that will last. . . . If you belonged to the world, it would love you as its own. Because you do not belong to the world, but I have chosen you out of the world—therefore the world hates you."

—John 15:16, 19

TEACHINGS

Q. It is through faith alone
that we share in Christ and all his benefits:
where then does that faith come from?
A. The Holy Spirit produces it in our hearts
by the preaching of the holy gospel,
and confirms it
through our use of the holy sacraments.

—Heidelberg Catechism Q&A 65

Some choices cannot be avoided. If you are holding a double-dip, peanut-butter-and-double-fudge-chocolate ice cream cone in bright sunlight on a hot day you have to decide whether to gulp it down or let it melt. You *have* to choose. You cannot refuse to decide. For that refusal is itself a decision—one soon dripping with melted ice cream.

The same goes for a gardener who refuses to decide whether to let his garden go to weeds.

The same goes for a confused sailor who has one foot on a dock and the other in a departing catamaran. In each of these cases, if you do not choose, the choice will be made for you. And you may not like the result.

When we reach our teens, we begin to understand how much the shape and happiness of life depend on our choices. True, some of our choices are small and innocent. Will we wear jeans or sweats? Ride or walk? Call or text? Study or take the night off? Small matters.

But some choices are very serious. They have to do with who or what will control us. A person may decide, for instance, to turn her brain to oatmeal by sniffing, smoking, or shooting certain drugs. In some cases a drug-ridden person can choose to get help before the damage is permanent. But sometimes an addiction that begins with a free choice to experiment ends up robbing a person of the power to choose anything but drugs. That's how frightening an addiction can be. It starts with a choice and ends with slavery. A person ends up mastered by chemicals.

Your most important choice is the choice of your master. You cannot refuse to choose: the refusal is itself a choice. For someone or something *will* master you. It might be God or it might be the devil. It might be your own changing moods or feelings. It might be the opinions of your friends.

If you say, "I refuse to choose," you will then be mastered by whoever and whatever happens to come along. Instead of having one master, good or bad, you will have many. There are people like that. They change masters as often as a square dancer changes partners.

To be a person grafted into Jesus Christ by belief and trust is to choose your master. It is to choose the only master who will never disappoint you. Instead of yourself, instead of evil, instead of friends or feelings or fondness for foolishness, you turn in faith to Jesus Christ and his promises.

You may do this very gradually. You may, year by year, *find* yourself believing in him. Or it may happen quite rapidly some winter week when things have broken down and friends have failed. You find one night that your prayers seem especially important to you. A part of the Bible suddenly speaks to you. You are strangely ready to do a painful thing that you know is right— confessing sin, for instance. A sermon one Sunday seems aimed at you like a shot to the heart.

In the midst of such things you turn to face Jesus Christ, your Master. "O Lord," you stammer, "now I give myself to you." And then, in one of the great and beautiful mysteries of faith, you discover something startling. You discover that it is not really you who has been doing the choosing. He has.

"You did not choose me," says Jesus. "I chose you."

How? By images and feelings and Bible stories that seeped into us when we were little kids.

By the sight of our parents on their knees in prayer. By the life of a person we admire. By a great joy or a shattering tragedy. Above all, by the silent, powerful work in us of the Holy Spirit. God has his ways. We cannot avoid him. God knows a thousand combinations that will unlock the treasure house in each of us where God has stored his goods.

> **Election:** God's choice of us for the gift of saving faith.

God chooses us to choose him. God's choice is called *election.* Ours is called *faith.* Both are a sheer gift.

FOR REFLECTION

How has the Holy Spirit worked (and how does the Spirit continue to work) in your life to give you faith?

PRAYER STARTERS

Thank the Lord for calling your name, for choosing you to choose him, for his wonderful gift of saving faith.

WEEK 14

WHY MUST WE MAKE A U-TURN? (REPENTANCE/CONVERSION)

TURNING

SCRIPTURE

"Repent, therefore, and turn to God so that your sins may be wiped out, so that times of refreshing may come from presence of the Lord."
—Acts 3:19-20

TEACHINGS

Q. What is involved
in genuine repentance or conversion?

A. Two things:
the dying-away of the old self,
and the rising-to-life of the new.

—Heidelberg Catechism Q&A 88

A driver reaches for his ringing cell phone and turns the wrong way onto a one-way street. He tools along for a hundred feet and then sees two lanes of cars coming straight at him. He slams on the brakes, skids to a stop, flips the gear selector into reverse, lurches backward into a driveway, waits for traffic to pass, and then drives off in the opposite direction.

A hiker tries a shortcut through a patch of woods. She keeps bearing left, as she thinks she should, but the path disappears, the woods get thicker, and the hiker begins to feel waves of panic washing over her. So she turns around and heads out the way she came in.

A father watches his prodigal son stride off down the road to a far city. Day after day the father walks out to the gate and peers down that road. He keeps watching and aching and hoping. He keeps praying that if his son is lost in the far city, he will not lose the memory of his home. And one day, perhaps years later, shading his eyes against the late afternoon sun, the father spies a figure in the distance. The approaching figure droops and hesitates, but there is no mistaking who it is. Overwhelmed with need, arms extended like a finishing sprinter, the father rushes toward the son he wants home.

The son and the hiker and the driver all repent. Repentance is more than simply turning a corner or turning over a new page. To repent is to stop in your tracks, pivot one hundred eighty degrees, and head back. To repent is to *turn completely* around. Sometimes it happens quickly; sometimes it takes years.

Most of us have heard of repentance. We may have the feeling that it is somewhat unpleasant. We are wrong. It is entirely unpleasant. Repentance is no fun at all. And yet we have to do it. In fact, as the great Christian writer C. S. Lewis once said, repentance is a special problem to us because only bad people *need* to do it and only good people *can* do it.

What is this turning and why can't we forget about if it's so unpleasant?

Repentance—or *conversion*, as it is often called—is the complete turnaround of our lives. Because of original sin we have a tendency to do wrong—to lie, to envy, to think of ourselves as the best thing to ever walk the earth, and so on. We also tend to avoid doing what's right—working hard, for example, or encouraging a person we don't like very well. We are like a small outboard fishing boat headed downstream toward a ruinous waterfall. Our tendency is to let the stream carry us. That's easiest, especially if we don't know or don't care about the danger. We tend to go with the flow.

Repentance in such a situation is a hard and delicate move. We have to see our danger, shift into reverse, plow stern-first backward till we get upstream to quieter water. Then we have to turn carefully around and head against the current.

These descriptions of repentance are all pictures. They tell what repentance (conversion) is *like*. Repentance is like a U-turn in traffic. It is like a hiker's retreat or a runaway's homecoming. Repentance is like an outboard backing upstream, full-speed astern.

> **Repentance:** the complete turning around of our lives. Repentance is like dying and then being born again. Repentance is sometimes called *conversion*. Some conversions, such as the apostle Paul's, are sudden and dramatic. Others, like Timothy's, are more gradual.

There is, as a matter of fact, one more thing that repentance, or conversion, is like. It is like dying and rising. It is as though an old person within us—one that cheats and struts—is killed off and a fresh new person—one that is clean and straight—is born. Repentance is the conversion, the turning of a person from old to new, from death to life. Repentance is like being born again.

What does this mean in detail? As we shall see, it means feeling the pain of those we hurt. It means running away from evil. It means taking delight in what's right. It means starting to think of ourselves as being driven by a new engine, by the power of the Holy Spirit.

Why do we have to do these things? Because without them we will drown or crash or get lost or die in some far-off pig pen.

Without repentance we will be without God.

FOR REFLECTION

If you are already committed to Christ, how did the turnaround of repentance (conversion) happen in your life? Was it sudden and dramatic, or did it happen more gradually, perhaps still going on or still in the future?

PRAYER STARTERS

Talk to God about the process of repentance/conversion in your own life. Ask for God's Spirit to enter your life in a powerful way and help you live as a brand-new person.

DYING-AWAY

SCRIPTURE

Godly sorrow brings repentance that leads to salvation and leaves no regret, but worldly sorrow brings death.

—2 Corinthians 7:10 (NIV)

TEACHINGS

Q. What is the dying-away of the old self?

A. To be genuinely sorry for sin,
   and more and more to hate
   and run away from it.

—Heidelberg Catechism Q&A 89

People say it all the time.

You get a wrong number because of your machine-gun speed with your phone. "Sorry," you say to the stranger who answers. You walk down the hall at school and accidentally conk someone on the head with your overloaded backpack. "Sorry," you say. You reach for the dinner rolls and drag your cuff through your brother's mashed potatoes. "Sorry."

These are all apologies. They are small sorrows for small errors. They are the oil that cuts down friction in the turning of life's little wheels. Politeness means saying you're sorry.

So does repentance. But a repentant person who uses these words means something far more serious by them than does the person who is only being polite. In his book *Forgive and Forget* Lewis Smedes, a fine Christian writer, has helped us understand this.

Suppose, for instance, that another student has suspended himself by his knees from a chinning bar. You think it would be fun to swing him like a hanging side of beef. So you give him a shove. Suddenly he flips off the bar and lands on the back of his head. He doesn't move. The principal calls an ambulance, which speeds the injured student to Emergency. Eventually he recovers, but meanwhile he suffers through several weeks of blurred vision, headaches, and time lost from school.

An apology is not quite good enough. You need to do more. You need to feel the other person's pain. You need to feel sadness and concern. You need good grief. After all, you hurt someone. You may want to bring him a gift, trying somehow to make up for your bad behavior. You will certainly apologize profusely. You will want him to know how bad you feel and how much you wish you hadn't pushed him. Finally, you solemnly promise yourself never to do something that stupid again.

You repent.

Our whole life needs repentance. The old self we are born with is tempted to push and shove. It likes to stand in the winner's circle while crowds roar and bands play. It wants deliciously to chew on a juicy morsel of gossip that will bring another person down. And it shrinks from the honest praise that will build another person up.

To tell the truth, the old self in us shrinks from God. We know God is there. There are times, like some late night on a camping trip, that we have almost felt the breath of God. But because we want to drive our own life, run our own show, hoist our own flag, we find that God becomes a kind of embarrassment to us. We ignore God. We neglect Jesus Christ. We do not pray unless we have to. We daydream through church services. Though we are radiant, pulsing images of God, we try to become instead images of some human jock, or clown, or queen, or star, or fool.

Repentance (conversion) means turning away from all this. It means feeling the pain of those we hurt or ignore. It means feeling the pain and fearing the anger of the God of the universe. Repentance includes a softening of our hearts and a turning toward the Father who waits by the gate for us to come home. He is the only person in the world who can open a door and welcome us *inside*.

To repent is to muscle aside familiar habits. You have to beat down old attitudes. You have to try to kill somebody—the old self with all its warts and ways. This is hard work. Old selves die hard. You might put out a contract on your old self but find that it takes a long time to get up the nerve

to go through with the act itself. It is humiliating to be your own hit man.

> **Dying-away:** the killing of the old self. Our old self is the person we are by sin, original and actual. Dying away includes fighting sin and fleeing from it.

But it can be done. Over time repentance works. God is at work in this painful, holy suicide. Like the last notes of a filthy song, like the freight-train rumble of a killer tornado, like the roar of a lynch mob, the old self slowly dies away.

It can still be heard from time to time. But each time its voice begins to sound more and more like the voice of a stranger.

FOR REFLECTION

Why is repentance (conversion) so difficult and painful? Have you experienced it that way yourself?

PRAYER STARTERS

"To repent is to muscle aside familiar habits." Think about habits or attitudes you have that need pushing aside. Confess these to God and ask for specific help in beating them down.

DYING-AWAY CONTINUED: FIGHT OR FLIGHT

SCRIPTURE

But you, man of God, flee from all this, and
    pursue righteousness, godliness,
faith, love, endurance and gentleness. Fight the
    good fight of the faith.

—1 Timothy 6:11-12 (NIV)

TEACHING

Q. What is the dying-away of the old self?
A. To be genuinely sorry for sin,
    and more and more to hate
    and run away from it.

—Heidelberg Catechism Q&A 89

In certain ways animals are a lot like humans. They will respond to a threat either by facing it or by running away from it. They fight or flee. Hunters know that a startled deer, for instance, will run. A deer, hearing the crackling of underbrush, turns up its tail so that the white underside shows, and bounds off. That is, a deer usually responds to a threat by hightailing it out of danger. But an injured animal, particularly a cornered one, responds to danger by becoming dangerous itself. It may attack. Savvy hunters know this and take precautions. They tell each other tales of men being slashed or gored by the sharp antlers of wounded bucks.

And humans are like animals. Homeowners who are tormented by repeated vandalism will stay up at night in the dark with a telephone or even a shotgun. Some do that; others simply move out of the neighborhood. Fight or flight. Similarly, a person who is unfairly criticized might face and speak up to the critic. Or she might just walk away and seek a place to pout. Fight or flight.

Look at the quotation from the catechism on this page. Repentance includes dying away. Dying away, in turn, includes sorrow for sin (which we thought about last time) and two other things— hating sin and running away from it.

Let's think of these as fight and flight. Part of dying away means hating sin enough to want to fight and kill it. Somebody wrecks a family by causing a divorce. A Christian will hate that sin, even if he loves the sinner. Somebody is tempted again and again to brag about imaginary accomplishments. The bragging and lying regularly get her into trouble with her friends. She comes to hate that sin. She wants to attack and kill it before it does more damage. Or suppose a person likes to bully smaller and weaker people. As he begins to turn toward God, he begins to hate his own bullying. He wants to root out this tendency in himself. For this (and all sin) is an enemy that corrupts and destroys.

Part of repentance is coming to feel a hatred of sin and its power to hurt. Repentant people especially hate and fight the sin over which they have some control. They level their biggest guns at their own sin.

But sometimes the right response to the temptation of sin is to run away from it. Suppose you are alone on a dark street late at night. Three young gentlemen swinging bicycle chains start walking toward you. You'll feel like a fool if you run, but the truth is that only a fool would stand and fight against those odds.

It is the same way with some sins. We are not strong enough, or wise enough, or old enough to fight some of them—and we know it. These may be sins that are especially tempting to us, sins especially fear, or sins that are brought to us as temptations by others. Suppose, for example, that a group wants to play a truly humiliating prank on a weak or unpopular person. You cannot stop them. You are afraid even to try. Perhaps you ought to have more courage. Maybe someday you will. But, for now, you can at least walk out. You can hightail it out of there. If someone accuses you of being afraid, the right answer would be, "Yes, I am. I'm afraid of what this will do to Ben (or whomever). And I also don't like what it's going to do to us."

The fact is that sin is frightening. Fools will pretend that it isn't—just as fools will play with live grenades. More mature people have the same healthy fear of sin that they have of a wounded wild animal. They do not snuggle up to it.

You have your choice with sin: fight or flight. Dying away "is to be genuinely sorry for sin, to hate it more and more, and to run away from it."

We have to die before we can be born again.

FOR REFLECTION

What kinds of sins might you actively fight? Flee from?

PRAYER STARTERS

Ask God for the courage to fight sin when you can, and for the wisdom to run away from it when you have to.

COMING-TO-LIFE

SCRIPTURE

Restore to me the joy of your salvation
and sustain in me a willing spirit.

—Psalm 51:12

TEACHINGS

Q. What is the rising-to-life of the new self?
A. Wholehearted joy in God through Christ
and a love and delight to live
according to the will of God
by doing every kind of good work.

—Heidelberg Catechism Q&A 90

Many of us know what it's like to feel a stab of joy when reading fantasy. A writer named Frederick Buechner (BEEK-ner) talks about the reasons for that feeling in one of his books.

In fantasies we read of places different from our own: a far-off country, or a forbidden forest, or a dark and fearful castle, or a boarding school for teaching magic to young witches and wizards. A person from ordinary life, often a child, enters one of these strange places. She may wander into the forest or come upon the castle at the end of a yellow-brick road. She may step into a wardrobe to hide from friends and find herself moving clear through it to an icy land ruled by an evil queen whose face is as white as death.

Fantasies often include danger. There may be a great and terrible wizard. There are forks in the path where a wrong choice means lostness or death. There are witches who cackle and drool over plump children. Above all, there are deceptions. Things are not as they appear. A gingerbread house is really a trap. A beautiful queen is a disguised witch. A great and terrible wizard is only a hairless little man with a microphone. A lion, in the end, appears to be someone like God. A stuttering, ineffective professor is really sharing his soul with the most terrible dark wizard of the century.

Fantasy almost always includes a "turn" too. After wild events and frustrating setbacks, after confusion and threats and dangers and battles, things take a turn for the good. A sleeping beauty awakens. An ugly duckling is transformed into a stunning white swan. Children who had been treated terribly by a cruel stepmother are rescued by their kind father. Cinderella's "wicked sisters with their big feet and fancy ways . . . repent in the end and are forgiven." The children and animals in *The Lion, the Witch, and the Wardrobe* celebrate and sing for joy because Aslan has conquered. A brave young wizard named Harry Potter defeats the traitorous Professor Quirrell by the power of love.

We rejoice with them. J. R. R. Tolkien (the man who wrote The Lord of the Rings trilogy) says that when the turn comes we feel "a catch of the breath, a beat and lifting of the heart." In fact, many of us feel like weeping—but not for grief. We cry for joy at the triumph of good. We weep because this triumph has a beauty as sharp as a northern wind.

Something old and deep in us is born again when we read of Aslan or of Mrs. Whatsit or of Professor Dumbledore or of the Velveteen Rabbit. Christians are especially open to these things because the coming-to-life of the new self in repentance includes "wholehearted joy in God through Christ." There is that stab of joy again. I think we can begin to understand it when we think of the gospel as *fantasy come true.*

The gospel is the story of a son coming home from a far country. It is the story of a sheep rescued from a dark and fearful wilderness by the strong arms of a fierce shepherd. It is the story of children released from prison, of demons unmasked, of the crushing of lethal snakes, and of the triumph of the Lamb of God. It is the story of all heaven breaking loose, the stars singing together and the sons of God shouting for joy.

For things are not as they seem. There is a turn. The dying Jesus, nerves stretched over nails, rises to kill death and to live for good. It happens this time not in a fantasy but in the Bible; not in fantasy land but in Israel; not once upon a time but on the first day of one week in about A.D. 29. The Son of God awakens.

Coming to life: the arising of the new self. The new self is the person we are by justification, faith, and repentance. The new self is Christlike and full of joy.

For us the stab of joy, the catch of the breath, is not only for our dead Lord who comes alive. It is also for ourselves. For in our baptism and in our repentance we die and rise with him, rejoicing in the triumph of God, a triumph with beauty as sharp as a northern wind. Once more, as when Adam awoke and when Jesus arose—once more God blows into us the breath of life.

Repentance is the dying away of the old self and the coming to life of the new.

FOR REFLECTION

How is the gospel like a fantasy come true?

PRAYER STARTERS

Think about the role of joy in your life as a Christian. Are you experiencing the deep and satisfying joy of being a new person in Christ? In your prayer today, thank God for the joy you already experience in your Christian walk. If joy is lacking in your life, ask the Spirit to awaken you to what it means to be a new person in Christ.

WEEK 15

**CAN WE REALLY BECOME
LIKE JESUS? (SANCTIFICATION)**

LIVING THE NEW LIFE

SCRIPTURE

As you therefore have received Christ Jesus as Lord, continue to live your lives in him, rooted and built up in him and established in the faith just as you were taught, and abounding in thanksgiving.

—Colossians 2:6-7

TEACHINGS

We believe that . . . true faith . . .
     makes us . . . new . . .
causing us to live a new life
     and freeing us from the slavery of sin.

—Belgic Confession, Article 24

Things can belong to a person in more than one way. A public library, for instance, belongs to all the citizens of a town or city. But only some of them actually use the library. They consult its reference works, browse through its stacks, borrow its books and videos. These people "make the library their own" in a way that others do not. The library really belongs to those who use it.

The same goes for sports equipment and musical instruments. You may receive a set of golf clubs or a trumpet as a gift, but if you never learn how to hit a straight iron shot or play a scale, you do not really possess these gifts. Such things must be used before they fully belong to you.

Something like that is true in our Christian faith. In justification God forgives our sins and credits us with the righteousness of Christ. We receive these gifts by faith and repentance.

But how can we use them? How can we actually begin to live like Christ and think like Christ? How can we learn to treat our friends as valuable persons made in the image of God instead of as stepladders for our own ambitions? How can we learn to spend time with shy or boring persons? How can we firmly resist going against what we know is the will of God? That is, how can the righteousness of Jesus Christ get injected into our bloodstreams so that it circulates through every part of our lives? How can the righteousness of Christ actually start to *belong* to us?

The answer lies in what Christians call *sanctification*. Justification is like the gift of golf clubs or a trumpet. Sanctification is like the long process of learning to play well.

Even in this process much must be done by God. Just as a musician has to be given a talent and an instrument and good lessons, so God must justify us and fill us with faith and show us the example of Christ, our Master. In addition, the

Holy Spirit must energize us with breath and new life before we can play a single note.

But there's also something we must do. Perhaps you have noticed that in the Bible we are sometimes treated as children and sometimes as adults. We must be childlike in our faith—mouths and hands and hearts wide open to receive nourishing life and breath from the Holy Spirit. But as adults we are to do what *we* can in sanctification. Christians who have been grafted into Christ by faith and who have died and risen with Christ in repentance are then told to go to work. We are told to fight the good fight, run the race, finish the course. We must put off old habits and put on new ones. We are to strive, sow, reap, follow, obey, take up our crosses. In other words, we are to become holy.

That may seem disappointing. We may think of holiness as boring or weak.

But if so, we are mistaken. In hiding Jews from Nazis, people in the Second World War were doing something dangerous—and holy. In fighting to liberate African Americans in the U.S., Martin Luther King Jr. was doing something risky—and holy. In struggling to obey his Father when he felt like backing out, Jesus, our Lord, was doing something painfully difficult—but holy.

To be holy is to be like Jesus Christ. Sanctification is the long process—partly painful, partly joyous—of learning to live well. That is, sanctification is the process of learning how to live like the holy Christ.

Look back at the Bible text for today. "As you therefore have received Christ Jesus as Lord,"

says Paul, now "continue to live your lives in him."

Receiving a gift is one thing. Learning how to use and live with our gift is another. Only then will the gift really belong to us.

FOR REFLECTION

What is there about becoming holy, learning how to live like Jesus, that appeals to you? That raises questions or concerns for you?

PRAYER STARTERS

You may want to play or sing the chorus of the song "Sanctuary" as your personal prayer. You can listen to it performed by numerous artists on YouTube.

WHAT DRIVES YOU?

SCRIPTURE

"I am the vine, you are the branches. Those who abide in me and I in them bear much fruit, because apart from apart from me you can do nothing."

—John 15:5

TEACHINGS

It is impossible
	for those grafted into Christ by true faith not to produce fruits of gratitude.

—Heidelberg Catechism, Answer 64

Q. What are good works?
A. Only those which
		are done out of true faith . . .

—Heidelberg Catechism Q&A 91

Watch just about any crime drama on TV and you'll know what's meant by "motive." Let's say someone has murdered his boss. One of the first things the good guys ask is why someone would want to do that. What could possibly be his or her motive?

A motive is anything that drives or moves us to do or say something. For instance, a murderer may be motivated by envy. That is, a murderer may hate and want another person's success so badly that he feels driven to kill him. People do not usually act randomly. There is something *behind* what they do or say. Ordinarily, bad motives such as greed or envy produce bad deeds. Ordinarily, good motives produce good deeds.

What are some motives behind good deeds? Or, to ask the question another way, what are motives for holiness? (After all, good deeds, as we shall see, are only one part of holiness.)

There are three main motives behind the Christian life of holiness. Three main things drive us forward in sanctification.

One of these is our desire for God, something we read about way back in week one. We hunger and thirst for God even when we don't know it. And just as hunger for food motivates us to eat, so hunger for God drives us to do good and to be holy. Why? Because acting like God is a way to get close to God. You have seen people imitate sports heroes or film stars. You have watched a small child try to act like an older brother or sister. These people are using imitation to try to get close to someone, to share his or her life. So it is with us and God.

Another motive for holiness is gratitude, or thankfulness. Suppose a person you admire takes an interest in you. This person asks about you, wants to spend time with you, tries to build up your strengths. You feel pleasure and appreciation in all of this. You are grateful for this person's interest and want to show it.

But suppose that in an emergency the person you admire actually saves your life in some spectacular way. You might feel gratitude toward him or her for the rest of your life.

Gratitude is a main motive in the Christian life. Our lives have been saved by the powerful rescue work of Jesus Christ. This must always be in the back of our minds. We could have been wrecked. Instead we have been accepted and loved. We ought to be grateful to God for the rest of our lives.

But there is one other motive. In striving for holiness, a Christian is motivated by faith. Faith tells me that I belong to Jesus Christ and am justified. I really do need faith to believe this. After all, it sometimes seems as though I am making little progress in repentance. If I had to judge by how I act, I might doubt my justification.

But suppose I do actually believe I am a saved child of God. Suppose I trust Jesus Christ for rescue. Then this belief and trust make me try to act like a saved person. Faith drives me to act in accordance with who I am.

You recall Don Quixote's noble lady. She thought she was only a whore. But when she began to trust Don Quixote, she began to act like a noble lady. Why? Because he accepted her and called her noble. And faith made her act in accordance with the new person she was in the eyes of her savior.

It's like that with us. By faith we believe God when he calls us his saved children in the Bible, in our baptism, and in the eyes of our loved ones. We believe this even when we don't feel very close to God and have not been acting very much like God's children. We must keep reminding ourselves who we are. We must remember who accepts us and calls us noble. We must then begin to act once again in accordance with the new person we are in the eyes of our Savior.

FOR REFLECTION

Reflect on your own life and what really drives you to live a holier life.

PRAYER STARTERS

Ask God to make you want to be close to him, to really hunger and thirst for God. Ask God to help build up your gratitude and faith so you may be driven to act in Christlike ways.

GETTING IN SHAPE

SCRIPTURE

Depart from evil and do good;
so you shall abide forever.

—Psalm 37:27

For while physical training is of some value,
godliness is valuable in every way, holding
promise for both the present life and the life to
come.

—1 Timothy 4:8

TEACHINGS

Q. What is the rising-to-life of the new self?
A. Wholehearted joy in God through Christ
and a love and delight to live
according to the will of God
by doing every kind of good work.

—Heidelberg Catechism Q&A 90

In week 7 we learned that original sin includes
guilt and corruption. These are humanity's
oldest and deepest problems. Now we're ready
to understand the solution to these problems.

Justification is God's solution to the problem
of guilt. To people who have broken God's law
and deserve punishment God brings instead
forgiveness and alien righteousness.

Sanctification is God's solution to the problem of
corruption. Corruption, you recall, is the seeping
power of sin. Corruption is like an overflowing
sewer that pollutes all we think, say, and do.
Sanctification is the gradual process of getting
unpolluted. In sanctification God goes to work
with us to clean the grime off and to polish us up
as God's images.

It begins when we are old enough to feel really
sorry about our sin. Soon we gain enough
experience of sin's destruction to hate it and to
want to get away from it. Then, perhaps suddenly
one summer, or gradually over a period of years,
our faith in God's forgiving love sharpens and our
joy in God himself deepens. All of this, we know,
is repentance, or conversion.

Sanctification is the word we use when we think
of conversion stretched out across a whole life.
After all, it takes a long time to unlearn habits
that are old and deep. The righteousness for
which Christians hunger and thirst is not fast
food. It needs time to simmer into something rich
and savory.

Let's think of another comparison. An athlete
trains. He or she will eat right, get to bed on time,
and take on the daily discipline of practice. Certain
muscle groups will be worked in thousands of
repetitions till they have mass and flexibility. Certain moves will be practiced again and again till
they become second nature: a one-on-one fake,
for example, or an overhead smash, or a flip turn.

Each time the athlete trains, he gets a little better. Each time she works out, some sloppy old habit dies a little and some disciplined new one begins to come to life. That is, each training session causes a tiny conversion. But it is only after many seasons of such training that a person can perform his or her skills by second nature. The mini-conversions repeated thousands of times add up to the change of one's life. A duffer becomes a disciplined athlete.

The Christian life is almost exactly like that. We have to be *trained* in godliness, or holiness, till it becomes second nature. Every time we pray, every time we resist a temptation, every time we bring a gift to a lonesome person, every time we make ourselves think of the needs of others—each time we do these things our old self dies a little and our new self comes more to life. Add up all these mini-conversions across years of training and you have a spiritual athlete. A flabby and clumsy Christian becomes a trim and graceful one. A polluted person gets sanctified. Sanctification is lifelong conversion.

> **Sanctification:** the lifelong conversion by which Christians become gradually holier—that is, more like Jesus Christ. Sanctification is the solution to the problem of pollution. We want to live the life of holiness because of our desire for God, our gratitude to him, and our faith in him.

We know its motives. We also know that in sanctification the Holy Spirit must decontaminate us who have been radioactive because of sin. So what must we do?

We must do good. Besides joy in God, the life of holiness includes "a delight to do every kind of good as God wants us to." The content, the "stuff," the material of the new life is doing good.

I know, of course, that some Christians are not terribly big on the idea of doing good. They think it's too hard or too boring. Some sneer at "do-gooders." Others do good—but sullenly, as though it's a joyless chore.

These folks are out of shape. They have broken training. They have forgotten what athletes know: you need discipline in order to be free. Trained people have fun. It takes hard work to be able to *play* well.

Doing good is the very stuff of the Christian life. We are not saved *by* doing it; we are saved *to* do it. We are saved to go into training and do our stuff.

FOR REFLECTION

"We have to be trained in doing godliness, or holiness, till it becomes second nature." Where do you see such training going on in your life?

PRAYER STARTERS

Use this prayer or one of your own:

God, coach me and train me to do good. Make me fit to serve you and your children. May I find joy in you. May I delight to do every kind of good, as you want me to do. Amen.

SHINE ON

SCRIPTURE

"In the same way, let your light shine before others, so that they may see your good works and give glory to your Father in heaven."
—Matthew 5:16

TEACHINGS

Q. What are good works?
A. Only those which
      are done out of true faith,
      conform to God's law,
      and are done for God's glory;
   and not those based
      on our own opinion
      or human tradition.
—Heidelberg Catechism Q&A 91

Anybody can see reflectors at night. Joggers wear reflecting tape on their shoes and shirts. Bike pedals and wheels show us moving circles of reflected light. Lane dividers, roadside mileage indicators, traffic signs, guardrails, bridge piers, the eyes of deer and raccoon—all these things reflect. Even the moon acts as a giant reflector of the hidden light of the sun.

A reflector is something that returns, or bends back, energy from a source. Wall tiles, for example, can act as reflectors of sound. If you sing in the shower, the sound waves of your voice hit hard surfaces and come bouncing back to you. "Bathroom baritones" like to make and hear those reflected sounds. Other family members might not.

The main thing about reflectors, whether they return sound or light, is that they do not produce energy themselves. The light must come from a car's headlights, or from the sun, or from some other power source. Sound waves must come from your larynx, or your radio, or your alto saxophone. A reflector does not produce energy. It only deflects or returns it.

But reflectors can do something else to light or sound. They can transform it. They can change its color or focus, for instance. Depending on the color of the reflector, light from your car's headlights can come back to you green or red instead of yellow. A spherical mirror (like the side-view mirrors on some cars, or the "shoplifter mirrors" in stores) can focus light so that a particular part of what's reflected can be seen especially well.

Christians are reflectors of God's glory. In sanctification we become clean mirrors, or polished images, of the glory of God.

What is glory and how do we reflect it?

Glory really means two things. One of them is "light." A sunset, for instance, may be described as "glorious" because it is brilliant, because it lights up the whole western sky.

One thing we mean, therefore, when we talk of the glory of God is that God appears dazzling to us: hot and pure and brilliant. In the Bible we read of persons meeting God and comparing the experience to walking into the center of the sun.

The other meaning of glory is something like "weightiness" or "worthiness." A glorious person is one who is centered, weighty, important. You cannot push such a person around. He has, so to speak, a low center of gravity. He is a kind of heavyweight. He is a person of important reputation. The glory of Solomon or the glory of ancient Greece, for instance, had to do with the weightiness of their reputation for wisdom.

The Christian life of sanctification has three main parts. One part is its motives: desire, gratitude, faith. Another is the content, or stuff, of holiness: doing good. The third is its purpose, or goal. What are we trying to achieve by doing good? What's the point?

The point, or purpose, is to glorify God. But how could mere humans glorify God? We are not like the sun in energy. Surely we do not all have dazzling reputations.

True. But we can reflect. Powerful energy from God—energy like dazzling light—can come from God and be reflected back to him from human beings. When this happens, we "color," or transform, such energy as reflectors always do. Energy from God goes back to him colored by the personalities of millions of God's children.

> **Glory of God:** the light of God and God's weighty reputation. Christians glorify God by reflecting his energy back to him in good deeds. These actually increase God's reputation among humans. To glorify God is the goal of the Christian life.

One more, almost unbelievable, thing: God's reputation is actually made greater when we act like Christ. By doing good we have the power to focus the reputation of God so that people can see it especially well and be awed. As Jesus said, "Let your light shine before others, so that they may see your good works and give glory to your Father in heaven."

A saint, said C. S. Lewis, is a person who makes God believable. A saint—a sanctified person—is a good reflector.

FOR REFLECTION

"To glorify God is the purpose of the Christian life." Do you think this would be a good answer to give to someone who asks why you're a Christian? Why or why not?

PRAYER STARTERS

Silence before God can be a form of prayer. In silence, kneel before the greatness and holiness and glory of our awesome God. Let God's glory fill your thoughts and your heart. Then raise your hands, palms out, in a gesture of reflecting some of that glory to others.

WEEK 16

HOW CAN WE KNOW WHAT'S RIGHT? (THE LAW)

INSTRUCTIONS FOR NEW DRIVERS

SCRIPTURE

Then God spoke all these words: "I am the Lord your God, who brought you out of the land of Egypt, out of the house of slavery; you shall have no other gods before me."

—Exodus 20:1-3

TEACHINGS

Q. What are good works?

A. Only those which
>   are done out of true faith,
>   conform to God's law,
>   and are done for God's glory;
>   and not those based
>   on our own opinion
>   or human tradition.

—Heidelberg Catechism Q&A 91

About three months after God rescued the Hebrew slaves out of Egypt, he gave them his law. Of course, the Israelites had known law before. They had been up against the Egyptian law of bricks and straw, a law for slaves. But now they were free. And the same God who had freed them, the same God who had originally created them—this God gave them a set of instructions for the new life of liberty.

It happened at Mt. Sinai. Out of the fire and smoke and the mystery of his glory God spoke.

Moses went up the mountain to listen. Up and down he went. But when Moses came down a final time, he had with him God's instructions: a set of Ten Commandments, as well as smaller rules that explained them.

> **Law of God:** the statement of what God wants from us. The law of God is a training guide for the new life of liberty.

These and other requirements from the rest of the Bible together make up the law of God. The law of God is a statement of what God wants from us. God wants us to do justice and love kindness and walk humbly with him. God wants us to love him above all and our neighbor as ourselves. That is, God wants his people to do good.

But what is good? What do we do that is good? Whatever is motivated by desire for God, by gratitude, and by faith. Whatever has the reflection of God's glory as its goal. These are things we have already learned. Let's now add a third item: what's good is whatever is in accord with God's law. The law is a kind of recipe for the right stuff of the Christian life.

Think of it this way. When people get to be a certain age, they may apply for a driver's license. Most teenagers can hardly wait. Beyond the sheer fun of driving, the reason, of course, is that the person who can drive is free. When you learn to drive, you can zip into town or across town. You can visit somebody two towns away. You can go to the drive-through window at a fast-food joint. You can drive yourself to school. You can pick up friends and cart them around. When you learn to drive, you are free.

But, as you learn in driver's education, you need guidance in order to use your new freedom well. You need a set of instructions for your new life.

First, you need an owner's manual for the car you drive. The manufacturer may have designed the engine to run on diesel fuel, for instance. You may personally prefer to fill the tank with leftover vegetable oil, but then the car won't run. It's wise to know that before trying it. In general, you need to know how your car operates and how to operate it that way.

Second, you need to learn a set of traffic laws so that you can pass your driver's exam and get along with other drivers out on the road. Laws for stopping, turning, yielding, and merging are instructions allowing a whole town-full of people to drive at the same time.

The law of God is something like instructions for new drivers. Part of it tells us how to run our own cars: You shall have no other gods before me. Do not make an image to worship it. Do not swear. Keep the Sabbath. These first four commandments (the "first table" of the Law) are summed up in the first great commandment: You shall love God above all.

The first great commandment is a kind of owner's manual. It tells us that we were designed by our manufacturer to run on love for him.

Another part of the law is like traffic regulations. It tells us how to get along with other drivers: Do not kill. Do not commit adultery. Do not steal. Do not bear false witness. Do not covet. These last six commandments (the "second table" of the Law) are summed up in the second great commandment: You shall love your neighbor as yourself.

The law of God is a set of instructions for all of us new drivers who find ourselves in possession of a new life of liberty.

FOR REFLECTION

Read Psalm 19:7-11. In what ways does God's law benefit you personally?

PRAYER STARTERS

Reflect on your personal attitude toward God's law. Then say a prayer that reflects your attitude. If you sense that you need help in seeing God's law as a good thing, pray about that. Ask God to help you live the new life of liberty he has given you.

DO JUSTICE

SCRIPTURE

He has told you, O mortal, what is good;
   and what does the LORD require of you
but to do justice, and to know kindness,
   and to walk humbly with your God?

—Micah 6:8

TEACHINGS

We reject any doctrine which . . . sanctions in the name of the gospel or the will of God the forced separation of people on the grounds of race and color.

We believe

- that God has revealed himself as the one who wishes to bring about justice and true peace among people;
- that God, in a world full of injustice and enmity, is in a special way the God of the destitute, the poor and the wronged;
- that God calls the church to follow him in this, for God brings justice to the oppressed and gives bread to the hungry.

—Belhar Confession

The family of a murder victim troops grimly into the courtroom on the day the killer is to be sentenced. The wife of a man who has run off with another woman makes an appointment with a lawyer. A bank manager forces an embezzler to pay back every cent he stole. A judge punishes a witness for perjury. A government takes away some of the earnings of rich people and distributes the money to poor people. A panel awards first prize to the best entry in a photo contest. God disciplines his people for their idolatry.

In all these cases persons are seeking or doing *justice*.

> **Justice:** what persons have coming. The first table of the Law tells us what God has coming from us. The second table tells us what other humans have coming.

Justice means giving others what they have coming. For example, we owe God our worship and total obedience. As our Maker and Savior, God has a right to these things. Justice means giving God what he has coming. As we saw in week 9, we have covenant obligations to God. Justice requires that we fulfill them.

The Ten Commandments tell us how. They are a set of instructions for the new life of justice. The first four commandments tell us what justice toward God amounts to. First, God alone has a right to our worship: we must have no gods instead of or in addition to him. Second, human beings are the only images of God that have God's patent on them: we must make no other images of him. Third, God has a right to our reverence: we must not abuse his name. Fourth, God has a right to our celebration of his great acts in the creation and exodus: we must not abuse his holy day.

The owner's manual tells us that God has these things coming from us. If we offer them, we are doing justice. If we withhold them, we deserve a penalty. Penalties for unjust acts are themselves just. For when we are disobedient, we have punishment coming.

The second table of the law is a recipe for doing justice to other human beings. As persons in the image of God, others have a right to our respect. They have a right to be treated fairly—to be given a fair share of the earth's food, for instance. They have the right not to be forcibly separated on the grounds of race and color, a right written into the Belhar Confession (see Teachings, above). If they are our parents or civil authorities, they also have a right to our obedience (fifth commandment). Other people have a right to many additional things.

For example, others have a right (sixth commandment) to life: we may not murder. They have a right (seventh) to loyalty and promise keeping in marriage: we may not commit adultery. They have a right (eighth) to keep some private property: we may not steal. They have a right (ninth) to the truth: we may not falsely accuse them. In fact (tenth), all our desires for God, property, and persons should be shaped by God's law.

We can now see how the second table of the Law is like a set of traffic regulations. These commandments tell us how millions of people can live together in justice. They tell us what rights others have and what obligation we, therefore, have to respect those rights.

The Bible also tells us of God's penalties for those who act unjustly, those who trample on the rights of others. God is jealous of his own rights as God (third commandment). But he is also jealous of the rights of his children—especially the widows, the orphans, and the poor. The great Old Testament prophets tell us about this.

Judges, courts, and prize panels all deal with rights and justice. But God's justice is blended with love and thus goes beyond them. If you look, for example, at the little rules (Ex. 21-23) that follow the Ten Commandments, you will find some special provisions. For instance, it is unlawful to charge interest on a loan to a needy person (22:25). It is unlawful to keep a person's overcoat overnight (22:26). Why? Because such acts lack compassion. Further, if you are a farmer, you must harvest in a way that leaves food for the poor. Why? Because such acts show compassion.

God's laws are a recipe for justice. Beyond that they are a recipe for love. When you put justice and love together, you have what we call "doing good."

FOR REFLECTION

Where do you see a real need for "doing justice" in your community?

PRAYER STARTERS

Pray for persons/groups who are treated unjustly in your community, nation, and beyond.

LEARN TO LOVE

SCRIPTURE

He [Jesus] said to him, "'You shall love the Lord your God with all your heart, and with all your soul, and with all your mind.' This is the greatest and first commandment. And a second is like it: 'You shall love your neighbor as yourself.'"

—Matthew 22:37-39

TEACHINGS

We believe that this unity of the people of God must be manifested and be active in a variety of ways: in that we love one another; that we experience, practice and pursue community with one another; that we are obligated to give ourselves willingly and joyfully to be of benefit and blessing to one another.

—Belhar Confession

People are more likely to *talk* about love than to understand it or do it. People talk about love all the time. They mention books or movies they love. They confess to being in love with another person. Kids claim to love peanut butter. In the U.S. patriots place one hand over their heart and sing, "God bless America, land that I love."

All this talk about different kinds of love can be misleading, because, really, all these variations can be boiled down into two kinds of love: need-love and gift-love. Need-love is the kind of love we feel when we think we cannot get along without another person. We *need* this person to fill us, to complete us, to make us feel whole and happy. The classic case of need-love is romance—what a man and woman feel for each other when they fall in love.

> **Need-love:** a powerful yearning for others. Need-love wants others to adorn us with something they have. Need-love is created by God and comes naturally to us.
>
> **Gift-love:** the power of caring for others. Gift-love wants to adorn others with something we have. Gift-love is created by God but has to be learned by us.

Gift-love, on the other hand, is almost the opposite. Gift-love is the kind of love we feel when we want to bring something of value to another just to make that person feel whole or complete or happy. Need-love cares about its own needs; gift-love cares about the needs of others. Need-love is empty and wants to be full; gift-love is full to overflowing and wants to fill someone else who may be empty. Need-love wants to receive; gift-love wants to give. Need-love is a powerful yearning for others; it wants others to adorn us with something they have. Gift-love is the power of caring for others and of wanting to adorn them with something we have.

Healthy relationships have some of each. In fact, both kinds of love come from God. Take need-love: we are created to need others. It is not good for us to be alone. When a person hungers and thirsts for God, or for family or for a person of the opposite sex, this hungering is an appetite that God made. And whatever God makes us want is good.

Gift-love also comes from God. In creation God makes room for others and welcomes them into life. In incarnation God sends his only Son as a Christmas gift to the world. In atonement God gives up his only Son as a sacrifice for sinners. God's love is the original gift-love. Ours is a human copy.

But how important a copy it is! Our gift-love is so important, in fact, that Jesus summarizes the whole law of God by means of it. We are to love God above all; we are to love our neighbor as ourselves. The Ten Commandments tell us how.

How do we love God above all? By giving God what he has coming—our obedience, our loyalty, our very selves. In our relationship to God justice and gift-love are the same thing. We owe all that we have and all that we are to God. We cannot give more than this.

But to other human beings we can give more than we owe. The last six commandments tell us how. To love others means two things: it means being just to them; it also means caring for them and wanting to adorn them with something we have. Love goes beyond justice.

Think of three examples. The sixth commandment says I must not murder. Justice means respecting my neighbor's right to life. The priest and the Levite who passed by a wounded stranger in the ditch acted justly (Luke 10). They did not harm him. But the Samaritan showed love. He cared for the stranger. He gifted the stranger with time, energy, and money.

Justice keeps me from stealing (eighth commandment). Love goes beyond justice by giving to those in need. Justice keeps me from telling a damaging lie (ninth commandment). Love goes beyond justice by leading me to tell people the truth in a way that is tender toward their feelings.

Need-love comes naturally. You do not have to tell people to fall in love. They just do. But gift-love must be learned. That is why God commands it.

FOR REFLECTION

Think about one realistic, uncontrived way in which you could show "gift-love" to another person. Then make a commitment to do more than just think about it—to act!

PRAYER STARTERS

One way of showing "gift-love" to someone is to pray for them—not just once or twice, but faithfully, over a period of time. Pick one person who, in some way, needs your prayers. Gift-love that person by praying faithfully for him or her every day this week—and beyond, if you wish.

WALK IN FREEDOM

SCRIPTURE

I will always obey your law,
for ever and ever.
I will walk about in freedom,
for I have sought out your precepts.

—Psalm 119:44-45 (NIV)

TEACHINGS

Looking for life without God,
we find death;
grasping for freedom outside the law,
we trap ourselves in Satan's snares;
pursuing pleasure,
we lose the gift of joy.

—*Our World Belongs to God,* paragraph 14

Jesus once said, "Those who want to save their life will lose it, and those who lose their life for my sake will find it" (Matt. 16:25). This statement is a paradox; that is, a statement that looks as though it contradicts itself but really doesn't.

In the verse from Matthew, Jesus means that if you try to hang on to earthly money, power, or popularity—if you want to "save your life" in these ways—you will be cold toward your real Savior. Your life will end in ruin. But if you give up the idea that earthly things can save you—if you are willing to be a loser in this world—you may find yourself open toward your real Savior.

Your life will end up in glory, in heaven, and in unspeakable joy. Losers are winners.

Our text from Psalm 119 also states a paradox. It says that if we obey God's laws, or statutes, or precepts, we shall be free. For God's laws are statutes of liberty.

That sounds paradoxical. How can laws make us free? Don't they do just the opposite? Don't laws hem us in, cramp our style, reduce our options? Doesn't obedience to God's law make us slaves to God?

In a way, yes. The whole Bible declares that we are to be slaves, or servants, of Jesus Christ. We are to do what he wants, not what we want. We are to obey God rather than ourselves.

But just here is the paradox. For the truth is that we are never as free as when we are obeying God. Perfect slavery to God means perfect freedom for us.

How can this be so?

Let's think again of some comparisons. In the reading about sanctification I said something every athlete knows: it takes discipline to be free. The same could be said for musicians, drug addicts, and even trees.

An athlete trains. A basketball player, for instance, learns not only the rules of the game but also the rules for getting the most out of her body. If she trains long enough, she will have dozens of options on the court. She can go left or right. She can shoulder-fake or head-fake. She can stop and pop a jump shot or drive straight to the hoop. She is free to do any of these things. She is free because she is disciplined by rules and practice.

But she doesn't think of these rules in the middle of a game. That's because the rules have all become second nature to her by now. All she wants to do in a game is to play.

A musician practices. When you hear a great concert artist perform, you are impressed with his freedom. He looks as though he could play his piece backward if he felt like it. He soars. He is free because he is disciplined by the basic rules of his art.

But he doesn't think of these rules in the middle of a concert. That's because the rules have all become second nature to him. All he wants to do in a concert is to play.

Think of a sapling. When a tree is young and tender, you have to stake it with guy ropes. You do this to protect the tree from strong winds and to "train" the sapling to grow straight. But one day you can remove the stakes and ropes. Why? Because the tree has matured. It now grows straight and tall by second nature. And the tree is free to bend any way it wants because it has been well trained.

Drug addicts who have been saved by Jesus Christ will tell you that when they were doing dope, they were slaves. They will also tell you that by obeying God's law they have become free at last. They are free *from* drugs; they are free *for* life and joy.

> **Freedom:** the removal of things that drag us down and the opening up to joyful life in God. According to the Bible, we are never so free as when we are slaves of God.

Isn't it odd? Why are we never so free as when we are obeying God? The reason is that God made us. He knows how we work. God also saved us. He knows what gives us joy. The law is intended, like guy ropes or training rules, to teach us to do what's right and to do it by second nature.

Then we no longer have to think of the law at every step. For we are free.

FOR REFLECTION

"For the truth is that we are never so free as when we are obeying God." Have you experienced this freedom for yourself?

PRAYERS STARTERS

Consider saying the prayer of David in Psalm 119:44-45, quoted at the beginning of this reading.

WEEK 17

HOW CAN WE BUILD A
RELATIONSHIP WITH GOD?
(PRAYER)

THANKSGIVING

SCRIPTURE

Rejoice always, pray without ceasing, give thanks in all circumstances; for this is the will of God in Christ Jesus for you.

—1 Thessalonians 5:16-18

TEACHINGS

Q. Why do Christians need to pray?

A. Because prayer is the most important part of the thankfulness God requires of us.

—Heidelberg Catechism Q&A 116

It's one of the first prayers a small child learns. Over some days and weeks a parent teaches the words. Gradually the child learns them and puts the sentences together. The family sits around a table, savoring the blended aromas of a six-pound, golden-brown roasting chicken with pan gravy, buttered corn, fresh bread, garden salad with bacon dressing, and other good things. The child speaks: "God is great. God is good. Let us thank him for this food. Amen."

The child is taking her place with godly people around the world and across the centuries. Christians thank God for food received, thus distinguishing themselves from animals and TV families who simply graze.

But Christians are thankful to God for many things besides food. We thank God in the morning that we have awakened in our right minds. We thank God in the evening that we may fold our bodies between the covers and shut down our minds while God himself stays awake and on duty. If we are alert, we thank God for brothers and sisters to enjoy and to quarrel with; for parents who care about us more than they can say; for the breakup of winter and the promise of tennis and baseball in spring. If we have our wits about us, we thank God for teachers who inspire us, for good neighbors who trust us, for our church that turns us toward God. We thank God for a special friend who understands and accepts us.

In a quiet mood, we may give thanks for a stand of trees we like, or for a hill or valley where we seem to belong. We may thank God for a red fern that grows in a special place, or for a red-boned coon hound that bawls in a deep voice against the trees and across the fields.

But there is much more. If we have started to come alive to Jesus Christ, we go further in our thanks. For we know in thunder and in stillness, in sickness and in rosy health, in good complexion and bad, that we are loved by him. We know that when we are weary or strong, guilty or innocent, popular or temporarily out to lunch—we know we have been loved to the point of death. The supreme thanksgiving of Christians is for the mighty suffering of Jesus, our Savior.

Prayer is a way of saying our thanks for all these things. Besides doing good out of gratitude, we also *say* what's good, especially when God has done it. Prayer is any attempt to address God. Thanksgiving is our attempt to address God out of gratitude.

> **Prayer:** any attempt to address God. Our prayers include thanksgiving, confession, intercessions, and petitions.
>
> **Thanksgiving:** a kind of prayer that flows out of gratitude. We are thankful for many things, but especially for the mighty work of Jesus Christ, our Savior.

Why do it? Surely we don't give thanks just to keep the gifts coming. Little kids may try this with their grandparents, but even grandparents aren't fooled by it. Neither do we give thanks as a way of paying God back—as if we were to say, "We like gifts. God likes thanks. So we're even."

No. We give thanks to God because it is *fitting* to do so. Just as fans cheer a spectacular shot, just as grieving relatives cling to each other, just as people rest after work, so all of us give thanks to God for his gifts. It is right and proper and appropriate. It fits.

There is a side benefit. When we pray our thanksgiving, we ourselves feel somehow rich and complete. We notice how many wonderful things we have from God, and how good they really are, and how good God is. A grateful person is happy. An ungrateful person is miserable. It's as simple as that.

According to the catechism, prayer is the chief part of thanksgiving. But thanksgiving, we may add, is also one of the chief parts of prayer.

FOR REFLECTION

Why do *you* pray?

PRAYER STARTERS

Take a little time out of your busy schedule today to give sincere thanks for the gifts—big and small—that God has given to you.

CONFESSION

SCRIPTURE

Have mercy on me, O God,
        according to your steadfast love;
according to your abundant mercy
        blot out my transgressions.
Wash me thoroughly from my iniquity,
        and cleanse me from my sin.
For I know my transgressions,
        and my sin is ever before me.

—Psalm 51:1-3

TEACHINGS

Q. What does the fifth request mean?
A. "Forgive us our debts, as we also have
            forgiven our debtors" means:
        Because of Christ's blood,
        do not hold against us, poor sinners that
                we are,
            any of the sins we do
            or the evil that constantly clings to us.
        Forgive us just as we are fully determined,
            as evidence of your grace in us,
        to forgive our neighbors.

—Heidelberg Catechism Q&A 126

Ned was the sort of guy who could never admit he was wrong. For instance, he would needle his brother Leroy mercilessly till Leroy got irritated and told him to stop. This always offended Ned. "You telling me to stop?" he'd ask. "You trying to tell *me* what to do, boy?" Then Ned would try to smack Leroy right in the chops. So Leroy would shove him. War would rage through the room till a parent appeared to break it up. When questioned, Ned would claim that the fight had started when Leroy had suddenly shoved him for no reason at all.

In school, Ned would claim that he had handed in missing assignments and that his teacher must have lost them. If Ned's test answers were exactly the same as those of a top student at the next desk, Ned always insisted that he hadn't cheated. In fact, he would suggest that maybe the other student was trying to copy from *him.* When Ned borrowed money or sports equipment or CDs from friends so foolish as to lend anything to him, he often forgot to return them. When reminded, he would protest that his friends were picking on him.

People like Ned are exasperating. They protect themselves with layer upon layer of lies that are all twisted around each other. You can't tell where one lie ends and another begins. Trying to reach out and take a firm hold on Ned is like trying to take hold of a large mound of spaghetti.

The uncomfortable truth is that there is some of Ned in each of us. We all deceive ourselves about who we are and what we do and what we have failed to do. Probably no one is truly honest with him- or herself. It's too painful. For the same reason, few of us are completely honest with God. For in order to be totally honest with God we have to be honest with ourselves. And that is just what we would like to avoid.

And yet we must face up to our need for such honesty. We cannot be spiritually healthy without it. We are like alcoholics in this way. At meetings of Alcoholics Anonymous members of the group stand up to speak one at a time. Each begins the same way. She mentions her first name and then admits her condition: "My name is Mary. I am an alcoholic." When an alcoholic tells his story at a meeting, he is never allowed to get away with excuses or denials. That's because alcoholics know that nobody can hope for help or healing without frankly admitting his or her weakness. Confession is the first important step toward wholeness and health.

> **Confession:** a kind of prayer in which we own up to who we are, what we have done, and what we have failed to do. In confession we also admit our dependence and our weaknesses.

It is the same for all of us. Besides thanksgiving, our prayers in church and by ourselves must include *confession.* To confess in prayer before God is to own up to who we are: "My name is Ned. I am a liar." To confess is to admit what we have done and what we have failed to do: "God, I have purposely deceived people who have a right to the truth"; "God, I had a chance to stop a damaging lie about another person, and I failed to do it."

Confession is painful. It digs beneath our surface, pulls off our masks and disguises, and lifts up the truth. The truth includes not only our sin but also our dependence on God for health, and breath, and life itself. Confession includes mentioning our weaknesses.

Confession is like cleansing a wound. It hurts to do it thoroughly. But if you go ahead and clean it, the wound may heal without getting infected. It is part of the dying away of the old self and the coming to life of the new.

FOR REFLECTION

Is confession of sin a regular part of your prayers? Is it more than just a quick "and forgive me all my many sins" at the end of your prayers?

PRAYER STARTERS

"To confess . . . is to own up to who we are . . . to admit what we have done and what we have failed to do." Think about that, and then offer a sincere prayer of personal confession to the God who loves you.

INTERCESSION

SCRIPTURE

Then Jesus said, "Father, forgive them; for they do not know what they are doing."
—Luke 23:34

Then he knelt down and cried out in a loud voice, "Lord, do not hold this sin against them." When he had said this, he died.
—Acts 7:60

TEACHINGS

God wants us
> to love our neighbors as ourselves,
> to be patient, peace-loving, gentle,
> > merciful, and friendly toward them,
> to protect them from harm as much as we can,
> and to do good even to our enemies.

—Heidelberg Catechism, Answer 107

Someone has thought of a way to remind us to pray for others. You look at your hand. The thumb is closest to you. It therefore reminds you to pray for people who are close to you. We pray for family members, for instance. We bring before God a parent who is unemployed, perhaps, or a brother who feels left out of things.

Your index finger is used to point. It therefore reminds you of people in authority. We must pray for teachers, pastors, employers, and others in authority.

Your middle finger is highest. It reminds you to pray for presidents, prime ministers, governors, mayors—for all who are in *high* authority.

The ring finger is weakest, as all pianists know. It reminds you to pray for weak people—for people crushed by poverty or ignorance or sickness or cruel governments. Weak people can be found in our own schools and neighborhoods. They can be found in some of our own families. These may be people Jesus calls "the least of my brothers." He says that they especially need our help and care. He even says that helping them counts as helping him.

Finally there is the little finger. It comes last and reminds you, at last, to pray for yourself.

Four out of five of these prayers are for other people. We call them *intercessions.* To intercede is to act as a "go-between," standing between a neighbor and God. In such prayers we play the part of priests, speaking on behalf of, or for the sake of, another person.

> **Intercession:** a kind of prayer in which we play the role of a priest by pleading the case of someone else. Our intercessions are helpful not only to others but also to us who pray them.

You can find intercessory prayers throughout the Bible. Moses pleads for the children of Israel. Job prays for his friends. Paul intercedes for his young churches. Our Lord pleads for the very people who are killing him: "Father, forgive them; for they do not know what they are doing."

Intercessions are wonderful prayers because they have a sort of double effect. When God hears and answers an intercessory prayer for good, our neighbor is blessed. Pastors pray for such blessings every week in congregational prayers. We pray that God will comfort a grieving person, heal a sick person, save the life of somebody in grave danger. So one good effect of an intercessory prayer is that God may help a neighbor.

The other effect, strange to say, is that an intercessory prayer helps us. When we set aside our own concerns and lift before God the needs of somebody else, we are improved. For example, our anger can be softened by praying for the persons who anger us. Our pride is reduced when we make ourselves focus on the hurts and struggles of others. Our envy shrinks when we pray our gratitude to God for gifts given to someone else.

Look at your hand. Four of five fingers remind us to pray for others. That is, they remind us to love.

FOR REFLECTION

Last week we suggested that you show "gift-love" to someone by praying faithfully for him or her. How are you doing on that? This week continue your prayers for the person you've chosen.

PRAYER STARTERS

Use your hand, as explained in the reading, as a guide to your own prayer of intercession.

PETITION

SCRIPTURE

"Ask and it will be given you; search, and you will find; knock, and the door
will be opened for you."
—Matthew 7:7

TEACHINGS

Q. Why do Christians need to pray?

A. Because prayer is the most important part
   of the thankfulness God requires of us.
   And also because God gives his grace and
   Holy Spirit
   only to those who pray continually and groan
   inwardly,
   asking God for these gifts
   and thanking God for them.

—Heidelberg Catechism Q&A 116

A petition is a solemn request. Somebody gets an idea about a plan or event that needs to be pushed forward or held back and draws up a petition about it. The petitioner may want to save whales from harpoons or babies from abortion. She may want a governor to permit casino gambling or to forbid it. People sometimes petition a government to release a prisoner. In a petition we ask someone in power to *act*.

You may be asked to sign a particular petition. Many others are asked as well. Finally the petition, signed by thousands of people, is delivered to the right person, and everybody waits to see what happens. Sometimes we get what we petition for; sometimes not.

> **Petition:** a kind of prayer in which we make a solemn request of God. Petitions may be for others (intercessions), for the whole world, or for ourselves. Denied petitions sometimes raise a problem in our minds.

In prayer we petition God. Along with thanksgiving, confession, and intercession, we include solemn requests for God to act. We may ask God to do something for a neighbor—to heal an injury, for example, or to protect our neighbor in his travels. Then our petition really amounts to an intercession. But at other times we pray for the whole world. When we pray as our Lord taught us, we say, for instance, "Your kingdom come, your will be done on earth as it is in heaven." These are petitions for God to move his great world plan forward.

Sometimes we pray for ourselves. These are our little-finger prayers. We ask God for comfort when we are humiliated, for forgiveness when we are guilty, or for a friend when we are lonely. We may pray in faith for a place on a team, for a job, for a relationship, or for a decent performance on a test.

We pray for all kinds of things. But almost at once we face a problem with petitionary prayer. Jesus promises, "Whatever you ask for in prayer, believe that you have received it, and it will be yours" (Mark 11:24). The problem is that sometimes we receive something very different from what we asked for. Sometimes we seem to receive nothing at all. And we wonder what is going on.

A famous passage in Mark Twain's *Huckleberry Finn* describes this problem in a memorable way. In this passage Huck is getting "civilized"; Miss Watson is trying to teach him to pray:

> Miss Watson, she took me in the closet and prayed, but nothing come of it. She told me to pray every day, and whatever I asked for, I would get it. But it warn't so. I tried it. Once I got a fishline, but no hooks. It warn't any good to me without hooks. I tried for the hooks three or four times, but somehow I couldn't make it work. By and by, one day I asked Miss Watson to try for me, but she said I was a fool. She never told me why and I couldn't make it out no way. I set down one time back in the woods and had a long think about it. I says to myself, if a body can get anything they pray for, why don't Deacon Winn get back the money he lost on pork? Why can't the widow get back her silver snuffbox that was stole? Why can't Miss Watson fat up? No, I says to myself, there ain't nothing in it.

What must we say to this? *Is* there anything in it?

Yes, there is. But what we can say about God's response to our petitions is not easy and not at all complete. We can say this: probably God does not give us what we ask sometimes because we ask him to do something wrong. Suppose someone prays, "Smash my enemy to smithereens, O God." We can see why that petition might be turned down. Or perhaps we ask God for something that would harm us: "Reward me with a ski trip and a subscription to *Playboy,* O Lord." No. Or suppose that two teams both pray to win. Not even God can grant both requests at the same time.

Sometimes we can understand why God sometimes denies our requests. Our requests might be wrong, or dangerous, or impossible to grant. But at other times what we ask for seems to be perfectly good and right. We ask that someone's life be saved, for instance, or that separated parents be reunited. Suppose we then get only terrible silence from God or the sound of a door being slammed.

Why? Why would that happen? To tell the truth, nobody knows. We believe that God has his reasons, but we cannot claim to know what those reasons are. All we can do at such times is to cling to the God we do not understand.

FOR REFLECTION

How do you personally handle a firm "no" from God for something for which you have been earnestly and faithfully praying?

PRAYER STARTERS

Talk to God about big and small things you truly need. Then trust God to do what is best for you.

UNIT 4

OUR PLACE IN CHURCH AND KINGDOM

WEEK 18

WHAT IS THE CHURCH AND WHY DOES IT MATTER?

DAY 1

THE CHURCH IS PEOPLE

SCRIPTURE

But you are a chosen race, a royal priesthood, a holy nation, God's own people, in order that you may proclaim the mighty acts of him who called you out of darkness into his marvelous light.

—1 Peter 2:9

TEACHINGS

I believe in . . . the holy catholic church.

—Apostles' Creed

We believe in one holy, universal Christian church, the communion of saints called from the entire human family.

—Belhar Confession

In the middle of a busy workday in New York City, a woman walks up the steps of a cathedral and enters the hush of the great sanctuary. There she kneels to pray to the God who alone can keep her sane in a mad world. In the middle of a silent night in Chicago, three refugees from a Latin American country slip into a church in which they seek refuge and protection. At the end of a long and bitter war, the bells in a thousand churches clang and peal to celebrate the return of peace. At the beginning of their new life together, a man and a woman step into the sunshine from a building in which they have promised to love each other till death. On a regular Sunday in North America, millions of people stream in and out of church.

What is the church, and why does it matter?

The word *church* can simply mean a particular building that is used for worship, weddings, and refuge. When someone says, "Our church burned down last year," this person is speaking of a structure of wood or brick.

But *church* can also refer to what goes on in such a building. When people whose church burned down gather for worship in a gymnasium, they can still speak of "going to church." They do not mean they are heading over to the gym. They mean they are getting ready to attend public worship.

Church can refer to a building. It can refer, too, to what God's people do when they gather. But the word *church* also has a wider, more important meaning: when we stand up to say the Apostles' Creed, we confess that we believe in "the holy catholic church."

When we use *church* in this sense, we are referring to a certain group of people. This group or community is the most important meaning of *church.* The church is the community of all those who truly believe in Jesus Christ: it is believers as well as their children. The church is the group of people who are justified and sanctified. These are people with faith and repentance. Among them you can find prayer and reverence for the law of God. In fact, all the Christian "things of the faith" that we have been learning for weeks—all these things happen in and to the church. That is, they happen in and to people who belong to Jesus Christ.

We often think of the church in too small a way. We think of it as the group we worship with on Sundays. But that's like looking east from Miami Beach and calling the twenty miles of water you see "the Atlantic Ocean." So it is. But the Atlantic is more—much more—than the little stretch of sea you say you can see.

So with the church. The church of Jesus Christ is incredibly vast and colorful. It includes high-tech Japanese Christians from Tokyo and dignified African tribal chiefs from the bush country of Kenya. It includes high-powered businesswomen from the boardrooms of great corporations and timid young fishermen from tiny villages in Portugal. The church contains ripe old Christians who have believed the gospel for eighty years and infants so young they do not yet believe anything at all.

Church: the group of people who have been "called out" of the world for true faith in Jesus Christ. Even though the members of this group—across the world and across the centuries—are often different from each other, they still belong to only one group.

The church stretches not only across continents and seas and occupations and races but also back across time. Martin Luther belonged to the same community as you and I do. So did C. S.

Lewis and Bach and John Calvin and Augustine and Paul and even Abraham and Sarah. All these belong to the same church we do because all of us belong to the same Lord. As Abraham was called out of his country to serve God in a new land, as Paul was called out of his blindness to serve the Lord he had persecuted, so you and I are called out of the darkness and into the light. We are called out of a fallen world and into the warmth of the Christian community. In fact, the word *church* in the New Testament really means "those who are called out."

The key question for each of us is whether we will answer this call. On this our growth, and the growth of God's work in the world, depends.

FOR REFLECTION

Go online to find out about how many Christians are in the world today. Then find one area of the world where Christians are persecuted for their faith. As an alternative, read up on one missionary your church sponsors.

PRAYER STARTERS

Pray for one area of the world where you know Christians may be persecuted or struggling. Or pray for the needs of a missionary sponsored by your church.

CALLED TO BE HOLY

SCRIPTURE

But just as he who called you is holy, so be holy in all that you do; for it is written: "Be holy, because I am holy."

—1 Peter 1:15-16 (NIV)

TEACHINGS

The church is a gathering
of forgiven sinners called to be holy.
Saved by the patient grace of God,
we deal patiently with others
and together confess our need
    for grace and forgiveness.

—*Our World Belongs to God,* paragraph 39

The church is God's gift to sinners. It is like a mother for orphans, or an ark in a flood, or a hospital in an epidemic, or a wayside inn on the road from Jerusalem to Jericho. In the community of the church those who have been hurt may be comforted. People can be inoculated against certain types of sin. Those who have been drowning in their own misery can be pulled aboard. All of us may be nourished and fed by the Word of God and the sacraments.

At least that is how things are supposed to go. In the church we are supposed to learn sanctification so that our sin may be gradually scoured away and our pollution controlled. Then we are supposed to go back into the flood to pull other swimmers into the ark, or out onto the robber-infested roads to carry other wounded travelers to the wayside inn. Christians, who are called out of the world, are then sent back into it with their new equipment and training.

Because a holy God wants us to become holy, we are to come together in the church. Because God then wants to set us apart for rescue work in the world, we are to be trained in compassion and strong love. Being holy means not only *being* good but also *doing* good. This is what the church is for. We believe in the *holy* catholic church.

> **Holiness of the church:** the sanctification of the church in doing good and becoming more Christlike. To say that the church is holy also means that it is set apart for doing rescue work in the world.

Is it hard to believe that the church is holy in these ways? Is this so hard to believe that we have to keep saying it over and over in the Apostles' Creed?

A lot depends on where we look. In some parts of the great universal church we can find striking holiness. It can make us feel humble before God and at the same time proud to be Christians. For example, some Christians visit prisoners once a week. That's hard work. After all, some prisoners are dangerous people. Some prefer four-letter words. But others are hungry for the gospel of Jesus Christ. Many deeply appreciate the care and concern a visitor may bring.

Other Christians minister in other ways. They may try to bring joy to a lonesome old person or friendship to someone whose mind has gone dark. Every day across the world Christians struggle to teach peasants to farm, or adults to read, or beginners to pray. Wise and strong Christians assist pregnant teens. Streetwise believers spend time helping drug abusers get unhooked. Some Christians lead protests against tyrannical governments. We look at all this and much more. Then we say, "I believe in the holy catholic church."

Many Christian teenagers have gotten the idea. With their youth groups they participate in service projects that assist those in need close to home and far away. They serve meals in homeless shelters, tutor persons with mental impairments, raise money for good causes, conduct worship services in nursing homes, and much, much more.

I once read of a high school student who had leukemia. He became very sick—not only from the disease but also from the cure. The killer chemicals that doctors aimed at his cancer made him retch and throw up and lose his hair. Being sick was bad enough, but the thought of returning to school bald filled him with horror and dread.

But he did it. He went to school on the day he was expected back. Walking timidly into his first class, he was astonished to see a whole group of his friends with their hair shaved down to their scalp! Their shaved heads told him that they cared about him and wanted to share his burden. Those bald heads that day became reflectors of the glory of God.

The church can be like that! It can show a beauty of holiness that makes you gasp.

Why is it, then, that in some Christian communities sleek and handsome people are celebrated while plain and ordinary people are on the fringes? Why in some churches are wealthy people respected and poor people ignored? Why in some schools are sports heroes turned into teenage gods for whom hundreds cheer—even if their god isn't a very good person?

Is this holiness? Or is it a small reminder of hell?

FOR REFLECTION

"The church can be [holy] like that! It can show a beauty of holiness that makes you gasp." Have you seen that holiness expressed in your church? If so, how?

PRAYER STARTERS

A few readings back (page 155) we suggested that you sing the chorus of the song "Sanctuary" as your personal prayer, or listen to it performed by numerous artists on YouTube. You may want to do that again today. Or offer your own prayer for holiness.

THE CHURCH IS CATHOLIC

SCRIPTURE

Make every effort to keep the unity of the Spirit through the bond of peace. There is one body and one Spirit . . . one Lord, one faith, one baptism; one God and Father of all, who is over all and through all and in all.

—Ephesians 4:3-6 (NIV)

TEACHINGS

We believe that this unity of the people of God must be manifested and be active in a variety of ways: in that we love one another, that we experience, practice and pursue community with one another . . . that we share one faith, have one calling, are of one soul and one mind; have one God and Father, are filled with one Spirit, are baptized with one baptism . . . are obedient to one Lord . . . that [we] together serve God in this world; and together fight against all which may threaten or hinder this unity.

—Belhar Confession

Ordinary, non-electronic letters have ordinary addresses. You write a person's name, street and number, city, state or province, postal code, and, if necessary, country. That's it. That should be enough to get the letter properly delivered.

But suppose one day you are really thinking big. You address your letter as follows:

Mr. Homer Klankenfelder
1665 Pennybrook Lane
Sheboygan, Wisconsin 53081
U.S.A.
North America
Northern Hemisphere
Earth
The Solar System
The Milky Way
The Universe

You see immediately that each item fits into the next larger one. You move from smaller to larger, from more specific things to more general ones. You don't want just any old Klankenfelder; you want Homer himself. You don't want just any number on Pennybrook; you specify 1665. You want Sheboygan out of all cities, Wisconsin instead of West Virginia, and so on. Obviously, you need to know what you want and to say so on your envelope. Your chances for hitting the target with a letter addressed simply to "Homer, the Universe," would be on the slim side.

The church is structured in a similar way, smaller to larger. If you are a baptized person, you belong to a particular congregation—call it Friendship Community Church. Your congregation probably belongs to a denomination—say the Christian Reformed Church. This denomination belongs to a group of churches that follow Calvin's

Reformation teachings more than Luther's. This group is called Reformed churches. Reformed and Lutheran churches are Protestant instead of Roman Catholic or Greek Orthodox. But all Protestants, Catholics, and Orthodox belong to Christianity instead of Hinduism or Islam.

Your church address, then, might look like this:

Vanessa Klankenfelder
Friendship Community Church
Christian Reformed Denomination
Reformed Churches
Protestantism
Christianity in the Twenty-first Century
The Universal Church

> **catholic church:** the church in its biggest, most universal form. The catholic church is like a great hall. Denominations and congregations are like rooms off this hall.

When we say "I believe in the holy catholic church," we are saying that all true believers in all congregations and denominations and branches of the Reformation; all true Protestant and Catholic and Greek Orthodox Christians of all times and places—all these add up to a church, one church. We call it "catholic," meaning universal. We believe it is the "one body" that Paul describes in Ephesians. Just as a human body is made up of many parts, so the universal church is like a body of which Jesus Christ is head.

In this body your congregation is a square millimeter of northwest thumbnail, left hand.

"I believe in the holy catholic church," we say. We need to *believe* there is only one universal church, for it is hard to see unless you look for it.

And we need to join with other Christians in doing Christ's work in the world. All the parts of the body, however different, are intended to fit and work together.

Of course, the part of the church we know best is our own congregation. Here we are baptized and taught. Here we listen and sing and give. Here we have pancake breakfasts, retreats, and Christmas programs.

C. S. Lewis once used a helpful picture. The universal church is like a great hall. Along the hall are doors to rooms. Everybody in the hall is a true believer in Jesus Christ. But it is when you leave the hall and enter a room that you can have fires and chairs and meals.

Naturally, we may like our own room best. We are used to it. But it is not polite to criticize the rooms of others. What would be the point? What would be the point when so many people are not yet even in the hall?

FOR REFLECTION

When do you most feel a part of your congregation? Of the larger church in the world?

PRAYER STARTERS

Thank the Lord for giving you a place in his universal church.

HOW TO FIND THE TRUE CHURCH

SCRIPTURE

The Spirit clearly says that in later times some will abandon the faith and follow deceiving spirits and things taught by demons. Such teachings come through hypocritical liars.

—1 Timothy 4:1-2 (NIV)

For myself I feel certain that you . . . have real Christian character and experience, and that you are capable of keeping one another on the right road.

—Romans 15:14 (Phillips)

TEACHINGS

We believe that we ought to discern
    diligently and very carefully,
    by the Word of God,
what is the true church—
    for all the sects in the world today
    claim for themselves the name of "the church."

—Belgic Confession, Article 29

People go out to eat a lot more than they used to. People used to have restaurant meals only at special times, such as the day before a wedding. But now, especially in families where two parents work outside the home, people eat out more often.

People care about restaurant quality. For instance, they want food to be fresh: lettuce ought to be crisp; bread should be soft and fragrant. People want restaurants and their workers to be clean: if a restaurant worker handles money and then immediately palms your hamburger, you can lose your appetite. People also want service that is reasonably fast and always courteous: rude waiters don't last long in restaurants. Finally, people expect fair value in food for their money.

These are all marks of a good restaurant: fresh food, cleanliness, courteous service, fair value. They are qualities, or characteristics, that will show up in any well-managed place to eat.

The Christian church also has marks. Across the world one can find over two billion Christians and hundreds of thousands of congregations. Where, among all these, do you find the church true to its nature? Where do you find the church doing what it's supposed to do? Where is the church obedient to Jesus Christ, its head? In other words, what are the marks of the true church?

> **Marks of the true church:** the qualities you can find in the church when it is true to its nature and obedient to Christ. These include good preaching, sacraments, and discipline.

The church is true to its nature wherever it faithfully preaches the Word of God, offers sacraments in a pure way, and keeps up the discipline of the group. Good preaching, sacraments, and discipline are the marks of the true church.

Let's take each of these in turn. What makes preaching good? It ought to be interesting. And you ought to be able to understand a sermon. In addition, a well-preached sermon might make you laugh, or wonder, or feel like weeping. It will *get* to you. You may also learn something new from it. Over time, good preaching can actually change your life in important ways.

But these things, necessary as they are, do not finally make preaching good. For the most important thing has been left out—namely, that a sermon ought to become a carrier of the Word of God. God ought to *speak* to you and me in a sermon. A minister who preaches faithfully is God's voice to us. This voice tells us of sin and salvation. It speaks of forgiveness and compassion, of hope and courage for dark days. This voice brings the gospel of Jesus Christ.

Faithful biblical preaching is a mark of the true church. So is proper offering of the sacraments. I'll say more about these next week. For now, recall that whenever a child is baptized, people make promises within the whole gathered congregation. A minister doesn't just go to a shopping mall and start baptizing every kid within reach. People must make promises within the covenant of grace and in the gathering of the church. Sacraments must be done right.

Group discipline is a third mark of the true church. We have already seen how we need to be trained in sanctification. We have to become spiritual athletes, training out sloppy habits and adding trim, dynamic spiritual muscle.

This is true not only for individual Christians but also for the whole church. The church is like a baseball team in spring training, or an orchestra in rehearsal. Pastors and consistory members act like player-coaches, reminding us of the Ten Commandments and other training rules. They keep motivating us to do better in the Christian life. On rare occasions they may suspend someone for missing practice too often. All of this is church discipline.

But we also discipline each other with encouragement and warning and support. We try to keep each other "on the right road."

Good preaching, sacraments, and discipline are marks of the church that people have talked about for centuries. If you look back at the reading for day 2, can you think of some others?

FOR REFLECTION

What are some of the strengths you see in your congregation (or that you would like to see in any church)?

PRAYER STARTERS

Ask God to bless your church and make it strong. Pray for the pastor(s) and others who lead.

WEEK 19

HOW CAN THE SACRAMENTS GROW OUR FAITH?

RITUAL

SCRIPTURE

For as often as you eat this bread and drink the cup, you proclaim the Lord's death until he comes.

—1 Corinthians 11:26

TEACHINGS

We believe that our good God,
mindful of our crudeness and weakness,
has ordained sacraments for us
>   to seal his promises in us,
>   to pledge his good will and grace toward us,
>   and also to nourish and sustain our faith.

—Belgic Confession, Article 33

Some rituals are so common that we hardly notice them. You are introduced to someone new, for instance, or you greet your pastor after a service. Each of you extends one hand. You then clasp them and begin to wave the locked pair of hands up and down for a few seconds. Then you stop.

Or maybe you greet a friend at school. Instead of a handshake, you do high fives or just give each other a big hug. In fact, friendship hugs—in a variety of cool moves and styles—have become a hugely popular, nonromantic greeting among today's generation.

Handshakes, high fives, and hugs are rituals, pieces of behavior that tie life together and help people act out deep feelings or important promises.

Hands are often important in rituals. A person swearing an oath in court, for example, raises his right hand or places his left hand on a Bible or both. These rituals act out promises to tell the truth. People getting married join hands while repeating their vows; then each places a ring on the other's hand. These rituals act out their promise to be faithful for life. Boxers touch gloves. Volleyball players do high fives. Church elders lay hands on the shoulders of young people leaving on a mission trip. Soldiers salute. Patriots place their hands over their hearts.

Rituals say things with actions. They say such things as "You are my friend," or my country is important to me" or "I respect your authority" or "I promise to tell the truth, the whole truth, and nothing but the truth—so help me, God."

> **Sacrament:** a sacred ritual, a sign and seal, by which God binds himself to us and we bind ourselves to God.

Some rituals say even more than that. This is true not only of wedding and funeral rituals but also of the two most important rituals of Protestant worship, the sacraments of baptism and the

Lord's Supper. What really goes on in these rituals? Why do we do them and what do they mean?

To understand sacraments we will need a comparison. U.S. citizens celebrate Independence Day on the Fourth of July. People set off fireworks and shoot cannons. Some dress up in eighteenth-century costumes and pretend to sign the Declaration of Independence all over again. At certain ceremonies citizens take the solemn vow of loyalty by placing their hands over their hearts and saying, "I pledge allegiance to the flag of the United States of America. . . ."

Fourth-of-July observances in the U.S. are ritual celebrations of a past event—colonial victory in the war for independence. But they are more than that too. Besides acting out the main events by signing documents or shooting off cannons, people also try to *include* themselves or *identify* themselves with the history and nation begun by the Declaration of Independence. They do this by parading, by waving flags, by pledging allegiance, and by singing "The Star-Spangled Banner." By these acts such people are saying, "We are the people who come from the war of independence. We are the people of that event and of all that it means." They are saying, "This is our event and our nation and our history. I am a part of these things. They are part of *my* history, even though I wasn't born till much later."

Fourth-of-July rituals celebrate a past event and identify people with the history that began back then. Such people feel as though they belong to this history and this event.

Church sacraments are something like that but are far more important. By dipping in water, by breaking bread and pouring out juice or wine, we "act out" the central event of our Christian existence. That is, we act out the saving death and resurrection of Jesus Christ, the event that won our independence from sin and Satan. In sacraments we identify ourselves as the people of this double event and of all that it means.

We do this by gathering as the church, the covenant people of God. We reenact the main event to recall it to God and to ourselves, to give thanks for the gift it brings, and to pledge our allegiance to the Lord of this event.

We are saying, "We are the people of the war for redemption. This victory has made us who we are. We belong to this history and this Christ."

Ritual sacraments tie life together for us— because they tie us to Jesus Christ.

FOR REFLECTION

What are some examples of rituals from your everyday life? Why do we say the sacraments are church *rituals*?

PRAYER STARTERS

Thank God for the gift of the sacraments. Express your feelings about belonging to Jesus and to each other.

SIGNS AND SEALS

SCRIPTURE

For if we have been united with him in a death like his, we will certainly be united with him in a resurrection like his.

—Romans 6:5

TEACHINGS

Q. What are sacraments?

A. Sacraments are holy signs and seals.
   They were instituted by God so that
        by our use of them
   he might make us understand more clearly
        the promise of the gospel,
   and seal that promise.
   And this is God's gospel promise:
   to grant us forgiveness of sins and eternal life
        by grace
        because of Christ's one sacrifice
        finished on the cross.

—Heidelberg Catechism Q&A 66

Human life is full of signs. You know the obvious ones: a metal rectangle with a number painted on it indicates the legal speed limit on a freeway. A billboard displays a huge photo of a succulent, crosshatched, medium-rare, charbroiled steak—a sign of the good food you can expect at a particular restaurant.

When you get off the freeway you find other signs. A trousered figure on a door indicates a men's room; a skirted figure, a women's room (don't mix up the signs!). If you see 4/4 printed into a staff of music, you know that in that composition each measure will have four beats, and quarter notes will be worth a beat apiece. The composer *signs* this information by simply writing a pair of vertical 4s.

A sign *points to* or *indicates* something. A traffic arrow points out which way to turn. A first crocus in March indicates the coming of spring. A thumb jerked out to one side indicates either that the signer wants a ride or else that he has just called a base runner out. Your name written by your own hand indicates your identity: only you sign your name in just that way.

Without signs many things would drag on a lot longer, and life would seem much poorer and less interesting. For signs have great power. Making the sign of the cross, for instance, reminds millions of Roman Catholics of the central event in the life of Jesus Christ. The straight-armed Nazi salute told millions of Germans that Hitler was god.

Sometimes a sign becomes a seal. Your signature doodled all over your history notebook is a sign of your identity (and maybe your boredom), but it doesn't mean much more than that. However, if you sign a $500 IOU, you are sealing your promise to pay back this amount. A wedding kiss indicates love between a bride and a groom, but it also seals their wedding promises; it confirms their covenant with each other. A handshake after a business deal is not only a ritual sign of human politeness or trust; it is also a seal on the deal.

A seal *confirms* or *certifies* something—often an agreement or a promise.

Sacraments sign and seal our closeness to Jesus Christ, our "union with Christ." This union is like the union between a grafted twig and a well-rooted receiving plant. Or it is like the covenant union between a man and a woman in marriage.

How do sacraments sign and seal? In many ways. When we gather within the covenant community for the Lord's Supper, for instance, we break bread and pour out wine or juice. We are then acting out the crucifixion of Christ that atones for our sin. The breaking and pouring are *signs* of this terrible and splendid event. When Christians then eat the bread and drink the wine or juice, they are indicating that they want to get as close to Jesus Christ as they possibly can. In a reverent, spiritual way they want to *take him into* the center of their lives. These Christians are acting out, or signing, their union with Christ—and actually making the union stronger at the same time.

> **Sign:** a pointer or indicator. Breaking bread and pouring wine are signs of the death of Christ. Dipping a person in and out of the water (or sprinkling a person) is a sign of the death and resurrection of Christ.
>
> **Seal:** something that confirms or certifies. The sacraments sign and seal our union with Christ.

But these signs, like a signature or a handshake or a kiss, also become seals. For with these sacramental gifts God confirms that his promises of salvation are good. They can be trusted. God *binds* himself to us with these rituals. A sacrament is in fact a binder. That is what the word *sacrament* means.

But when we take and use the sacraments, we also bind ourselves to God. We seal our obedience and faith as though with a signature, a handshake, or a kiss.

Sacraments are church rituals in which we act out the central events of Christ's life and in which our union with Christ is signed and sealed.

FOR REFLECTION

What does it mean to you to "be close to Jesus Christ?" Have the sacraments helped you do this?

PRAYER STARTERS

You may want to say this prayer or use one of your own:

Thank you for showing us through simple things like water, bread, and wine that we can trust your promises of salvation. Help me see and believe through Christ. Amen.

HOLY BAPTISM

SCRIPTURE

When you were buried with him through baptism, you were also raised with him through faith in the power of God, who raised him from the dead.

—Colossians 2:12

TEACHINGS

Q. Should infants also be baptized?

A. Yes.
   Infants as well as adults
       are included in God's covenant and people,
   and they, no less than adults, are promised
       deliverance from sin through Christ's blood
       and the Holy Spirit who produces faith.

—Heidelberg Catechism Q&A 74

We believe that this unity of the people of God must be manifested and be active in a variety of ways: in that we . . . are baptized with one baptism.

—Belhar Confession

During a Sunday morning church service two parents walk up to the baptismal font. They are carrying their eight-week-old daughter. In a solemn ritual, the parents confess their faith and promise to raise their child as a Christian. The congregation then promises to help care for this child's instruction in the Christian faith.

Meanwhile, the minister states God's promise to surround this child with love.

Then, several times, the minister dips a hand into the font and drips water onto the child's head. The child flinches. The minister says words from Matthew 28:19: "I baptize you in the name of the Father and of the Son and of the Holy Spirit. Amen." In some congregations, a minister then takes the child in his or her arms and blesses her, as Jesus used to do. In many congregations the ritual is concluded with a hymn about children and the significance of baptism.

We have all witnessed this event many times. What is going on during baptism, and why does it matter?

Children are not baptized at a kitchen sink. The event happens before a worshiping congregation. Why? Because baptism is a ritual of the whole church, not just of children and their parents.

Let me explain this further. Baptism signs and seals union with Christ. As Christ went down into death and rose up into life, so a child in baptism gets washed by going down into water and coming back up. Baptism acts out Christ's death and resurrection.

> **Holy baptism:** the church ritual in which a believer or the child of a believer is sprinkled with or dipped in water. Baptism identifies us as members of the people of God.

I admit that sprinkling a child isn't a very good sign of this. Dipping would be far better. But, then, most of our churches aren't equipped to dip.

Baptism is a sign of the events of Christ and of our union with Christ. For by acting out the Christ events, we say, "We are the people of the cross and resurrection and of all that they mean." They mean the washing away of sin. They mean justification and sanctification. They mean faith and law and prayer. They mean compassion for unpopular people and mercy for leukemia victims. We place ourselves, identify ourselves, include ourselves within this history and these meanings of it.

But we especially place ourselves within the people who have come from that history. Baptism is a church ritual because in it we say that a new person has been accepted into the holy catholic church and into one of the rooms off its main hall. In this room Jesus Christ will be worshiped and the people will be shaped into spiritual athletes and will become good reflectors of the glory of God.

Of course, an infant cannot place *herself* within this history of these people. She's too young, too weak, too helpless. But that's just when God wants us accepted. That's just the point of infant baptism and the grace that flows in it. God reaches for us and marks us as his children and as heirs of his fortune *when we don't even know what's going on!* When our minds are still being formed and our movements are still random, God grasps us and says, "my child."

In infant baptism God promises that we will be included in the history and people of Jesus Christ. The gospel of Christ will be taught to us, preached for us, learned by us. Parents and others will try to be models of what it means to live like Christ. People will show us how to pray, how to give, how to treat others with kindness even when we don't feel like it.

In other words, people around us will try to make Christian history *our* history, the Christian community *our* community. Baptism is the start. In your baptism God says, "my child."

What everyone is waiting for is the day, years later, when you walk back into the same church on your own two feet. You stand before the same worshiping community that witnessed your baptism. And to the God who years ago said, "my child," you now say, "my God."

FOR REFLECTION

Read Psalm 63:1-4. Have you made the commitment to God mentioned in this psalm and in the last paragraph of today's reading?

PRAYER STARTERS

Pray Psalm 63:1-4 as your personal prayer of commitment to God.

THE LORD'S SUPPER

SCRIPTURE

The he took a loaf of bread, and when he had given thanks, he broke it and gave it to them, saying, "This is my body, which is given for you. Do this in remembrance of me."

And he did the same with the cup after supper, saying, "This cup that is poured out for you is the new covenant in my blood."

—Luke 22:19-20

TEACHINGS

Q. What does it mean
    to eat the crucified body of Christ
    and to drink his poured-out blood?

A. It means
    to accept with a believing heart
        the entire suffering and death of Christ
    and thereby
        to receive forgiveness of sins and
          eternal life.
    But it means more.
    Through the Holy Spirit, who lives both in
        Christ and in us,
    we are united more and more to Christ's
        blessed body.
        And so, although he is in heaven and we
          are on earth,
        we are flesh of his flesh and bone of his
          bone.

And we forever live on and are governed
    by one Spirit,
    as the members of our body are by
        one soul.

—Heidelberg Catechism Q&A 76

We believe that this unity of the people of God must be manifested and be active in a variety of ways: in that we . . . eat of one bread and drink of one cup . . .

—Belhar Confession

Everyone knows you have to eat and drink to live. A person can last only a few days without water, and can last only a few weeks without food. Death from hunger or thirst is unimaginably slow and painful.

Yet in the short time it takes to read this devotional, a number of people across the world will die in these ways. That is why we have relief agencies. Fear of starvation is one obvious reason we ourselves eat and drink: we don't want to die.

Eating and drinking not only nourish us, however; they also nourish others. When we share a meal with others, we are saying we don't want *them* to die. We want them to flourish and thrive and be alive with us. We want the same food and drink that nourish us to nourish them too.

That is one reason people eat together. Of course, sometimes—maybe more than sometimes—you have to grab a bite by yourself. But people usually try to avoid that kind of self-serve filling of their tank. Done often, it can be downright lonely. There's no chance to share food and good talk with others.

That's why people make a ritual of meals. Christians surround their meals with prayers and readings and unhurried conversations. They serve and pass and offer each other good things to eat and drink.

Christians and others also celebrate important events with meals. The festive Lord's Day gets celebrated with special Sunday dinners or brunches. Parts of Christmas and Easter and Thanksgiving are spent in leisurely meals with people we care about. People eat together after weddings. This is a way for the bride and groom to share their happiness with others. People often eat together even after a funeral. This is a way of saying to bereaved people, "We are the ones who share this sadness with you."

Eating and drinking, in other words, are not only for nourishing bodies, but also for nourishing *fellowship*.

The Lord's Supper (holy communion): the church sacrament in which members eat bread and drink juice or wine. This sacrament binds us not only to Christ but also to each other. That is, it nourishes the whole church.

The Lord's Supper is a meal of this kind. In this ritual meal we act out the death of our Lord by spilling wine or juice into a cup and breaking a loaf into pieces. Then, by eating and drinking, we identify ourselves as people of the cross and of all that this means. And by taking nourishing bread and refreshing drink into the center of our bodies, we sign and seal our union with Christ.

In the Lord's Supper we are also doing something else. We are nourishing the body of the Lord, the church. We are sharing the gifts of food and drink as a way of building up our fellowship together.

As believers lift the cup and take in a piece of broken bread, they also serve and offer and pass these good things to other Christians. They are saying, "We don't want your faith to die. We want you to flourish and thrive and be alive to Jesus Christ with us. Here, take and eat. Here, take and drink this cup."

FOR REFLECTION

If you currently participate in the Lord's Supper, how does taking communion benefit you and help you as a follower of Jesus? If you don't currently participate in communion, how do you think doing so would benefit your faith?

PRAYER STARTERS

Say a prayer of thanks to Jesus for his supper, for reminding us of his death for our sins, and for binding us close to him and to each other.

WEEK 20

WHEN WILL GOD'S KINGDOM COME?

THE RETURN OF THE KING

SCRIPTURE

"The time has come," he said. "The kingdom of God has come near. Repent and believe the good news!"

—Mark 1:14-15

TEACHINGS

Jesus Christ rules over all.
To follow this Lord is
to serve him wherever we are,
without fitting in,
light in the darkness,
salt in a spoiling world.

—*Our World Belongs to God*, paragraph 43

We believe that God's life giving Word and Spirit has conquered the powers of sin and death, and therefore also of irreconciliation and hatred, bitterness and enmity.

—Belhar Confession

The universe is at war. We cannot see all the fighting or measure it. But it goes on every day. Beyond the wars everyone knows—civil wars and world wars, rebellions and revolutions, terrorist attacks and border skirmishes—beyond all these the whole universe itself is at war with God.

The war began before the dawn of human history in a revolt so mysterious and unthinkable that the Bible only whispers of it. A powerful nonhuman creature, one made by God and loved by God, rebelled against God the King and challenged others to join him. This "evil one" set up a rival kingdom whose inhabitants prefer darkness to light, cruelty to tenderness, deception to truth.

We call this evil power "Satan" or "the devil" because the Bible does. We do not have a great deal of information about him. We don't even know how to interpret much of what the Bible says about him.

But we do know this: the evil one is a rebel. And we know that his rebellion has spread like a disease into the human race. In this rebellion and in its spread, war has been declared against God, the King of the universe.

Where do we see signs of this war?

We see them in the fall of humanity, as the great deceiver turns human beings into great pretenders. We see them in students who casually ruin the reputation of others at school or online, and in drug dealers who peddle their poison to kids on the street. We see them in a man who threw gasoline on a woman cowering in the corner of an elevator in New York City and then set her ablaze. We see signs of war and rumors of war in cheating and invitations to cheat, in lying and temptations to lie. We see signs of war, in short, wherever we see sin and the misery that results from it.

All the Bible, all Christianity, and all world history is the story of this universal war between sin and holiness, evil and good, the kingdom of darkness and the kingdom of light. The warring is not just on the side of the rebels. God the King doesn't simply hand over his world to them. God doesn't just give up on his rebel children and say, "To hell with you." For the universe belongs to God. Our world belongs to God. He wants it back. And he has taken certain steps to get it back.

The Bible traces these steps. God makes a covenant with Abraham and seals it with Moses and the law. God rules his people Israel through priests and judges and kings and prophets. Later God establishes "a new Israel," the church, among whom the gospel may be preached, sacraments celebrated, and people shaped to look and act like God.

For the whole universe is God's kingly realm. And all these things—covenant, prophets, law, church, sacraments—are the tools of God's kingly reign. They are all part of what could be called God's reelection campaign. God wants the whole world to acknowledge again that he is King and that our world belongs to him.

Why? Is God so weak and insecure that he needs lots of praise and acknowledgment to build him up? No. God wants us to recognize his kingship because it's true: he is King, and our world does belong to him. And he wants to protect us from falling under the rule of other kings who will sooner or later destroy us.

The gospels tell us the most important part of this story. They tell us of the turning point in this universal war: when a man from Nazareth leaves his home, moves out into Galilee, and begins to preach. "Repent," he says. "Lay down your arms. For the kingdom of God is coming near."

The world has become enemy-occupied territory. It has become the kingdom of the evil one. "Christianity is the story of how the rightful king has landed, you might say landed in disguise." Now is the time for sabotaging the kingdom of darkness and reelecting the King of light.

FOR REFLECTION

How does looking at the world as a battleground between good and evil impact you? How does it affect your faith?

PRAYER STARTERS

Read Psalm 47. Then say a prayer of praise to the King of all the earth.

SABOTAGE AND REELECTION

SCRIPTURE

Then comes the end, when he [Christ] hands over the kingdom to God the Father, after he has destroyed every ruler and every authority and power. For he must reign until he has put all his enemies under his feet. The last enemy to be destroyed is death.

—1 Corinthians 15:24-26

TEACHINGS

To follow this Lord is
to serve him wherever we are. . . .
[in]
our sexuality . . .
marriage and family . . .
education . . .
our work, even in dull routine . . .
rest and leisure . . .
science and technology . . .
politics . . .
for our world belongs to God.

—*Our World Belongs to God,* selections from paragraphs 43-51

We think of our religion as a devotional thing. When we pray or sing hymns or read the Bible—then we are being religious. When we have devotions, we are acting like Christians. When we attend church and observe the sacraments, we are being faithful.

And so we are. But the Christian faith is much bigger than these things, and being religious includes much more. After all, the whole universe belongs to God the King and Jesus the Lord. A thoughtful Christian once put it like this: Of every square inch in the universe, Jesus Christ says, "It is mine." In every square inch we therefore need a campaign to sabotage the kingdom of the evil one and reelect God the King.

What does this mean?

Let's look at some examples from various areas of human life. In *medicine and health care* Christians fight against drug abuse, including alcoholism, and try to help its victims with tough love. In the kingdom of darkness, athletes, rock stars, and actors sometimes celebrate the high life of drug abuse till it wrecks or kills them. But in the kingdom of God, one's body is a temple of the Holy Spirit. God lives in us, and we must keep his house clean.

In *earthkeeping* Christians fight against abuse of nature. Christians and others reclaim the earth with skillful animal care and with expert soil, water, and forest management. In the kingdom of darkness, people strip and rape the earth for profit. They foul clean air and pollute pure water. They neglect and abuse animals. But in the kingdom of God, the earth and its fullness are treated with respect. For they come from the hand of God.

In *sexuality* Christians fight against the attitude that women are men's inferior servants. Christians see men and women as equal partners serving God together and trying to build each other up. Christians also fight against the use of sex to trap, humiliate, or make money off people. In the kingdom of darkness, sexual partners are disposable tissues and bones. In the kingdom of light, sexuality is for imaging God in love and trust. It is a gift of such power and beauty that it is protected by the covenant of marriage.

In *education* Christians fight against the idea that learning is just for getting jobs and making money. In the kingdom of darkness, learning happens without the light of God's Word to shine on it. Learning is used to make people powerful but not to make them wise. But in God's kingdom, education is for deepening our wonder at the greatness of God and his world. It also prepares us to serve wisely all across the kingdom of God itself.

In *politics* Christians fight against the use of power to frighten other nations or to take advantage of the weak citizens of one's own nation. In the kingdom of darkness, citizens ride over elderly and poor people, children and minorities, and all those who don't matter except when they vote. But in the kingdom of God, governments protect the freedoms and rights of all citizens—and even make extra allowances for those who are disadvantaged.

Our religion is not just for devotions and worship. We also serve God when we take care of our bodies, care for animals and plant trees, respect the dignity of the other sex, learn a math lesson well, serve the poor and elderly—and do all of this because we are citizens of the kingdom of God. For all these acts and many more are ways of sabotaging the kingdom of darkness and reelecting the King of light.

After all, our world belongs to God.

FOR REFLECTION

How can you—in your everyday world—be an active kingdom member? What can you do to advance the kingdom of God in your part of God's world?

PRAYER STARTERS

Think of at least one Christian you know who is a model for you of how to serve God in business or politics or education or earthkeeping or parenting or some other area. Give thanks for that person and ask God to bless his or her work.

THE UPSIDE-DOWN KINGDOM

SCRIPTURE

"Blessed are the meek, for they will inherit the earth."
—Matthew 5:5

TEACHINGS

Our hope for a new creation is not tied
to what humans can do,
for we believe that one day
every challenge to God's rule
will be crushed.
His kingdom will fully come,
and the Lord will rule.
—*Our World Belongs to God*, paragraph 55

In one of her Mrs. Piggle-Wiggle stories, Betty MacDonald presents an upside-down house. Children come to visit this amazing place. Floors stretch overhead; ceilings lie underfoot. The piano that hangs from the floor above is very hard to get at; a person has to dangle from a trapeze in order to play it. Couches and chairs are also suspended from the floor overhead. This makes sitting in them extremely awkward. If someone wants to open a cupboard, or go to the bathroom, or even heat up some hot chocolate on the stove, he or she has to stop and think about the right approach. Nothing is, after all, quite where you expect it. Surprises wait for anyone who is careless.

The kingdom of God is like this house. Things in it seem upside-down. For instance, in our world it's pretty clear who the great people are. They are the people with power. Such people are presidents, prime ministers, and CEOs. They fly in private jets and issue electronic orders from their stretch limousines. They sneeze and the world reaches for a handkerchief. They order someone to jump and on the way up the person shouts, "How high?" These are the great people.

One day the disciples of Jesus Christ began to argue with each other about who would be the greatest. Jesus took a little child and had the child stand beside him. "Like this," said Jesus. "Try to be more like this." Then he said, "For the one who is *least* among you all is the greatest" (Luke 9:48, NIV). That's what the kingdom of God is like.

In our world it's pretty clear who the rich people are. They're the ones with money. They dine in swanky restaurants and sail in yachts. They dine; we eat. They sail; we row. The houses of the rich are large, their debts (presumably) small. Their wallets are fat, their bodies thin. They vacation in places where their every desire is fulfilled. They are the rich.

In his Sermon on the Mount Jesus gathered his disciples around him and began to preach: "Blessed are you who are poor," he said, "for yours is the kingdom of God. . . . But woe to you who are rich, for you have already received your comfort" (Luke 6:20, 24, NIV).

In our world it's pretty clear what you ought to do to enemies. You clean their clock, fix their wagon, take 'em to the cleaners, string 'em up and hang 'em out to dry. You do it to others before they do it to you.

Jesus says, "Love your enemies, do good to those who hate you . . . pray for those who mistreat you. . . . Do to others as you would have them do to you" (Luke 6:27-31, NIV). This is, incidentally, just what Martin Luther King Jr. did in his great civil-rights movement. It drove racists crazy.

And so it goes. In the kingdom of darkness, loving enemies, living modestly, trying to be great in service—these things are for suckers. In the kingdom of light, they are signs that one has been with Jesus Christ.

It's all a kind of upside-down house. The worldly-wise with their PhDs turn out to be fools in the kingdom of God—unless they know how to be saved. Bluebloods are simply passed by—unless they are washed in the blood of the Lamb. The person who wants to save his life will lose it, but the one who flings his life away into the service of Christ—that person will *find* his life and find it abundantly.

Somehow this seems all wrong. It's all upside-down by the world's standards.

Or is it the world that is upside-down and the kingdom of God that is really right-side up?

FOR REFLECTION

Read Matthew 5:1-12. Select one of the "upside-down" values of kingdom citizens that Jesus lists. Keep that value in mind as you go through your day.

PRAYER STARTERS

Ask God to help you live by the upside-down values of the kingdom, so that your values become more like those of Jesus Christ.

THE SECRET OF THE KINGDOM

SCRIPTURE

He put before them another parable: "The kingdom of heaven is like a mustard seed that someone took and sowed in his field; it is the smallest of all the seeds, but when it has grown it is the greatest of shrubs and becomes a tree, so that the birds of the air come and make nests in its branches."

—Matthew 13:31-32

TEACHINGS

Q. What does the second petition mean?

A. "Your kingdom come" means:
Rule us by your Word and Spirit in such a way
that more and more we submit to you.
Preserve your church and make it grow.
Destroy the devil's work;
destroy every force which revolts against you
and every conspiracy against your holy Word.
Do this until your kingdom fully comes
when you will be
all in all.

—Heidelberg Catechism Q&A 123

At the heart of the Christian religion is the claim that God is the cosmic King and Jesus Christ the Lord of the whole universe. The world belongs to God.

Sometimes this is hard to believe. A pastor tells about a time during World War II when he was minister of a church in Germany. One night he came to meet his Bible class. They were going to discuss one of Jesus' magnificent sayings: "All power in heaven and earth has been given to me." For this discussion of Christ's great power only three people showed up—two very old women and one trembling old man.

Outside the church Hitler's storm troopers marched. Crowds cheered and searchlights crisscrossed. Bands and banners and salutes and marching orders all said, "Hitler is king. All power in heaven and on earth has been given to Hitler."

Inside the church two very old women and one trembling old man tried to believe instead in the power of Christ. It must have been uphill work. For everything they could hear and see said to them, "There is no king but Hitler."

Christians today sometimes struggle with the same problem. Cities seem to move through each noisy day without thinking of Christ. Cocktail parties glitter, nightlife fades into dawn. The big universities hum, the great stadiums roar, the factories belch and smoke. All the busy people in all the busy places work and eat and play and rest. Then they do it all over again. How many of them know that Christ is Lord? How many know that the kingdom of God is coming? How many care?

Jesus' disciples were already worried about the kingdom's progress way back at the beginning. They believed that Jesus was the promised Messiah. They believed that he would make things right in the land and turn people back toward God. But progress seemed so small and so slow.

Every once in a while the disciples would ask about it. "Lord," they would say. "Lord, if it isn't too much to ask, when *will* you restore the kingdom?"

The disciples had their doubts. Of course, they knew Jesus had done some good things. But it didn't seem like enough! Shaping up a few ragged beggars—that wouldn't budge King Herod. Healing some sick folks, befriending a prostitute, or having dinner with a weasel like Zacchaeus—that wouldn't shake up a man like Caesar!

Looking at the Roman army and the Roman tax system and all the arrogant Roman power, the disciples must have struggled hard to believe that Jesus was King. Everything they could hear and see told them there was no king but Caesar.

> **The kingdom of God:** God's reign over his universal realm. Covenant, prophets, priests, human kings, and the church are all tools, or instruments, of the kingdom of God. Like a mustard seed, the kingdom starts out small but grows and grows. The things that kingdom people cherish and value—like humility, forgiveness, kindness—seem "upside-down" to people of the world.

For such doubts Jesus tells one of the secrets of the kingdom. The kingdom of God, he says, is like a mustard seed. A man reaches with two fingers into his seed pouch and draws out a tiny seed. The seed is so small you can hardly see it. But the man sows this seed into the ground.

Slowly, over the months and years, the seemingly lifeless seed grows into a ten-foot shrub.

The kingdom is like that. At the time of sowing, progress may look small and slow. But one day there is the tree.

That is God's way in history with his kingdom. Who would have thought that God could make a great nation out of Abraham and Sarah—two barren people old enough to be on Medicare? Who could have known what God would do with one man named Luther—a monk who nailed some protests to the door of a church and thus launched the Protestant Reformation? Who would have thought that a weary black woman named Rosa Parks could start a movement that would help millions of people?

On Good Friday who could have predicted what God would do with the dead body of Jesus, our Lord—a seed sown in the ground for three days? Only somebody who knows the secret of the kingdom.

FOR REFLECTION

Is it hard for you to believe that God really is the ruler of this world? Why or why not? Where do you see God's kingdom growing in your world—even if it's currently as small as a mustard seed?

PRAYER STARTERS

Pray that God's kingdom will soon be complete and perfect. Use your own words or those of Q&A 123 (see the top of this reading) as your prayer.

UNIT 5

OUR FUTURE HOME WITH GOD

WEEK 21

WHAT WILL HAPPEN WHEN CHRIST RETURNS?

THE SECOND COMING

SCRIPTURE

For the Lord himself, with a cry of command, with the archangel's call and with the sound of God's trumpet, will descend from heaven.

—1 Thessalonians 4:16

TEACHINGS

He ascended to heaven,
and is seated at the right hand of God the Father
     almighty.
From there he will come. . . .

—Apostles' Creed

Predicting the future can be big business. People try to make money from it. People bet, for example, on who will win the World Series or the Super Bowl. They lay wagers on boxing matches and horse races. People predict who will win these contests and by how much. Then they stake money on their predictions.

People predict other sorts of things too. They try to guess, for instance, whether stocks and bonds will rise or fall in price. They stake money on whether oats and soybeans will gain or decrease in value. These money-backed predictions are sometimes called "futures."

People also try to predict the future when they're deciding whether to train for one occupation or another. For example, most folks today would

doubt there's much future in stagecoach repair or crossbow manufacturing.

Some people spend their whole lives studying signs and trends of the future and making guesses about it. Those who gaze into crystal balls are called fortune-tellers. Those who have degrees and write books are called "futurologists." Some of those who appear on the local TV news are known as weather forecasters.

But one problem plagues all these people. Bettors, investors, fortune-tellers, and other predictors of the future all suffer from one drawback. Nobody knows the future. We can predict, of course. We can make educated guesses. We can even form intelligent opinions backed up by pretty good evidence. Still, we don't really know. Except for death coming sometime—and taxes—we can never be sure. We never know exactly what's coming.

But we do know *who's* coming. Christians know that in the future lies the third great event of history. We have had two of them so far: the creation and the first coming of Jesus Christ, our Savior. What we are waiting for is his second coming. In this great supernatural event history will come to its climax. God will triumph completely over sin and misery, and the new age of peace in a new heaven and a new earth will begin.

We call the second coming, together with the events attached to it, the *consummation.* By this name we mean the "summing up," the "completing," of all history. We mean the end of the human story as we now know it.

> **Second coming:** the event at the end of history in which Jesus Christ returns in a special way to earth. In the second coming history comes to its climax.
>
> **Consummation:** the second coming and the events attached to it—the resurrection of the dead, the last judgment, and the beginning of everlasting life.

Christians do not know very many details about the second coming. The Bible says that Jesus will return "on the clouds of heaven." The Bible talks of shouts and the sounds of trumpets. It says that Jesus will reappear with angels "in blazing fire." But we don't know how much of this language ought to be understood literally. Neither do we know how Jesus could reappear to a whole globe simultaneously. Nor whether people will know right away who he is. Finally, we don't know just when this remarkable event will occur.

Certain Christians do attempt to figure this out. They work up charts and timetables and calculations. At various times in history small bands of Christians have been so sure of their predictions that they have staked everything on them—quitting their jobs, pulling out of school, selling all their furniture. But the times they pinpointed have always come and gone without the return of our Lord. As a matter of fact, the Bible tells us, in effect, that the time of the second coming is none of our business. We are simply to watch for it and be alert (Mark 13:35-36). We are to do our work and look forward in trust.

We know who's coming. But we don't know just when or how. But the fact of our Lord's return does shape our future. We know that life has a goal. We know that work and play and good relationships have purpose. No kindness, no prayer, no small act of friendship is lost. It all counts. For these things are signs of the coming of the kingdom of God.

And the coming of the kingdom will be complete with the second coming of the King.

FOR REFLECTION

"The fact of our Lord's return does shape our future." In what ways is that true for you personally?

PRAYER STARTERS

Say your own prayer of trust in Jesus, or use this prayer:

Give us trust, O God, that our future is with you and with Christ. Let us look forward with hope to the coming of Christ, the Lord of history. In his name, Amen.

THE RESURRECTION OF THE BODY

SCRIPTURE

Listen, I will tell you a mystery! We will not all die, but we will all be changed, in a moment, in the twinkling of an eye, at the last trumpet. For the trumpet will sound, and the dead will be raised imperishable, and we will be changed.

—1 Corinthians 15:51-52

TEACHINGS

I believe . . . the resurrection of the body.
—Apostles' Creed

Q. How does "the resurrection of the body" comfort you?

A. Not only will my soul
>> be taken immediately after this life
>> to Christ its head,
> but also my very flesh will be
>> raised by the power of Christ,
>> reunited with my soul,
>> and made like Christ's glorious body.

—Heidelberg Catechism, Q&A 57

People spend a lot of time fixing their faces. A lot of men these days are going for the five o'clock shadow look—a short, scruffy kind of beard, favored by many athletes and movie stars, that nicely covers facial blemishes and projects a rugged look. Other men—especially those in a losing battle with baldness—may shave off their remaining hair and present a polished dome that can look sharp and, sometimes, a little intimidating.

Women may apply a liquid-base "foundation" to even out facial skin color and cover up small blemishes. Lips get color-coated by brush, fingers, or tube. Teeth get whitened, gaps in them cleaned and flossed. Hair gets washed, rinsed, styled, combed, and brushed.

Eyes get outlined with one pencil while another is used to shape and darken eyebrows.

Neither pencil comes with an eraser.

People fix their faces because, of course, faces draw more attention than, say, backs or elbows. That, in turn, is because one's face is a communications center. Flared nostrils and tight lips can reveal anger, for instance. Broad smiles and twinkling eyes can show joy or mischief. Sagging jowls can indicate old age. Eye shape, nose shape, lip shape, muscle firmness, skin color and clarity—such things can signal a person's age, health, people group, and emotional condition.

Christians believe that faces and bodies are important. They are closely connected with who we are. But bodies, including faces, ought not to become idols, the way they sometimes do on TV and in advertisements.

Christians actually take a place between those who worship bodies and those who despise them. We all know body worshipers. They're the ones who mistakenly believe they ought to spend most of each day in some body shop—fixing, shaping, painting. They're convinced they have to be pretty or handsome in order to be happy. Not so. Most people, in fact, are neither pretty nor handsome by Hollywood standards. They just look like themselves. They just look like who they are. And they get along fine.

On the other hand, some people lack respect for bodies. They may neglect or abuse their own bodies. They may think sex isn't nice—just because it's done with bodies. Or they may foolishly believe that work done inside one's head is more important than work done with one's hands. All this is a mistake.

Bodies are important. God made them. Jesus Christ became incarnate in one of them. And we ourselves are souls, or selves, that are *embodied.* Soul *and* body make up a complete person. True, we believe that when we die we will be with Christ without our bodies, in a kind of conscious "intermediate state" between this life and our resurrected life once Christ returns. But this intermediate state—when our souls or selves but not our bodies are with Christ— is an incomplete and unnatural kind of existence for us.

One of the clearest signs that bodies are natural to us is that at the second coming we shall be resurrected like Jesus Christ. That is, we shall have renewed bodies like his. Once again, we will be complete persons, souls or selves that are "embodied."

Receiving renewed bodies is marvelous enough for those of us who are healthy. But think what this means for those of us whose bodies now need repair. Think what it means for a person with cerebral palsy or muscular dystrophy or blindness. Think what it means for those who have been spine-injured in accidents.

> **Resurrection of the body:** a consummation event in which, at the second coming, dead people are reunited with their bodies. Those who belong to Christ shall be given bodies like his.

The Bible promises that we shall have bodies like Christ's. "The Lord Jesus Christ . . . will transform our lowly bodies so that they will be like his glorious body," says Paul in Philippians 3:20-21 (NIV). C. S. Lewis once encouraged his readers that, if the body they are now driving is a junker, they can take heart. One day God will give them a new one.

FOR REFLECTION

The Bible says that our resurrected bodies will be like Christ's. What might this mean? Luke 24:36-43 and 1 Corinthians 15:42-44, 53 will give you some ideas.

PRAYER STARTERS

Thank God for caring for our bodies enough to raise them from the dead and renew them when Christ returns to this earth.

THE LAST JUDGMENT

SCRIPTURE

When the Son of Man comes in his glory, and all the angels with him, then he will sit on the throne of his glory. All the nations will be gathered before him, and he will separate people one from another as a shepherd separates the sheep from the goats, and he will put the sheep at his right hand and the goats at the left.

—Matthew 25:31-33

TEACHINGS

From there he will come to judge the living and the dead.

—Apostles' Creed

Then the books (that is, the consciences) will
    be opened,
and the dead will be judged
    according to the things they did in the world,
    whether good or evil.

—Belgic Confession, Article 37

At the end of history our Lord shall return. We do not know just how or when he will come. But we do know that he is coming. We also know two things that will happen. One is the resurrection of our bodies. The other is the last judgment.

What is a judgment? A judgment is a determination that a thing is good or bad, or that an act is right or wrong. In some cases, as we know, persons are judged to be right or wrong, good or bad, guilty or innocent.

Of course, we think at once of courts. A man or a woman wearing a robe enters a courtroom and mounts the bench. This person, when no jury is present, makes judgments of guilt or innocence. This person has the power to find you guilty of driving a car without a license or of hacking into someone's computer to obtain private information.

Of course, other people make judgments too. Teachers judge whether your term paper merits an A, B, C, or worse. Your boss judges your performance at work. Contest judges determine who submitted the winning drawing or photograph. Umpires judge whether an infield throw beat a runner to first base and whether a pitcher is guilty of a balk.

You yourself make judgments every day. When driving you constantly judge safe distances and appropriate speed. You judge which items on your daily schedule take priority and whether to order a burger or a salad. You determine what books to read, what music to listen to, what clothing to wear. You decide who you want as friends.

A judgment is a determination, or assessment, of some act or thing or person. We deal with judgments all the time. The trouble is that human judgments can be flawed. Sometimes they are plain wrong or even wicked. More often they are at least partly slanted by our own prejudices.

Most courtroom judges, for example, are honest and wise. But a few can be bribed to help criminals go free. Most teachers are skillful and caring. But a poor teacher might have it in for you just because he didn't like your older brother. Bosses and contest judges can be prejudiced. Umpires sometimes need a visit to an optometrist. You and I sometimes make wrong judgments about distances, schedules, food, books, music, clothing, friends, and countless other things.

The Bible says that at the end of history there will be a perfect judgment, a last judgment, a final judgment. All those who are then raised from the dead, plus those who are still alive at the second coming—billions of people—will be judged. The judges will be Jesus Christ and God the Father. The God of the universe and the King of history will judge.

> **The last judgment:** a consummation event in which all the people of history are judged by God the Father and Jesus Christ according to whether they have done good or evil. Though many of our works may be judged evil, we face as judge the same Christ who died to save us.

This time there will be no slip-ups, no bribes, no prejudices, no slanted judgments. In this final, perfect judgment the loose ends of the world will be tied up and the friends and enemies of Jesus Christ exposed. The sheer truth of all history will be publicly revealed.

We don't know exactly how it will go. There are great mysteries here. But the Bible makes one thing clear: people will be judged according to whether they have done good or evil. Compassion, kindness, fairness, and other things will count for good, especially when done to "the least" of Jesus Christ's brothers and sisters. Hard-heartedness, meanness, cruelty, and dishonesty will count for evil, especially when done to the least, the poorest, the most vulnerable.

Of course, we are not saved by our good works. We are saved by grace and through faith. But we are judged according to works. For works are the evidence of faith. People sometimes have more faith than they think they do. Their works show this. And sometimes people have less faith than they think. Their lack of works shows this.

In other words, we can expect surprises at the last judgment.

FOR REFLECTION

Should Christians fear the final judgment? Look forward to it? Not think about it? What should our attitude be?

PRAYER STARTERS

Bring any concerns you have about the last judgment—and the future in general—to the one who knows you, loves you, and will find you "not guilty" on the day of judgment.

THE LIFE EVERLASTING

SCRIPTURE

"Then the King will say to those at his right hand, 'Come, you who are blessed by my Father, inherit the kingdom prepared for you from the foundation of the world . . . . ' Then he will say to those at his left hand, 'You that are accursed, depart from me into the eternal fire prepared for the devil and his angels.'"

—Matthew 25:34, 41

TEACHINGS

I believe . . . the life everlasting.

—Apostles' Creed

Q. How does the article
concerning "life everlasting"
comfort you?

A. Even as I already now
experience in my heart
the beginning of eternal joy,
so after this life I will have
perfect blessedness such as
no eye has seen,
no ear has heard,
no human heart has ever imagined:
a blessedness in which to praise God
forever.

—Heidelberg Catechism Q&A 58

Christians believe that Jesus Christ is coming. We believe that he is coming to judge the living and the dead. We also believe in the resurrection of the body and the life everlasting.

Because life everlasting comes in two kinds, the final judgment divides humanity into two groups. In his parable our Lord calls these groups the sheep and the goats. The goats receive everlasting punishment, the sheep everlasting bliss. To the goats God shows his dark justice, to the sheep the brightness of his mercy. We need to understand that the sheep are naturally no better than the goats. Their good works have come from faith and from the warm glow of the Holy Spirit working within them. And both faith and the Spirit are sheer gifts from God.

> **Everlasting life:** the eternal state of those who are judged. Some face everlasting punishment, while others—because of the mercy of God—are given everlasting bliss.

Let me admit that the whole arrangement feels uncomfortable. Anyone who thinks about it very long will have questions. Many Christians wonder whether we correctly understand our Lord about everlasting life and death.

Still, here it is in the Bible. We must do the best we can with it. Leaving behind our questions and agonies about everlasting punishment, let's think for a bit about everlasting life with God.

Let's be honest. You may not think of everlasting life very often or even want it very badly. The idea of "going to heaven," or living with God, may seem strange, remote, and not very inviting.

Why? Why is that so, even for some older adults who have been Christians all their lives?

Two reasons occur to me. First, if God has blessed you with a loving family, good health, plenty of food and clothing, and a good friend or two, you already have some of the benefits of life with God. These are gifts of the King. These are inheritances of the kingdom. If in addition you are reading the Scriptures, trying to obey Christ, and praying as honestly as you can—if you are doing these things, you are already living with God in a way. So perhaps heaven doesn't seem like much of an improvement.

Things are very different, of course, if you are sick or poor or have been badly hurt by the cruelties of others. Then you may want the life everlasting very much. You hunger and thirst like Oliver Twist, who longed for God to fill his emptiness and show him the love and acceptance he did not feel from others.

There is a second reason that heaven often seems so remote: none of us fully understands what the joys of the life everlasting will be like.

My family and I once spent some time living in Cambridge, England. Neither I nor my family members had ever before visited England. Some of us didn't even want to make the trip. After all, when you live abroad for some time, you leave behind good friends, familiar places, and everyday ways of doing things.

Before we left the United States, we consulted with some people who had lived in England. We asked them questions. They told us what we could expect there, what life would be like. They described wonderful things to see and do there. That helped. It made living abroad sound more like an adventure than an inconvenience.

But we have no one to consult about life everlasting—no one who's been there. We have no one to talk with personally who can answer our questions. We do not therefore really understand the joys of everlasting life, even after reading what the Bible says.

C. S. Lewis once made a helpful comparison. We don't know what we're missing, he said. We are like a small child who insists on staying in his sandbox because he cannot imagine what is meant by the offer of a day on the beach.

The life everlasting is like a day on the beach—a day there that never ends.

FOR REFLECTION

What is your attitude toward "life everlasting" and about living with God in heaven? Similar to that described in this reading, or different?

PRAYER STARTERS

Thank God for the resurrection of the body and the life everlasting. You may want to ask God to make the life to come more real for or more appealing to you.

WEEK 22

WHAT WILL HEAVEN BE LIKE?

THE NEW HEAVEN AND NEW EARTH

SCRIPTURE

Then I saw "a new heaven and a new earth," for the first heaven and the first earth had passed away, and there was no longer any sea. I saw the Holy City, the new Jerusalem, coming down out of heaven from God, prepared as a bride beautifully dressed for her husband. And I heard a loud voice from the throne saying, "Look! God's dwelling place is now among the people, and he will dwell with them. They will be his people, and God himself will be with them and be their God."

—Revelation 21:1-3 (NIV)

TEACHINGS

We long for that day
when our bodies are raised,
the Lord wipes away our tears,
and we dwell forever in the presence of God.
We will take our place in the new creation,
where there will be no more death,
or mourning or crying or pain,
and the Lord will be our light.
Come, Lord Jesus, Come.

—*Our World Belongs to God*, paragraph 56

Art museums often reserve one of their galleries for special exhibits. In this gallery artworks from other museums across the world are displayed. Every so often the exhibit changes. The paintings hanging in the exhibit gallery are removed and new ones hung in their places. And, of course, the gallery then looks remarkably different.

Our own imagination is like one of these galleries. In it hang various pictures—pictures of home and country and family and friends and school and even ourselves. Every so often the pictures have to be changed. Suppose, for instance, that some wonderful person tells you how interesting and likable you are. Your self-image changes. You pull down the old portrait of yourself and replace it with one of your likable and interesting self. On the other hand, suppose someone you thought was wonderful does something really cheap and mean. You would sadly remove the old, perfect portrait of this person and replace it with one that includes a mean streak.

Many of us have a small gallery of pictures of heaven. We have, perhaps, a few pictures of angels and clouds and harps. Maybe God and Christ sitting on thrones are pictured in our gallery. Possibly we imagine gleaming gold streets and a population of heavenly residents quite a lot like ourselves. We have pictures of churchgoing and hymn singing and resting. All of it is airy and high up and, to tell the truth, somewhat boring and unreal to us.

It's time to change the exhibit, to replace these pictures with others. For the Bible, especially in Revelation 21 and Isaiah 60, includes some pictures that are very different from those in our galleries. I once read a remarkable little book about heaven by Richard Mouw. It's called *When the Kings Come Marching In.* In these readings I want to take some of Dr. Mouw's ideas and pass them on to you.

When our Lord returns, he will judge those who are living and also those who have just been resurrected. Then will begin the life everlasting. But where will that life take place?

We usually think of heaven as up, way up. We think of spirits with airy bodies floating about on cumulus clouds. These pictures must come down. For in Revelation 21 John suggests that the new heaven and the new earth will be right here where we now live. This earth will be purified and renewed so that heaven can be on-site where we now live. We don't go to heaven; heaven comes to us.

Think about what this means. It means that Banff will be part of heaven. Toronto, especially Ontario Place, will be included. So will Miami and Montreal, Paterson and Vancouver. There is an outside chance for Grand Rapids.

Of course, things will have to be purified and changed. It's hard to imagine smog and sleet and floods and urban decay in the new heaven and the new earth. But it is this present earth that will be invaded by heaven—these forests, these mountains, this city and that one, these streams and rivers, lakes and lagoons.

New heaven and new earth: the place of everlasting life. This present earth will be cleansed and renewed, and heaven will come down to it.

Into this renewed earth, into the heavenly city on earth, into the new Jerusalem will come some familiar things, all of them changed to match God's perfect portraits of them. Whole nations will march in, not just individuals. Symphonies and bands will be as much a part of the throng as choirs. Not just pastors, but kings and presidents and ex-dictators and prime ministers will march in. Revelation 21 tells us there will be no temple. I guess that means no church. But sports will probably be plentiful in the new earth, for we will have new, free, powerful bodies. The new earth will be filled with friends and old enemies and humble apologies.

Above all, Jesus Christ will be there. And everyone will be drawn to him as though by a magnet, for he will be the center of the new heaven and the new earth. Whatever pictures change in the gallery of our minds, his portrait must remain.

FOR REFLECTION

Do you have some of the "old portraits" of heaven suggested by this reading? If so, what important changes do Revelation 21:1-2 and this reading suggest?

PRAYER STARTERS

Based on what you learned in this reading, let your imagination roam about what heaven will be like. If you're excited about it, give God some genuine praise for the great future in store for you.

THE REFILLING OF THE EARTH

SCRIPTURE

"Then you will look and be radiant,
 your heart will throb and swell with joy;
the wealth on the seas will be brought to you,
 to you the riches of the nations will come.
 Herds of camels will cover your land,
 young camels of Midian and Ephah.
And all from Sheba will come,
 bearing gold and incense
 and proclaiming the praise of the LORD."
—Isaiah 60:5-6 (NIV)

TEACHINGS

God will be all in all,
righteousness and peace will flourish,
everything will be made new,
and every eye will see at last
that our world belongs to God.
—*Our World Belongs to God,* paragraph 58

When God made the earth, he told people to fill it. We read of this in Genesis 1:28. God blessed the man and woman and said to them, "Be fruitful and increase in number; fill the earth and subdue it. Rule over it."

As Dr. Mouw says, God did not mean just that Adam and Eve ought to make a lot of babies and fill the earth with them. God meant that human beings were to produce culture and fill the earth with it.

What is culture?

Human culture is the sum of what humans produce and of the ways in which they are organized for life together. When humans are organized economically, for instance, they produce goods and services such as electric clippers and haircuts. When humans are organized politically they produce judges and presidents and lawmakers—together with their judgments and vetoes and laws. When humans are organized artistically they produce artworks and galleries to show them in. And so on.

Add all this (and much more) together and you have human culture. Culture is civilization plus its goods and services.

God wanted the first humans to order the garden, to tame and manage it. He wanted them and their children to produce goods and services so that people could live, and even live well, together. God wanted culture.

As we know, the fall intervened. And in the fall culture got twisted by sin. For instance, people discovered that if they could make a plow for splitting the earth, they could also make a sword for splitting a head. The same hand that turned out a pruning shears for trimming a rosebush could also, with a few new turns, fashion a spear for impaling an enemy.

Nowadays twisted culture fills the earth. Great scientists use their excellent minds to dream up mega-destructive intercontinental ballistic missiles. Filmmakers put a good face on divorce or godlessness. Some politicians try to become dictators, and some doctors get more interested in wealth than in healing. Some ministers preach sermons that are popular but not true.

What's more, people take pride in their bad or dangerous culture. Nations boast of their destructive might. Schools brag about their prestige. Racists pride themselves on their color. People everywhere accept with open arms and minds the products of a bad culture—products such as pornography, dope, gambling casinos, abortion mills, and terrorist training centers.

The earth is full, all right. But it's full of—well, of trash as well as treasure.

Isaiah 60 says that the new heaven and the new earth will be refilled. Isaiah uses ancient pictures, of course. He says the ships of Tarshish will sail into God's city. Herds of camels (the ships of the desert), flocks of sheep and rams, lumber from Lebanon and gold from Sheba—all these things will come into the holy city of the future. That is, the wealth of the seas and the riches of the nations *outside* Israel will all be gathered into the city of God.

Why? What's the point? These are, after all, products of pagan culture, of twisted culture. They are products of wealth and might that have made pagan nations proud.

Refilling of the earth: The new earth will be filled with purified culture (civilization plus its goods and services).

The point is that the earth—*and* its fullness—is the Lord's. God means to reclaim the fullness that is his. God means to transform all this fullness, to refill the earth, so that culture can serve him and his people the way it was intended to way back at the beginning.

In this great refilling, spears will be turned back into pruning shears and swords into garden rakes. Artists and teachers, business people and attorneys, animal trainers and filmmakers—all will use their skills and products to make God's name great and to serve his people.

Can you think of a good use for old machine guns?

FOR REFLECTION

What sounds good to you about the refilling of the earth described in Scripture and this reading?

PRAYER STARTERS

Read Psalm 24:1-2. Be silent before the one who owns and loves our world. Then say aloud "Our world belongs to you, O God." Repeat this phrase slowly and thoughtfully for a minute or so.

THE MARCH OF KINGS AND NATIONS

SCRIPTURE

"Your gates will always stand open,
    they will never be shut, day or night,
so that people may bring you the wealth of the
        nations—
    their kings led in triumphal procession. . . .
You will drink the milk of nations
    and be nursed at royal breasts.
Then you will know that I, the LORD, am your
        Savior,
    your Redeemer, the Mighty One of Jacob."

—Isaiah 60:11, 16 (NIV)

TEACHINGS

God will be all in all,
righteousness and peace will flourish,
everything will be made new,
and every eye will see at last
that our world belongs to God.

—*Our World Belongs to God*, paragraph 58

At the end God will refill the earth. The new heaven and the new earth will be filled with the pure culture of art and education, science and technology, law and commerce. Animals and animal trainers will be part of the new earth. So will gardens and garden keepers. So will computers and computer programmers. What used to be a source of human pride will become instead a reflector of the glory of God. For the earth and its fullness are the Lord's.

Isaiah mentions in particular two kinds of culture, both political. He mentions kings and nations.

Why kings? Why will kings come marching in?

In his book Dr. Mouw offers three reasons. First, in ancient times a king was not just a ruler. He also represented his nation's whole culture. A king provided for arts and learning. (That is why some colleges have been named "King's College.") A king sponsored business, law, and medicine. In fact, a nation's cultural treasures were, in a sense, all on deposit in its national ruler. When kings come marching in, therefore, so do their cultural deposits. They are part of the "filling" for the new heaven and the new earth.

Second, Isaiah says that when kings come into the new earth, they will not head the parade. Instead, they will be "led in triumphal procession." They will be followers rather than leaders. The tables will be turned on unjust kings. Those who once dominated people will now have to meekly follow their victims into the new city. Those kings and queens who once tortured people or crushed them will now have to bow low before them. For in the new heavens and the new earth, rulers will have to account for their use of the political power God lent them.

Should we think of Nero bowing before the Christians he torched? Will Hitler be led by Anne Frank? How about slaves leading slave drivers?

Perhaps. In any case the purpose of this turning of the tables is not mere revenge. The purpose instead is a public demonstration of the justice of God. History's wrongs must be righted. The truth must come out. Oppressors must be made to face their victims and repent.

Think what this will be like if both parties are Christian believers. Catholics and Protestants, heretics and orthodox, masters and slaves—all must face each other before the Lord they both confess.

Third, Isaiah mentions kings because he wants us to know that in the new heaven and the new earth politicians will serve people instead of using them. Rulers will nourish people instead of sucking them dry. Isaiah uses a strange and striking image for this. He says that people in the new city will be "nursed at royal breasts." The point is that those who rule will be people who nurture, like a mother. They will be like our Lord himself, who wanted to gather his people as a hen gathers her chicks.

Perhaps it seems like a disconnect to think of politics in heaven. But that is what Isaiah says. Even political discussions and debates might be part of life there. But this time all politics will be perfectly managed by him who is King of kings and Lord of lords.

Finally, Isaiah says that nations will come into God's city. Not just individuals, but whole peoples will stream into the holy city. What's the idea?

The idea is that God takes pleasure in the sheer *kinds* of people he has made and rescued. Red and yellow, black and white—all are precious in his sight, and all have their place in the new Jerusalem. Ethnic groups can bring in their ethnic treasures without sinful pride. Races may offer their gifts to God without racism. For as surely as Pentecost opens the door to people of every tongue and tribe, so the gates of heaven will swing wide for the multicolor procession of God's people.

When the kings and nations come marching in— this will be a parade not to miss.

FOR REFLECTION

Read Revelation 5, which describes a scene in heaven. Notice who is at the center of this scene and why.

PRAYER STARTERS

Pray the praise song of the angels that circled the throne of God:

"Worthy is the Lamb, who was slain, to receive power and wealth and wisdom and strength and honor and glory and praise!" (Rev. 5:12)

SEEKING THE CITY OF LIGHT

SCRIPTURE

"Arise, shine, for your light has come,
    and the glory of the LORD rises upon you."
—Isaiah 60:1 (NIV)

For here we do not have an enduring city, but we are looking for the city that is to come.
—Hebrews 13:14 (NIV)

TEACHINGS

Even as I already now
    experience in my heart
    the beginning of eternal joy,
so after this life I will have
    perfect blessedness such as
        no eye has seen,
        no ear has heard,
        no human heart has ever imagined:
    a blessedness in which to praise God forever.
—Heidelberg Catechism, Answer 58

A hundred years ago in Sweden, a country doctor came out to a farmhouse one night to help deliver a child. As the woman labored on the kitchen table, her husband assisted the doctor by holding up a lamp to illuminate the room. After a time of courageous labor, the mother produced a fine baby boy. Then, to the surprise of both parents, the doctor announced that a second child was on the way. And, indeed, before long the mother delivered a lovely daughter.

The father was already shaken by this unexpected turn of events, so you can imagine his astonishment when he heard the doctor say, "Hold everything, I think there's a third. I think there are triplets."

At this, the father began to move out of the room. "Hold it!" called the doctor. "Come back here with that lamp."

"Oh no," said the father. "It's the *light* that attracts them."

Something does indeed attract us to light. Keepers of great churches and other buildings know this. They know how to illuminate a magnificent building at night so that people can hardly keep their eyes off it. Other lights also attract. Lost miners or cave explorers, for example, long for the light at the end of a tunnel. Insomniacs yearn for morning light. Long-distance bikers lean forward in their saddle toward the bright lights that signal a village and the inviting end of a long day's trek.

We all crave light because something in us fears and mistrusts the dark. Darkness seems to be a cover for danger and disease. Darkness can make us feel depressed. And darkness makes it hard for us to find our way. Ancient people shared our dislike of the dark. In fact, since their methods of illumination were primitive and weak, they were probably more afraid of the dark than we are.

We can understand, then, why Isaiah 60 says that the city of God is full of light. Light represents safety in darkness. Light represents health against disease, guidance instead of lostness, warmth instead of the coldness of outer darkness. Indeed, in the new heaven and the new earth, says Revelation 21, there will be no more night at all.

Why? Think back to what we learned in lesson 15 about glorifying God. The glory of the Lord has to do with light and it has to do with worthiness. *Glory* means both "brilliance" and "good reputation."

The new heaven and the new earth will be a city of light because it will be filled with the glory of the Lord. What's more, it will be filled with millions of God-glorifying reflectors from every race and tribe and tongue—the whole of God's people reflecting his light back to him in their own way and color. Thus, whatever is brilliant; whatever is luminous and clean; whatever is soft and lovely and bright; whatever is radiant and glorious—think of these things as lighting up the holy city of God.

At the center is Jesus Christ, the light of the world and the lamp of the new heaven and new earth:

> The sun will no more be your light by day
>   nor will the brightness of the moon
>   shine on you,

> for the LORD will be your everlasting light,
>   and your God will be your glory.
> Your sun will never set again,
>   and your moon will wane no more;
> the LORD will be your everlasting light,
>   and your days of sorrow will end.

—Isaiah 60:19-20 (NIV)

That is why the kings and nations come marching in. It's the light that attracts them. Ahead is the city that people seek—some willingly, some almost in spite of themselves. For in this city the Lamb of God shines like a lamp, drawing people to his glory.

FOR REFLECTION

Read Revelation 21. What do you think it will be like to live in the city of God in the renewed earth?

PRAYER STARTERS

Pray the song of the angels once more (see the end of the reading for day 3).

WEEK 23

WHAT DOES BEING REFORMED MEAN?

SPEAKING WITH A REFORMED ACCENT*

SCRIPTURE

All Scripture is God-breathed and is useful for teaching, rebuking, correcting and training in righteousness.
—2 Timothy 3:16 (NIV)

TEACHINGS

We receive all these books
and these only
as holy and canonical,
for the regulating, founding, and establishing
of our faith.
And we believe
without a doubt
all things contained in them—
    not so much because the church
    receives and approves them as such
    but above all because the Holy Spirit
    testifies in our hearts
    that they are from God . . .
—Belgic Confession, Article 5

An American who lives in England gives himself away every time he opens his mouth. The English speak English. An American speaks English with an American accent. I say "half past nine." The English say "hahf pahst noin." I say "bitter." Some English say "bih-er."

Everybody speaks his or her language with an accent. If English isn't your native tongue, you might speak it with a Dutch or Korean or French accent. But even if English is your native tongue, you still speak it with an accent that tells people what region you come from. In the U.S., for instance, people from Boston and the deep South and the Midwest and Texas and Brooklyn all speak English. But they speak English with regional differences. Some of these have to do with pronunciation, some with rhythm, others with the length of vowels. People speak English with a regional accent.

Test yourself. A baseball fan who yells "Moida da bum on toid!" is from (a) Edgerton, Minnesota; (b) Brooklyn, New York; (c) Ripon, California; (d) Toronto, Ontario.

An accent is a distinctive way of speaking. But accents and accent marks are also used in music, poetry, and painting. An artist, for example, can use a touch of color or light to bring out one part of a design. A poet shapes a line of poetry by the rhythm of stresses on syllables. A composer shapes a line of music by indicating which tones are to be struck, or blown, or voiced, or bowed more sharply than others. The composer, painter, poet—all use accents.

Everyone who trusts in Jesus Christ alone for salvation is a Christian. "Believe in the Lord

Jesus," says the Bible, "and you will be saved" (Acts 16:31). But Christians of various kinds stress different things in the Christian religion. Catholics stress sacraments. Lutherans stress justification through faith alone. Many Methodists lay heavy stress on the need for a warm heart toward Jesus. Certain Baptists emphasize the need for being born again. Pentecostals stress the gifts of the Holy Spirit.

All sincere believers in the gospel of Jesus Christ are Christians. But, as we can see, people speak their Christianity with different accents. To be Reformed/Presbyterian is to confess the gospel with a Reformed accent. What does this mean? Where do we lay special stress?

First I should say that Reformed/Presbyterian people join other Christians in thinking that sacraments are important. We also believe in the importance of justification through faith alone, the need for a warm heart, the necessity of being born again, and the wonder of the gifts of the Holy Spirit.

> **Reformed:** To be Reformed is to confess the common Christian faith with a special accent. In particular, it means to accent such things as the authority of Scripture, the sovereignty of God, personal integrity in the life of holiness, and the need for a view of world integrity (sometimes called a "world-and-life view" or "kingdom vision").

But although we believe in the importance of all these things, they are not the places in our religion where we place special stress. We accent other things. Our accents lie more on the sovereignty of God; on the authority of Scripture; on the need for disciplined holiness in personal Christian life; and, finally, on Christianity as a religion of the kingdom. In fact, these themes should be familiar to you by now. One way or another, they have appeared many times in this book.

The basis of our stress on all of these themes is the authority of Scripture. For in the Scriptures we read of God's sovereignty and kingdom. There we learn the need for disciplined personal holiness. The Scriptures correct and improve people. They reform us. That, in fact, is one reason we are called "Reformed." We are people who have been reshaped according to the Word of God. We are Reformed. We go by the Book.

To lay a lot of emphasis on the authority of Scripture is typical of Reformed/Presbyterian people. It's one of the ways our Reformed accent comes through.

FOR REFLECTION

"The [Scriptures] reform us. We are people who have been shaped according to the Word of God. We are Reformed. We go by the book." Think about how your life is being shaped by the Word of God. How is it authoritative for you?

PRAYER STARTERS

Ask that God may always be reforming and shaping you through his powerful and authoritative Word. Ask God to help you give that Word a central place in your life.

*(This week's readings owe much to John Hesselink's On Being Reformed.)

THE SOVEREIGNTY OF GOD

SCRIPTURE

The LORD is king,
    let the peoples tremble!
He sits enthroned upon the cherubim,
    let the earth quake.
The LORD is great in Zion;
    he is exalted over all the peoples.
Let them praise your great and awesome name—
    holy is he!

—Psalm 99:1-3

TEACHINGS

Our world belongs to God—
not to us or earthly powers,
not to demons, fate, or chance.
The earth is the Lord's.

—*Our World Belongs to God,* paragraph 7

Some things are really too obvious to say: Pain hurts. Pleasure feels good. The Sahara is dry. For good eating, it's hard to beat food. Bachelors are unmarried. And so on.

The sovereignty of God might seem to fit in this category of obvious things. Sovereignty, after all, means superiority and control. A sovereign person is one who is a high and majestic ruler. To say that God is a high and majestic ruler seems all too obvious.

Still, God's sovereignty has meanings we may not think of at once or may not remember.

First, saying that God is sovereign means that the earth is the Lord's and all that is in it. This is true of the original creation. It is also true, as we have just learned, of the new heaven and the new earth. It follows that we have to treat the earth with respect. Farmers, miners, foresters—even hikers—must pay attention to God's sovereignty. The earth is the Lord's. He made it. We are only long-term guests.

God's sovereignty over creation also means that animals deserve proper respect and care. It means that other human beings, imagebearers of God, deserve proper respect and care. They belong to God. It means that we ourselves—our bodies, our minds, our consciences—deserve proper respect and care. Because all of these things, and all of us, come from the hand of God.

Second, God's sovereignty goes beyond creation to redemption. In the mystery of human salvation God is the main actor. We may think we have been wise to choose God; actually he has been merciful in choosing us. His will, not ours, moves us to seek him.

People sometimes get quite excited about their salvation, telling the story of it again and again to anyone who has the patience to listen. They describe what happened the day they got saved, how their pulses raced and their spines tingled as they gave themselves to Jesus. In fact, some people "get saved" anew each time they attend a rally or crusade. Perhaps it's not really salvation they are after; perhaps it's the feeling of getting saved.

Well, feelings are important. We all want good strong ones. But it is quite dangerous for us to think that what is important in Christianity is how it makes us feel. We are then asking, What can the faith do for me? How can I have an unforgettable experience in worship? How can my salvation be fun and exciting? That is, how can God make himself useful to me and my feelings and needs?

This is all backward. This is religion centered on human beings instead of on God. These questions and attitudes miss the whole point of the Christian religion. The point is that we exist to serve and thank God, not the other way around. God is sovereign, not I. It is he who saves us, not we ourselves. The point is that we must let God be God.

True, thankfully serving Jesus Christ does make us happy. Worshiping God does arouse powerful feelings at times. In his mercy God does stoop to serve us in Jesus Christ.

All true. But these things become real and pure for us only when we do not try for them too hard. Try too hard to remember something you've forgotten, and it won't come back. Move on to something else—and the thought you wanted comes to you.

In the same way we must not try too hard for salvation or happiness or fine feelings in our religion. These things may come to us—but only when we forget about them and strive to serve the sovereign God. They will come through the back door when we answer him who knocks at the front door of our lives.

God is sovereign in creation and redemption. To say this is to speak the Christian faith with a Reformed accent.

FOR REFLECTION

When are you most aware of God's sovereignty?

PRAYER STARTERS

In the Old Testament book of Job, Job argues with God as to why disaster after disaster has hit him and his family. Near the end of the book, God speaks directly to Job and presents himself as sovereign, the maker and ruler of all things. Read Job 40. Then simply be silent for a minute or two before our awesome God.

PERSONAL INTEGRITY

SCRIPTURE

I have been crucified with Christ and I no longer
live, but Christ lives in me.

—Galatians 2:20 (NIV)

TEACHINGS

The Spirit renews our hearts,
and moves us to faith,
leads us into truth,
and helps us to pray,
stands by us in our need,
and makes our obedience fresh and vibrant.

—*Our World Belongs to God,* paragraph 29

Reformed/Presbyterian people stress living a
disciplined life of personal holiness. Earlier in
this book we looked at training and discipline in
sanctification. We saw that in things like sports
and music and our faith only disciplined people
are really free.

Now I want to say this another way. We have
been created by the sovereign freedom of God.
God is hospitable enough to make room for us.
Suppose, moreover, that we feel within us the
stirrings of love for Jesus Christ. This means
that the Holy Spirit has already been at work.
Suppose, still further, that we are saved people,
ready to serve God with minds and hands and
energy. We know some of the pieces of this life

of service and gratitude: gathering to worship,
praying at home, setting aside part of our money
for church and the poor, honoring parents,
showing compassion to people at school or at
work who especially need someone to take an
interest in them. All these things we know about.
They are all pieces of the Christian life.

But what puts these pieces together? What
makes them not just pieces, but parts of a
whole life? That is, what gives our Christian life
integrity?

What is integrity?

Integrity is the strength that holds things together.
Engineers who plan bridges or airplanes worry a
lot about integrity because they understand the
forces that can make a thing collapse. A bridge,
for instance, must be both firm and flexible, like a
long steel spring. It has to be able to give a little
as the forces of wind and traffic move it. But it
can't give a whole lot, or it becomes unstable.

The same goes for airplanes. Jumbo jets, for
instance, can develop cracks in their ribs from the
force of thousands of landings. Safety requires
that such aircraft be planned and built to flex just
enough to absorb the force of landing but not so
much that they fall apart. (Think of flexing your
knees in preparation for a six-foot drop.)

Reformed/Presbyterian people care deeply about the integrity of personal Christian living. To keep our integrity we need two things: firm structure and inner flexibility.

The law of God gives us structure and firmness. It's like a set of ribs in an airplane or like the superstructure of a bridge. The law of God, obeyed according to the authority of Scripture, shapes our lives so that they have strong ribs. Our lives are firm and stable when we are disciplined by the law. People can depend on us. They know we won't lose our Christian shape when forces push against us or pull on us. People can predict ahead of time that we will not lie or steal. They can depend on us to show reverence for God and respect for parents. These are our ribs. This is our superstructure.

But we must also be able to flex a little. Sometimes laws and rules cannot be our final answer. We need in us a *person*—a living, guiding person to inspire us with energy and enthusiasm for vital Christian living.

For this we have in us the very Spirit of Christ. "I no longer live," says Paul, "but Christ lives in me." Elsewhere he speaks of the Holy Spirit living in us.

What does this mean? It means that at our center, in our "heart," beats the warm, personal life of God to inspire and guide us. We have the law as our skeleton. We have the Spirit of God as our vital life and breath.

Suppose you have to lie to save a life. Suppose you face a situation for which there is no rule at all. You can still adapt. You can flex a little. You can go ahead and act, if you have to, knowing that the Holy Spirit will guide you.

The Christian life needs both firmness and flexibility. It needs integrity. To say this is to speak the faith with a Reformed accent.

FOR REFLECTION

How do God's law and the Spirit affect your own sense of personal integrity?

PRAYER STARTERS

Consider praying this prayer of David from Psalm 51:

Create in me a pure heart, O God,
and renew a steadfast spirit within me.
Do not cast me from your presence
or take your Holy Spirit from me.
Restore to me the joy of your salvation
and grant me a willing spirit to sustain me. Amen.

DAY 4

WORLD INTEGRITY

SCRIPTURE

He is before all things, and in him all things hold together.

—Colossians 1:17 (NIV)

TEACHINGS

Jesus ascended in triumph
raising our humanity to the heavenly throne.
All authority, glory, and power are given to him.
There he hears our prayers
and pleads our cause before the Father.
Blessed are all
who take refuge in him.

—*Our World Belongs to God,* paragraph 27

Personal integrity is important. You can tell when a person has it. She has a strong, flexible Christian life. She can stand firm against an unholy act but love and help an unholy person. She does not change her opinions and her conversation whenever she moves to a new group or place. She is not a chameleon. She has integrity.

But personal integrity is not enough. Personal salvation isn't enough either. Of course, for a person to be saved by the grace of God and the poured-out blood of Jesus Christ is an unspeakably fine thing. If such a person possesses personal integrity as well, we rejoice.

But it is not enough. In addition to personal integrity Reformed/Presbyterian people try for *world* integrity. After all, God doesn't save just individual souls. No, "God so loved the *world* that he gave his one and only Son." And this Son, Jesus Christ, is not just my personal Savior. No, he is Lord of the whole world. He is the King whose kingdom is the universe. He is the one, says Paul, in whom "all things hold together." The world has integrity, in other words, only because it is ruled and preserved by the sovereign Lord, Jesus Christ.

What does this mean?

When we looked at the kingdom of God earlier in this book, we saw that we must obey God the King and Christ the Lord in every part of life. Let me now say this in a new way with the help of two examples.

John is a patriot. He loves his country. When his national anthem plays, John breaks out in goose bumps. When his country's flag is hoisted, John snaps smartly to attention. John would do anything for his nation. If the military of his nation is ordered to invade another nation, John assumes that his national leaders have good reasons for that order. He asks no questions; in fact, he joins the army to fight in that war. "My country may be wrong this time," John reasons, "but it's been right before. I've got to be loyal. My country needs me. I'll do anything I'm told."

John is a saved person. He also has personal integrity. But he lacks a view of world integrity. For John has not fit his country into a bigger picture of the whole world. Other countries, after all, are important too. We must respect them and not invade them for selfish reasons. They and the whole universe belong to Christ. We must seek first to be citizens of *his* kingdom.

Joyce is an anti-patriot. She hates her country. When her national anthem plays, Joyce breaks out in a cold sweat. When her country's flag is hoisted, Joyce slouches and yawns. Joyce would do almost nothing for her country. If her national leaders order an invasion, Joyce asks no questions. She assumes her leaders have bad reasons for their order. She would never support that war in any way. "My country may be right this time," reasons Joyce, "but it's been wrong before. I've got to be suspicious. I'll do nothing I'm told."

Joyce is a saved person. She also has personal integrity. But Joyce lacks a view of world integrity. For she has not fit her country into a bigger picture of the whole world. Other countries, after all, may be defenseless against the invasion of some murderous dictator. We have to respect those weak countries and sometimes fight to save them. For they and the whole universe belong to Jesus Christ. We must seek first to be citizens of *his* kingdom.

The gospel applies to my personal life—how I am saved and how my life holds together. But it also applies to the whole world—how the whole world is reconciled to Christ and holds together in him.

Deciding what is Christlike in the world may be terribly hard for Christians. Still, we have to try. Otherwise, for us the world has no integrity.

To speak of world *integrity* is to speak the faith with a Reformed accent.

FOR REFLECTION

What does having a view of "world integrity" look like in your life?

PRAYER STARTERS

"Praying the news" is one way to become more aware of the need for world integrity. Just take one item from the day's world news and pray about it, asking God to bring that area under the Lordship of Jesus Christ.

WEEK 24

HOW CAN WE LIVE OUT OUR FAITH?

HANDING OVER A TRUST

SCRIPTURE

Dear friends, although I was very eager to write to you about the salvation we share, I felt compelled to write and urge you to contend for the faith that was once for all entrusted to God's holy people.

—Jude 3 (NIV)

TEACHINGS

God gives this world
many ways to know him.

—*Our World Belongs to God,* paragraph 31

This is the first reading of the last week. We have covered a lot of ground. If you look back at the table of contents, you can see where we have been and which way we've come.

We began with God, as all proper religion does. We wanted to know who God is and how God speaks and acts.

Second, we thought about ourselves and our need for a Savior. We studied the human tragedy of the fall and what came from it. We discovered God's surprising rescue arrangement—a covenant of grace.

Third, in the heart of the course we looked at our way out of the mess caused by sin. We wanted to know how God has been at work to provide salvation, to salvage and to save. We were reminded of who Christ is and what saving work he does. We saw how the Holy Spirit makes this work "take" in us, and we talked about justification, faith, repentance, and sanctification. Within sanctification itself we studied the role of law and prayer.

Fourth, we saw how God organizes his people for nourishment and for doing his work in the world. That is, we learned something about the church, the sacraments, and the kingdom of God.

In the fifth and last unit we have been studying how history will end and what the new heaven and the new earth will be like. We also spent a week studying our own Reformed accent.

These five units of knowledge can be summed up as three things—God, the world, and their relation. We have learned about the triune God, about the world (especially the world of human beings), and about how God and the world are related to each other in creation, fall, and redemption.

We have come a long way in studying these things. Along the way we've encountered a number of concepts and terms. These are important, as I'm sure you realize, for understanding the Christian faith and being an informed Christian. With this book I've entrusted you with the most valuable information I have.

In effect, I've "handed over" the content of the Christian faith to you.

Of course, I'm likely not alone in handing over the Christian faith to you. You may have been blessed by parents who promised at your baptism to raise you to love the Lord, and who did exactly that. You may have been blessed by church members who prayed for you and taught you the faith as you matured. You may have been blessed by Christian brothers and sisters, by relatives, friends, teachers, and pastors. If you were so blessed, then all of these—and perhaps many others—have been handing over the Christian faith to you.

Suppose you hand over something valuable to a friend, to an internet site, or to a good family. People do this all the time. They leave the country and hand over their house to someone else. They place a child in the home of adopting parents. They share valuable personal information on a website. They tell a sensitive secret to a good friend.

What allows people to hand over a valuable person or thing in this way? How do they dare do it?

They do it because they have reason to trust those to whom they give the person or thing. What reasons might they have for such trust? An adoption agency would study the family who wishes to adopt a child. An internet user would look for a secure website before giving out valuable personal information. A homeowner would ask a tenant for references. A young person would know from experience whether a friend could be trusted with a secret.

Without trust and reasons to trust and things handed over in trust, human life would be terrifying. It would also be hopeless and godless. For the most valuable thing ever handed over in trust is the knowledge of Jesus Christ and salvation. Without this knowledge the world becomes a maze for us. Without the faith entrusted to the church, we are like reflectors with no light source to shine on us. We are like wilderness hikers who have lost their compass. We are like sailors without a centerboard or rudder. We are like sheep without a shepherd.

The Christian faith is unspeakably precious. It is the most precious thing you have. The faith is, in fact, a trust. God entrusts the Christian faith to the church. All of us in the church keep handing over the faith to younger brothers and sisters, sons and daughters.

You are now in line to receive what's handed over. Everything depends on whether you can be trusted to keep the faith.

FOR REFLECTION

In what ways has the Christian faith been "handed over in trust" to you? Who has God used to pass the faith along to you?

PRAYER STARTERS

Ask God to make you a good receiver and keeper of the Christian faith.

KEEPING THE FAITH

SCRIPTURE

Timothy, guard what has been entrusted to you. Avoid the profane chatter and contradictions of what is falsely called knowledge.

—1 Timothy 6:20

TEACHINGS

We live confidently,
anticipating his coming,
offering him our daily lives—
our acts of kindness,
our loyalty, and our love.

—*Our World Belongs to God,* paragraph 57

Europe is full of castles. Some tower majestically over the Rhine River in Germany or over the fields and dales of England. Castles speckle the land in France, Spain, Switzerland, and Belgium. Some of these great buildings have begun to crumble, but most are so well constructed that they look just as strong today as they did seven hundred years ago.

A castle was built as a fortress house. Nobles would live in one of their castles for a time, till they had eaten all the fresh food and fouled up the toilets and moat. Then they would move on to another castle and start over.

But castles were built especially to be fortresses, places of safety against attack. They were ringed by water-filled ditches to make it hard for an attacker to set up ladders or to get over the wall in any other way. The only entrance to a castle was the drawbridge let down from the guardhouse. The door at the entrance to the guardhouse was double-thick and iron-reinforced. If an intruder did manage somehow to force this monster door open, he would find an unpleasant surprise just inside. For most castles were outfitted with loopholes along the passage just beyond the door. From these holes archers and gunners could assail the enemy. This passage was often also equipped with "murder holes" in the ceiling. From these, the castle's defenders could rain down rocks, spears, bowling balls, cannon shot, boiling tar, rotting animal carcasses, and other things of wonder. The intruder might wish he had dropped in some other time.

But the strongest part of early castles was a huge main tower, called a keep. Here the noble family had its rooms and housed its treasures. Precious lives, precious jewels, precious art—anything valuable was kept in the keep.

The keeps of surviving castles are impressively strong. Walls are four or even six feet thick. They are also slitted with arrow and gun holes—tiny at the bottom, large at the top. The spiral staircase in a castle is cunningly built to place the castle defender at an advantage. The staircase winds counterclockwise down to the left so that when facing an upcoming intruder, the defender could brace his left arm against the center post, leaving his right arm free to swing a sword in the open area of the staircase. The attacker, on the other hand, was in trouble if he wasn't left-handed; if he used his right hand, his sword got all tangled up with the center post.

In fact, most castle sieges ended before anybody got to a staircase. Most castles were almost impossible to penetrate. An attacker's best hope was to outwait the defenders, finally starving the castle into submission. Next best was to hope for treachery in the ranks of defenders.

In our text today Paul tells young Timothy to guard, to keep the faith that has been entrusted to him. This is a word to us as well. For when the things of the faith have been handed over to you, your Christian life has only just begun. Now you will have to guard your faith against assaults. You will have to guard it because it is the most precious thing you have—more precious than life itself.

How do we keep the faith? By studying it and knowing it well, so that we are not defeated by ignorance. By regular habits of Christian devotion—poured-out prayers, persistent Bible reading, attentive church attendance. One of the strongest keeps for the faith is a pattern of good deeds. Paul tells Timothy to be "rich in good deeds," because he knows how we are built. We are built so that when we act badly, the faith starts seeming small and unreal to us. On the other hand, when we stretch out in kindness or reach out in intelligent care for someone, Jesus Christ seems to be at home in us.

Paul tells Timothy to keep the faith. He means to guard it. And he is speaking to you and me too.

FOR REFLECTION

What are some of the things you need to guard your faith *against*? What helps you guard your faith?

PRAYER STARTERS

Thank the Lord for entrusting the Christian faith to you. Ask for a strong inner "keep" so that what you have been given may never be taken away.

FAITH AND EXPERIENCE

SCRIPTURE

"You asked, 'Who is this that obscures my plans
    without knowledge?'
Surely I spoke of things I did not understand,
things too wonderful for me to know. . . .
My ears had heard of you
but now my eyes have seen you."
—Job 42:3, 5 (NIV)

TEACHINGS

The Spirit renews our hearts
and moves us to faith,
leads us into truth
and helps us to pray,
stands by us in our need
and makes our obedience fresh and vibrant.
—*Our World Belongs to God,* paragraph 29

Most things we hear about mean a great deal more to us if we experience them. Suppose you had to describe the taste of pizza to a person who had never tried it. You could use the word "good" and all its synonyms (delicious, delectable, delightful, mouthwateringly yummy, etc.), but none of the descriptions would really do the job. You would need to escort this person to a high-quality pizza place and have the person actually anchor her teeth in a steaming, freshly baked slice. Experience tells what the word *good* means.

The same goes for other items in human life. Violinists, for instance, have to learn bow techniques that are very hard to describe. Most of them, like pizza, have Italian names. A good teacher will attempt a description, giving directions for making the move, and the student will try and fail. Then, one day when the student isn't trying too hard, the technique clicks. The student feels the combination of upper-arm relaxation and lower-arm firmness that makes for crisp bowing. Experience is the best teacher once again.

One could multiply examples: the strength of a hurricane gale, the soft loveliness of a morning in late May, the satisfaction of smashing a baseball with the sweetest part of the bat, the grief of death in one's family, the joy of being praised by a person you admire, the fragrance of a freshly run-over skunk, the sharp sense of shame from being caught cheating, the pleasure of losing yourself in a truly fine story. All these things can be described. In fact, you've just heard them described. But only people who have experienced these things really understand what is meant by a description of them.

Sad to say, some things in human life can be understood best when you lose them. These are things we experience all the time but take for granted—things like good health, political freedoms, or the comforts of home. You may not appreciate what these things mean till they are removed.

If you have been raised in a Christian home and church—and maybe educated in a Christian school as well—you have heard a great deal about the Christian faith over the years. This course has added to the number of things you've heard.

Many of these things may have seemed empty to you—just words, just marks on paper that lack real meaning. I've been trying to describe the Christian faith to you—telling about justification, for example, and repentance and the wonder of God's grace. I have tried to interest you in the church, in the covenant, in the kingdom of God. But I know you may have found some of what I've said to be empty or puzzling or boring.

I know that. But I also know that if you keep on in the faith, much of what you've learned will come alive for you sooner or later. This can happen unexpectedly. You might one day be low and guilty and weak because of some foolish sin. You then experience the love of God that comes for us exactly when we are low and guilty and weak. You learn by experience the meaning of grace.

Or perhaps you join with others in a summer workshop or other service project and find, to your amazement, that you are enjoying the work, that it is important to you, and that you feel like a part of a great, living body. "Church" takes on new meaning for you.

It has always been like this. The disciples of Jesus Christ were like us in this way. For instance, they had heard with their ears the prediction of Jesus' resurrection. Maybe they half-believed these words. And maybe the words didn't mean much to them. But then, on Easter morning, in a meeting that must have stopped their hearts, the disciples met the risen Lord. They saw him. And they knew him.

We can hear with the hearing of our ears. One day, in the grace of God, we shall see.

FOR REFLECTION

What does it take to make your faith really come alive?

PRAYER STARTERS

Ask God to make your faith more than just words or knowledge—to make it really come alive to you through your daily experiences.

OPENING THE DOOR

SCRIPTURE

"Here I am! I stand at the door and knock. If anyone hears my voice and opens the door, I will come in and eat with that person, and they with me."

—Revelation 3:20 (NIV)

TEACHINGS

The Spirit . . .
opens our hearts to God's voice.

—*Our World Belongs to God,* paragraph 31

A famous Christian by the name of John Baillie once wrote about this famous verse from Revelation. I want to translate what Professor Baillie said into my own words and leave them with you as a last reading.

Every Christian is familiar with the picture in this verse. It's a picture that has inspired many drawings and paintings and even hymns. All of us know, deep inside, what the picture represents.

For we have no doubt about who is knocking at the door. This is the person for whom we are named. This is the person whom some worship and by whom others curse. Charles Lamb once said that if Shakespeare were to walk into a room, we would all rise to our feet. But if Jesus Christ were to come in, we'd all fall to our knees. For he is our Lord. And it is he who knocks.

Most of us have heard that knock for years. Every time a parent read Scripture, we were aware of that knock. Every time a talk or a reading or a sermon gripped us, we heard the knocking. Every time God seemed to be trying to get at us in our conscience, or in nature, or in some experience too deep to tell—well, there again was the knocking at our door.

We hear it. We do hear the knock. But we've been hearing it for so long that it hardly makes an impression at times. We can eat right through the sound of it without getting indigestion. We can sleep clear through it without stirring much. Sometimes when the music is turned up loudly enough, we hardly hear the knock at all.

And, in fact, it does get blended in with other noises, doesn't it? A workman is driving roof nails, perhaps, or breaking up pavement three blocks away with a jackhammer. The windows rattle as a truck passes. The shutters bang, and a loose gate creaks. We can almost persuade ourselves at times that we were mistaken about the knocking,

Almost. But not really. Deep inside we know who's there. Deep inside we know that when we are eating or sleeping, when we are studying or playing, when we are aching or rejoicing, there he is—knocking at our inner door in that sort of patient, persistent way. We hear the sound. We know what it is. We know we are wanted. And we know who wants us.

For many weeks and months I have been writing to you about Christ and the Christian faith. I believe that what I've written is true and that it is important for you to learn. But most of it is information. You do need information to be a mature Christian, but you also need more. You need a Savior. You need not only Christianity but also the Christ. You need the person who knocks. Nothing in this book finally matters, in fact, unless you get up and open that door. You have to give in and give up. You have to get up, lift up your head, walk over, and open that everlasting door. And the King of glory will come in.

FOR REFLECTION

Have you answered that knock and opened that door?

PRAYER STARTERS

Even if you've already answered that knock and opened the door, it's good to occasionally re-invite Jesus into your life. Do that in your own words now or use this simple prayer:

Come in, Lord Christ, and make your home in me. Amen.